Artificial

First published in Australia in 2008 by
New Holland Publishers (Australia) Pty Ltd
Sydney • Auckland • London • Cape Town

1/66 Gibbes Street Chatswood NSW 2067 Australia
218 Lake Road Northcote Auckland New Zealand
86 Edgware Road London W2 2EA United Kingdom
80 McKenzie Street Cape Town 8001 South Africa

A record of this book is held at the National Library of Australia

ISBN 9781741107043

Publisher: Fiona Schultz
Publishing Manager: Lliane Clarke
Designer: Natasha Hayles
Cover Photograph: Brad Harris
Production Manager: Linda Bottari
Printer: KHL, Singapore

10 9 8 7 6 5 4 3 2 1

Greg French

NEW
HOLLAND

Although many fly fishers devote themselves to 'matching the hatch'—in creating 'perfect' imitations of the things trout eat—the truth is that large nondescript flies are usually a better bet. In this regard, trout are like people. They find glitz bigger and better than real life—they prefer artificial things to natural ones. It is self-deception, to be sure, and they don't realise until it's too late that there is a sting in the tail.

Contents

Glossary

arbor knot The business end of a fly rig consists of a three- to four-metre length of thin clear leader, which, hopefully, the trout can't see. It is attached to about thirty metres of thick flyline, which has to be heavy enough to cast. This in turn is attached to fifty (or even a hundred) metres of thin Dacron backing, which provides insurance if a particularly strong fish wants to race off downstream or into the middle of a lake. The arbor knot is the one used to attach the backing to the reel.

augur A drill, manual or motorised, which can be used to make a hole in an iced-over lake.

beetle fall Flying terrestrial insects often drop out of the air onto lakes and rivers. A potpourri of such insects is referred to as 'windfall', but often the event is species specific, hence 'beetle fall'.

berley A bait spread over the water in order to attract fish.

berleying The act of spreading berley.

Chernobyl Ant A large, ugly dry fly which represents nothing in nature but is often irresistible to trout. The ultimate artificial insect.

copepod A very small crustacean which often gathers in large, dense clouds, especially in lakes.

daphnia A minute crustacean which, like the copepod, often gathers in large clouds. Also known as water fleas.

dry fly An artificial fly designed to sit on the water surface.

dubbing A collection of thin short fibres which are hand spun onto fly tying thread in order to make a thick cord which can then be wrapped round and round a hook to make the body of an artificial fly.

dun The distinctive sub-imago (sub-adult) phase of the mayfly. It hatches directly from the aquatic nymph and usually rests a while on the water surface before flying off and metamorphosing into a spinner (imago, adult). Mayflies are the only insects to have three distinctive phases in their life cycles.

emergers Aquatic insects that have migrated to the water surface in order to metamorphose into winged adults (or, in the case of mayflies, sub-adults).

EPIRB Emergency Position Indicating Radio Beacon.

Hydro The Hydro Electric Commission was the State Government authority set up to produce all of Tasmania's electrical power needs. It has since been split into several divisions, but the entity which retains responsibility for generating power (as opposed to transmission or billing) is still called 'the Hydro'.

inchman A large stinging ant, bigger but slightly less aggressive than the jack-jumper.

iwi A Maori community, something akin to a village or tribe.

jack-jumper A very aggressive Tasmanian ant famous for its painful sting.

jollytail A small elongate baitfish. In Tasmania the term is used exclusively for one species of native galaxias, *G. maculatus*.

leader A three- or four-metre length of clear monofilament line, usually tapered. A leader is necessary because the flyline itself is too thick to fit through the eye of a small artificial fly and too noticeable to the fish.

matching the hatch A firmly entrenched tradition whereby anglers try to fish with artificial flies which are as close as possible to perfect imitations of whatever the trout happen to be feeding upon at the time.

mayfly See dun.

milt The white milk-like secretion from the genital organs of male fish. Sperm.

mini-beasts Small animals such as insects, tadpoles and shrimps.

parr markings The distinctive colours displayed on the sides of juvenile trout and salmon.

redd A gravel nest made by a female trout in which eggs are laid before being abandoned.

riser A fish which takes food, especially insects, off the water surface.

sampling The taking of biological samples, including the collection of fish and aquatic insects from the wild.

sandies Small bottom-dwelling fish also known as freshwater flathead.

scud A small shrimp-like crustacean of the order Amphipoda.

smut A small mayfly of the family Caenidae.

tailer These days this term refers to a fish which moves in very shallow water such that its dorsal and tail fins cut through the water surface. Traditionally it referred specifically to a fish which was standing on its nose with only its tail waving out of the water.

tippet The thin end-piece of the leader.

wet fly A fly designed to be fished beneath the water surface.

Woolly Bugger A specific wet fly design.

Prologue

MOST STORIES seem to start in spring or summer. This one begins in autumn. Why? Because that's when Tasmanian anglers need to work hardest to find their quarry, and when we are most likely to gain new insights into the world around us.

Fantasy novelists know that you cannot begin to understand yourself unless you are prepared to look at your environment from a range of perspectives, including difficult and uncomfortable ones. Tolkien had Frodo Baggins peer into the Mirror of Galadriel, while Rowling ensured that Harry Potter reflected upon the Mirror of Erised (*desire* backwards). These mirrors did not confirm preconceived truths. Rather, they allowed the heroes to see beyond mere reflection into the blinding glare, revealing wonders and horrors that they scarcely believed possible.

In late autumn, the cooling of the air and water tempers the activity of most mini-beasts, and events like mayfly hatches and beetle falls become almost non-existent. Suddenly the trout have to search harder for their food, and they have to be less fussy about what they eat. Generally they end up consuming sub-surface stuff like stick caddis and aquatic nymphs.

With the general absence of risers and tailers, the angler himself has to learn to scan for his quarry. Many fly fishers I know learned to polaroid in autumn—even though visibility is much better when the sun is high in the sky during summer—simply because they were forced to look more closely at the water in order to see any fish at all.

Polaroid glasses open a whole new world. You can watch autumn fish swaggering along side to side, dipping down to open their jaws, briefly revealing the whites of their mouths. But since autumn trout are inclined to cast their vision far and wide, they notice things from a long way off and tend to take well. The novice polaroider, who may previously have devoted his imagination to 'matching the hatch', is often surprised to find that these nymphing fish rise freely to take an artificial fly from the surface. Suddenly the realisation: perhaps there is no need to match the hatch. Soon enough, such a novice will be forced to re-examine other truths, like the extent and relevance of the trout's field of vision, not to mention the fish's supposed sensitivity to bright clothing and noise.

A friend of mine, a stream enthusiast, used to say that lake fishing was too bland for his liking. In his mind, reading current comprised the very soul of fly fishing 'and everyone knows there are no currents in lakes'. But when he began polaroiding he began to notice trailing weeds, silt-lines, wind-lanes, long-shore drift and bizarre concentrations of food and fish. In time he came to recognise the intensity of 'stillwater' currents, and found the whole concept quite shocking. He confided it was hard to admit he was wrong, and even more difficult to atone for a lifetime of prejudice. He didn't know whether to praise his polaroids or curse them. In the end though, like most fantasy heroes, he demonstrated mettle and made something good of it all.

The fact is that many of us discovered polaroids a year or two after we had begun fly fishing in earnest, and we too had to cope with having our world-perspective turned on its head. The upside was, as Alice found when she stepped through the looking glass, that things unknown and weird usually ended up being a whole lot more real and beautiful than familiar 'truth'.

Spawners

JUNE IS notable for its short, cold days and long, colder nights. In the Tasmanian highlands you can expect snow and icy rain. Yet for all the morbid atmosphere, the swollen streams hint at birth and renewal. Each winter I don my backpack and head out into the backcountry— to the farthest corners of the Western Lakes—where big brown trout pack themselves into creeks, some of which are small enough to step over.

Frequently the water is so shallow that the fish are compelled to expose their backs as they make their nests. Despite the low, cloud-obscured sun, I can usually see the females shuffling from side to side, employing powerful thrusts of their tails to shift fist-sized rocks. It is impossible not to marvel at the way they use the current to advantage.

A big male will attend a female, waiting a metre or so downstream, ready to release milt the instant the eggs are laid, though despite his vigilance a precocious youngster, perhaps no longer than my hand, will sometimes race out from an undercut bank, squirt an urgent milky cloud and flee upstream as if his life depends upon it, which it probably does.

The depositing of eggs is generally considered the beginning of life. But if you are a trout, you are more likely than not to die from the rigours of the spawning run. If you survive spawning, then you will probably die as a result of the biochemical changes induced by maturity. If you are a Pacific salmon, and you are not a precocious year-old male, you will definitely die. So perhaps we should consider egg-laying to be the end.

Ah, I hear you say, what is to be gained by dwelling on tragedy? Surely it is best to look to the future?

Let me tell you something else: most of the eggs will not even hatch.

In many streams, quality gravel is scarce, and trout are commonly compelled to build redds in sites recently used by other fish. Consequently, eggs are continually disturbed, and many get carried away by the current, straight into the mouths of opportunistic trout, usually rogue males which have learned to lie in ambush immediately downstream of the most used nesting sites. I've even seen some clever old cannibals systematically digging up perfectly good redds.

This heavy diet of ova is well known. In places that permit fishing for spawning fish, the most popular flies are imitative patterns— weighted balls of synthetic wool coloured fluro orange or hot pink—which trundle along the shingle beds like the real thing.

The cannibalism doesn't stop with eggs. In spring and early summer, adult trout congregate in the spits where spawning streams enter lakes and charge about in shallows eating newly arrived fry and fingerlings with the same gusto that estuary fish target whitebait.

When I was in primary school, we were taught that books should have a beginning, middle and end. How about you? Perhaps you think of life as something cyclic? Or maybe something lineal, with an indefinite past and infinite future?

Wrigglers

MY POP had two small domestic-supply dams on his rural property at Woodsdale, about thirty kilometres inland from Tasmania's east coast. The dams were excavated just before I was born, and soon became home to all manner of mini-beasts. As small kids, we got quite used to drinking glassfuls of mosquito wrigglers, but the tadpoles were another matter—some of the bigger ones actually blocked the water pipes.

In search of a cure, Pop conscripted my dad (his son-in-law), and together they drove his ancient FC station wagon out to some backwater lagoons on the floodplains of the Little Swanport River at Stonehenge. It had been a long hot summer and aquatic plants had proliferated: the shallow lagoons were completely choked with strapweed. Unperturbed, the men armed themselves with circular sieves. These were of the sort used for screening cement, but to my impressionable mind they resembled ones used by goldminers when panning the rivers of the Yukon and Klondike.

Pop and Dad waded about in the shallows, pushing their sieves through the aquatic foliage and got not so much a flash in the pan, as a glistening turmoil of success. There were dozens of tench fry—barely three centimetres long—and a couple of nuggets four times that size. During the next hour or so they eked out other precious gems, notably a handful of redfin perch. These fish averaged seven centimetres and glittered madly. They had diamond-white sides, six black vertical bands and ruby-red fins.

I'd never seen redfin before, mainly because there were none in my home river, the Prosser. And I didn't realise that Pop's dams lay in the uppermost reaches of the Prosser catchment. What would happen if the dams were breached during a flood? It wasn't a question that entered anyone's head, and I doubt that it would have bothered us if it did.

The fry and fingerlings—hundreds of them—were transported back to Woodsdale in steel cream cans. Part-way home, the car began to make an obscure noise. It eventually became so loud that, fearing some sort of mechanical meltdown, the men pulled over. No engine problems—just dozens of fish, their snouts right out of the water, sucking air in desperate painful gulps.

Apparently this is more or less how the fishy invasion of land began. In the brackish reaches of freshwater rivers, with oxygen in limited supply, fish that could survive by gulping air when the oxygen content fell to critical lows were the ones that survived. Through successive generations, some fish developed pouches in their alimentary canals in which air could be stored, and these pouches eventually became rudimentary lungs. This is also how swim bladders evolved.

Pop had a brainwave. He got out the tyre pump and blew bubbles into the water until the fish stopped panicking and gradually subsided below the surface. This somewhat jocular activity had to be repeated several times en route, but the fish were delivered safely with scarcely any mortalities. The liberated stock immediately went to work on the wrigglers and tadpoles, and within a few months the water was running clear through the taps.

Aquarium

WHEN I was in late primary school, I started getting serious about aquaria. I upgraded from a glass battery case to a professionally built aquarium, a full one metre long. The first inmates were crayfish, *Astacopsis franklinii*, collected from Hobart Rivulet, the tiny brook on which Hobart was founded, near the Cascade Brewery. They didn't adapt well, judging from the way they kept pacing back and forth clawing at the glass. I wondered if they resented being confined to a constant depth of forty centimetres. In a fit of inspiration, I salvaged some closed-cell trays from a packet of sausages and sewed on a few ribbons of tulle. Then I set the tray afloat, like a lifesaver, and allowed the lace to fall like Rapunzel's tresses all the way to the bottom. The crayfish climbed to the top and lined up contentedly, returning to the water only to feed or wet their gills.

As interesting as crays were, I really wanted to keep fish. Not tropicals, which could be selected like lollies from glass jars, but real fish. Ones I could hunt myself from the local ponds and rivers. I shunned handbooks on fish husbandry, reasoning that such texts would be irrelevant to keeping wild fish, and anyway I wanted to discover everything for myself. (This arrogance has always been, in equal measure, a blessing and a hindrance.) Being a Luddite at heart, I would have liked to have avoided *all* the aquarium paraphernalia being pushed at the pet shop, but I was experienced enough to know that most fish wouldn't last more than a few hours without basic equipment like air pumps and charcoal filters.

So at age ten, after having properly fitted-out my aquarium, I went back to those dams of my earlier childhood with a bush pole, a small hook and some worms. After hours of trying I eventually hooked a tench of around twenty-five centimetres, which was too big for my metre-long tank, but I was so ecstatic that I refused to listen to logic, sense or compassion.

Tench aren't particularly energetic, and at first my trophy seemed relaxed enough, but within a few days it was covered in what looked like cottonwool. I worried that it was fungus, but on closer inspection it turned out to be slime. This time I had a brainwave: I planted some dense clumps of pin rushes in the gravel. The result was immediate: the tench swam vigorously backwards and forwards through the rushes until it had completely de-slimed itself.

Given how hard it was to catch fish from the dams, it was inevitable that I returned, with Dad, to Stonehenge, with the very sieves that he and Pop had used a decade beforehand. I didn't catch much, only a dozen or so see-through tench fry, too small to eat worms, and so small that I feared they would be eaten by other fish in the tank.

I resurrected my old glass battery case and furnished it with silt and weeds, hoping that they might contain enough tiny bugs to provide sufficient food for the fry. Surprisingly enough, the little fish thrived, and when they were five centimetres long I transferred them to the main tank. But I still couldn't bring myself to get rid of the big fella.

Eventually I managed to catch three redfin from the dams, the smallest being nine centimetres, the largest eleven. They established territories within minutes, the big one choosing the mouth of a cave I'd created by laying a flat rock atop two other rocks, a design which may have been subconsciously inspired by the new resident's place of origin. This cave also happened to be where the daily supply of worms rained down, so the dominant redfin soon outgrew the tank. When I let him go, the next biggest perch, which hadn't grown much at all in the intervening months, immediately took over the prime lie. Perch, it turned out, were going to be processed through my aquarium rather quickly.

Eels were easily caught in the Prosser on a conventional hook and line. They had the advantage of being almost totally indestructible. But they had an annoying habit of burrowing into the gravel and staying there, showing nothing more than a bit of head.

I also hooked sandies and tiny trout, which adapted quite well to their new life in the living room. As for galaxias, their hook wounds often struggled to heal, so I ended up making fish traps, about fifty centimetres long, from copper flywire, which I snuck from flyscreens on the least used windows of my parents' house. It was some months before I was discovered and reprimanded.

By now I was running out of fish to collect, and my enthusiasm was waning somewhat. On a trout fishing trip to Lake Sorell with Dad, I discovered dense schools—enormous clouds—of a completely different galaxias to the ones that lived in the Prosser. These turned out to be golden galaxias (*G. auratus*). I caught a dozen or so on small hooks baited with pieces of a worm I'd found under a rock, and ended up keeping them in a blackened billy. I had to change the water constantly while boating around the lake, and I held them on my knee all the way home in the car, supplying them with air via a tyre pump (what else?). Against all odds, my treasures arrived in perfect health. I tipped them into the aquarium, and they were promptly engulfed by the redfin perch—all gone in the space of seconds. The perch had never bothered the other galaxias: not the jollytails or mountain galaxias or climbing galaxias. I was devastated.

This piscivorous flurry might have helped to alleviate the one big problem in my aquarium: overstocking. But the perch were no match for my incessant collecting.

Copious quantities of fish poo resulted in the water becoming cloudy, and eventually it got to the stage where the tank required cleaning every couple of weeks. I emptied the rancid water straight out the window, frequently knocking the bucket against the sill, sloshing water all over the walls and floor. Then I'd snake the garden hose in through the very same window, and promptly forget to turn it off. First the carpet rotted away, then the same thing happened to the floorboards.

My mum never complained. She just asked, repeatedly, that I be more careful. Was she offering some compensation for the restrictions imposed on her children by our severely autistic brother? Was she somehow aware of the critical importance of this fishy stuff to my sense of self? Did she simply enjoy seeing the outside world delivered into her domestic prison?

In addition to putrefying the water, overstocking commonly resulted in stress-related diseases, most noticeably the dreaded cottonwool fungus. The galaxias were most susceptible, probably because when I lifted the fish trap from their home waters they would flail about all over the sharp copper fibres along the seams. Accordingly, I redesigned the traps. The new ones were made out of two clear-plastic fruit juice bottles. I'd cut the spout off one; I'd cut the bottom and spout off another and slide it a little way over the first; I'd invert one of the chopped-off spouts and jam it in the end. Finally I'd glue the joins together with roof-and-gutter silicone stolen from my father's workshop.

This stemmed the fungus, but there were still outbreaks from time to time, and I found them demoralising.

The only fish that contracted fungus and didn't die from it was my original tench, Mr Big. From the outset he had a small spot where my hook had penetrated his upper lip and, although it never healed, neither did it spread nor cause him discomfort. It stayed in the same place and remained the same size for eighteen months until I released him. Which makes me wonder if there's any truth in the old rumours about tench slime having medicinal properties.

Floundering

AFTER ONE big fungus attack in my freshwater aquarium, I decided that keeping marine animals might be an easier option. I released most of my healthy freshwater fish, and set up a saltwater tank. The nails rusted away before the new floorboards had the chance to rot.

The first specimens to occupy the marine tank were the salt-tolerant fish from my freshwater collection: sandies, jollytails, eels and trout. Despite everything I've since read, all these fish handled the changeover—a brutally immediate one, with no attempt at acclimatisation—with no observable ill effects whatsoever.

Catching wholly saltwater fish was easy. Since before I could remember, I'd been helping my father and brothers collect bait from the eelgrass flats in the Prosser estuary. We used a small cotton seine net with twelve-millimetre mesh. Normal practice was for one person to stay on the shore while the other waded out knee deep, and to pull the net along twenty metres or so of bank before drawing it up onto the shore. But collecting aquarium fish was an intensely private affair. I pushed a stick into the silt near the water's edge, tied one end of the net to this, and stretched the net along the beach. Then I waded out and around, scribing a full 180-degree arc. Delicate mid-water fish like prettyfish and mullet proved too fragile to keep, but thick-skinned bottom-dwellers—soldierfish, toad fish, pipefish, bream, leatherjackets, sea horses—fared remarkably well.

Reasoning that estuary fish would need to eat estuarine foods, I spent days on end gathering up sandworms from under rocks along the mudflats at low tide. The ones in the Prosser were relatively small, about the same length as garden worms, but they were aggressive blighters, with a pair of fearsome pincers on a retractable head. My favourite fish, juvenile greenback flounders, engaged in herculean battles with these odious worms. If they tried to eat them tail-first, the head would swing round like a hydra, and strike repeatedly at the flounder's protruding eyeballs. Sometimes, on the second attempt, the flounder would opt for a head-first approach, though as often as not the worm would battle its way out through the gill cover. Yet none of the flounder—not Hercules, not Sinbad, not St George—was ever beaten. Eventually you'd find them sleepily recovering from their repast, only their eyes and grossly inflated stomachs visible above the sand.

Despite their dogged battles, which never varied in style and always resulted in several of the dreaded eye-gouges, the flounder demonstrated an amazing capacity to learn. Within a day of being placed from the wild into the aquarium, they would associate me walking into the room with a meal, and swim over to the glass in anticipation. Within a few days I could train them to rise to the surface, slide up on my palm and take morsels from the fingers of my other hand.

Fish, I uncomfortably observed, display distressful responses to misery. Wrasses, like flounder, were clever and endearing. They liked to rest, and used rocks as pillows. Unfortunately, they were super-sensitive to water quality, and prone to skin ulcers. It is simply unbearable to watch a distressed wrasse fruitlessly trying to relieve itself of itch or pain by rubbing itself against its pillow for hours on end. All I could do was let them go and try to improve the water quality.

In an attempt to kill bacteria, I began boiling water in a tub with an immersion heater, before allowing it to cool and placing it in the tank. I also cycled the water from the aquarium through an old beer fridge—through thirty or fifty metres of coiled hose—in order to keep water temperatures low in summer. Some of my attempts may have had the potential to be beneficial, except any advantages were overwhelmed by my incessant overstocking.

What I learned, by age twelve, was that fish have memory and that they react to pain and discomfort in exactly the same way as humans do. Well, almost.

In addition to hunting fish for my aquarium, I was just as enthusiastic about hunting fish for the table. In summer, when river levels were low, I'd look for eels amongst the rock crevices and log jams in the mid-reaches of the Prosser. They proved easy to hook, but difficult to pull out. One eel, when finally extracted, was bejewelled with several different hooks, all mine, each one embedded in its upper lip within minutes of the last. By the way, I caught this eel on some green plasticine I found in my pocket. Except it wasn't really plasticine. On closer inspection, it turned out to be a piece of wallaby meat—eel bait from a previous fishing expedition a fortnight beforehand.

More recently I cast to a trout feeding on galaxias in Tooms Lake, only to have it break off the instant I set the fly. The trout carried on hunting as if nothing had happened. I tied on a new fly, waited for an inevitable eruption of baitfish to betray my quarry's whereabouts, and caught it again, first cast. The trout fought itself to exhaustion, and after removing both my flies from its mouth, I left it to recuperate in the shallows. It remained upright, but didn't swim away. It just sat there, periodically flaring its gills. A minute or so later, a school of baitfish swam into the bay and the trout shot off and began feeding again. I could have caught it a third time, but didn't have the heart.

A friend hooked an especially determined riser in the same lake. He played this large brown trout for a while, but it swam under a log, so he chose to let the line go slack and wait. Soon enough, the fish swam out from under the log and sipped a natural dun from the surface, apparently unaware of the fact that it was still well and truly hooked.

When sampling in the Western Lakes, I made a slender spoon that I could push down a trout's mouth and remove stomach contents. The hope was that we could find some way of getting the samples we needed without having to kill every trout in the process. I tried it out on thirty browns at the Salmon Ponds, and not one suffered any ill effects.

For me, these memories pose interesting questions. What would I have become if my mum had discouraged my early fishy endeavours? Can fish feel and remember pain? Should people be allowed to fish? Is it a sin to enjoy fishing? Would forsaking our primal impulses make us more human, or less so?

Bang!

IT PAYS not to forget that our fishing mates were children once, and that, like us, they never really grow out of it.

Calvin's extraordinary habit began innocently enough when, just a few weeks after birth, he farted in the bath and laughed his very first laugh. It was all downhill from there.

At age seven, his uncle showed him how to light farts, and soon afterwards he was revealing, to a highly amused aunt, fantastic theories about how one might collect 'fart gas' to make bombs.

For his eighth birthday this same aunt, somewhat out of character for a respected company executive, decided his ideas were not entirely impractical and presented him with a prototype 'Calvin and Mary's Fart Lighting Kit™' which, in addition to a generous supply of beans and onions, included a hundred-millilitre syringe, a clear glass jar and a rather splendid zippo lighter.

Within minutes of eating his beans, Calvin was lying on his back in a steaming-hot tub. 'I can feel a beauty coming on,' he declared enthusiastically to everyone in the lounge room, most of whom were doing their best to ignore him.

After a time, just as the rest of the family had drifted back into normal conversation, Calvin abruptly resumed his commentary. 'I'm sinking the jar and allowing it to completely fill with water… Now I'm turning the jar upside down and manoeuvring it towards my bum hole… My back is slightly arched… '

There was an improbably loud bubbling noise. Despite the best intentions of those in the lounge room, most laughed. Someone even tried to tell the what-about-a-water-bottle-Wardle joke, but Mary interrupted. 'Calvin, remember not to let the jar break the water surface or else the fart will escape. Have you got the syringe?'

'Check.'

'Is the plunger completely depressed?'

'I'm depressed,' sighed Calvin's mother, so quietly that scarcely anyone heard her.

'Check. I'm submerging the syringe now.' Calvin's voice was deep and solemn, as if he was involved in some dangerous scientific procedure which called for utmost delicacy and timing. 'I am allowing the nipple of the syringe to enter the glass and penetrate the bubble of fart held therein… I am slowly drawing back the plunger and extracting the air into the syringe… '

'The *fart* into the syringe,' said his little sister, getting into the spirit of things, sensing that this time she'd probably get away with saying naughty words.

'Houston,' Calvin declared triumphantly, 'we now have eighty cubic centimetres of pure methane and hydrogen-sulphide blend.' Even at this early age, his knowledge of chemistry and rocketry was quite precocious.

Everyone rushed into the bathroom, all except Mum, who resolutely stayed put.

Dad switched off the light, and Mary held forth the zippo.

Calvin placed the syringe within a centimetre or so of the flame… and pushed the plunger! A poisonous blue blaze shot across the room. There was another eruption of laughter. Applause. Tears of delight.

Ten minutes later, Calvin brought a particularly full jar to the surface of the bath, tipped the corner slightly and set fire to the whole jar in one hit.

BANG!

Mum ran in, expecting to find broken glass, blood and carnage.

The Kit was banned, but only temporarily, because the rest of the family loudly protested, ostensibly on Calvin's behalf.

Calvin got his powder-monkey licence when he was eighteen.

Big bang

I FIRST met Calvin when he was an adult, not a child, when I was posted to Strahan, on Tasmania's West Coast, to work as a Parks and Wildlife ranger. I arrived in the aftermath of the High Court decision that halted construction of the Gordon Below Franklin Dam in the Wild Rivers National Park.

'You're a fly man,' said Calvin, who happened to be one of the utility officers.

Observation or accusation, I wondered.

'Want to go fishing?' he added.

We used my car, an old HQ station wagon. Fred, another utility officer, claimed the front passenger seat, and Calvin climbed in the back. I turned the key. My thumb and index finger received a painful electric shock.

The boys began giggling uncontrollably. 'Funny, eh?' said Calvin. 'Give it another go.'

'Bugger off.'

'It's alright—what we did only works once.'

'*You* do it.'

So Calvin reached across and turned the key.

I received an electric shock to the bum, bigger and more painful than the first. The boys' laughter was now loud enough to deafen the dead.

When they regained some semblance of self control, Calvin showed me how he had fitted a wire to the ignition, fed it under the floor covering, all the way to the driver's seat, then left an exposed end right where I sat down.

'First turn of the key shorts out through your hand. Then, when *I* do it, it gets you in the arse. Works every time.'

More laughter.

The stream we were going to was beyond Melba Flats, near Zeehan.

The Forestry Commission had installed a bright-yellow boom gate across the access track, and protected the lock from the local blokes' hacksaws and bolt cutters by enclosing it in a steel cylinder, capped at the top, accessible with one hand only from underneath.

'Soon fix that,' said Calvin grinning. He retrieved his daypack from the car and pulled out a lump of jelly and a detonator.

I was alarmed—not because I seriously thought we'd hurt ourselves, but because I was a rookie ranger, sworn to uphold the law. I didn't want to lose my job.

'Reverse your car out of harm's way,' Fred advised. 'We'll shelter behind that boulder.'

BOOM!

The cylinder and lock had been blown apart, and the force of the explosion had conveniently swung the gate wide open.

'Let's go,' said Calvin, as if he had done no more than use an official key.

The 'stream' turned out to be the very upper reaches of the Little Henty River. It was way too small and overgrown for fly fishing. In fact, I doubted that it was ever fished by anyone. 'Can't cast here,' I said, somewhat annoyed.

'Wasn't intending on using flies.' Then I noticed that Calvin was playfully tossing a stick of jelly from one hand to the other. He put the explosives on a floating plank, and let them off. I helped clean up the carnage: dozens of slabby little brown trout, mostly half-pounders.

'Small,' Fred conceded, 'but they'll make good fish patties.'

'Some of them are already mashed up,' Calvin added brightly.

I realised that I had stopped feeling panicky or guilty, and concluded that I was going to enjoy my time in Strahan. 'I'll get the car,' I said, slapping Calvin on the shoulder.

I hopped into the driver's seat and turned the ignition.

Dead silence. Levitation. Darkness. Incomprehension. Ringing in ears. Outright fear!

This, it turned out, was a perfectly normal reaction to six enormous explosions from under your car bonnet. It's what happens when Calvin takes the spark plugs out of the engine, leaves them wired up to the distributor, and tapes each one into an oxyacetylene-filled condom.

Miraculously my car was undamaged, but I soon learned that that was not always the case. I was at one party when the bonnet of Fred's car ended up on the local police officer's back lawn.

The Taxman

EVERYBODY IN Strahan had a nickname, had to have a nickname. I got mine nine days into our first ten-day stint building boardwalks on Sarah Island, in the middle of Macquarie Harbour. We were living out of a twelve-foot by twelve-foot metal garden shed. We'd just spent a couple of hours fishing the mouth of the Gordon River, for sea trout, from an aluminium dinghy. It was dark by now, and drizzling, and Fred was serving up some of our catch.

'We can't just keep on calling you Greg,' Calvin insisted.

'Call me whatever you want.'

Calvin wasn't happy. 'Look, if you won't tell us your nickname...' Despite his own situation being proof to the contrary, he was perfectly convinced that no-one could manage life without a nickname. '... we'll be forced to give you one ourselves.'

I refused to be intimidated.

He looked around the campsite for inspiration and settled his gaze upon the lid of the esky. 'Okay, make your choice: Trout, Maggot or Slug?'

I noticed, much to my surprise, that there really were maggots on our trout. And a slug. I said nothing.

'Okay, Trout it is,' conceded Fred.

***

The Taxman got his name because of his unusual hobby, taxidermy, which he'd taken up in primary school.

'What do you think?' I asked expectantly.

He picked up a piece of exploded trout tail in one hand, and an almost complete head in the other, and shook his head despondently. 'You really want all this carnage mounted on a shield like a deer head?'

'It's for Calvin's birthday.'

'Ah!' He was excited now. 'Tell you what: what say we give this to him as a joint present and I don't charge you for the job. He'll *love* it.'

Drinking games

THE WILD rivers of the West Coast are addictive—bestial and ancient, inviting glorious disinhibition, like submitting to a lover. Back in Strahan after ten days of work on Sarah Island, Ric, a mate from Forestry, suggested we go straight back down the harbour and spend a long weekend fishing the lower Gordon River. 'We could even have a night or two with Jock.'

Jock was a fellow park ranger, a big amiable bloke with a flowing ginger beard, who spent his ten-day stints at the Sir John Falls Camp deep in the rainforested wilderness.

Sir John Falls Camp was originally built by the Hydro. It comprised a handful of cheap surveyors' huts and working-men's quarters, all relics from the 1970s. After the proposal to dam the Gordon below the Franklin junction was vetoed by the Federal Government in 1983, ownership and management of the camp was passed on to the Parks and Wildlife Service. The buildings were crude timber-framed things, under constant assault from mould, moss and riverbank erosion. There was no power, no hot water, no services of any kind. Without much to do except maintain an official presence, most rangers just relaxed, read too many pulp novels, drank too much alcohol, smoked too much dope, and became extraordinarily content.

Ric and I press-ganged Calvin from the Regatta Point Tavern and, using my four-metre dinghy, a fibreglass Islander with a twenty-horsepower outboard, we carefully navigated our way forty kilometres across Macquarie Harbour. After catching some sea trout at the river mouth, we made our way another forty kilometres upriver to Jock's little haven.

That evening, in the middle of cribbage, for no apparent reason, Jock demanded that we 'Look at this!' He was pressing a five-cent piece against his forehead, and he kept pressing until it stuck fast. Then he hit the back of his head with his right hand, once, twice, three times, until it fell off and rolled across the table. 'Anyone care to get it off their forehead in less than three hits?'

'Easy,' slurred Ric.

'If it's *that* easy, I'll put it on for you.' Jock held the back of Ric's head and used a thumb to press the coin painfully hard into Ric's skin.

'Enough, enough.'

'If you can knock that off in ten hits, I'll shout you a bottle of scotch.'

Everyone laughed. But not for the reason Ric thought we were laughing. What he didn't know was that Jock had already removed the coin. All that was left on Ric's forehead was an impression of the coin.

Ten progressively harder hits later, when Ric had lost his bet and our laughter had reached manic proportions, Ric started hitting himself over the head with the crib board—so Jock finally exposed the trick.

'Okay,' Ric chuckled, 'what say you let me hypnotise you.'

Jock could hardly say no.

'We need an enamel plate… Ah, here's one I prepared earlier.' In mock triumph, he picked up a plate that had been sitting on the table in full view of everyone all night.

We giggled like schoolgirls.

'Turn off the gas lamps and blow out all the candles bar the two at the back of the room,' Ric said smoothly.

Long ago, the masonite walls had been painted a pale green, and although tempered somewhat by years of accumulated grime, the candlelight still enhanced the sickly supernatural hue. Shadows flickered. The atmosphere became eerily dull.

'Hold this in your left hand,' said Ric, passing the enamel plate to Jock. 'Using the middle finger of your right hand, trace the bottom with a circular motion, spiralling slowly, slowly, slowly in from the outside to the very centre.'

Jock obeyed.

Ric kept talking. Soothingly. Authoritatively. 'Breathe deeply, slowly, and allow all thoughts to disappear. Concentrate only on your breathing and on the movement of your finger. Do not smile. Allow your face muscles to relax. That's the way. Good, good. Feel your cheeks. Are they relaxed? Good, *good*. Trace the bottom of the plate again. Breathe. Relax. Trace a circle around your eyes. Are you relaxed? Good, *good*.'

The monotonous chant was certainly having an effect on the rest of us.

'When I light up the gas lamps,' Ric continued in his lilting, calming tones, 'you will feel happy, you will say something of your own invention that will make everyone laugh, and then you will make us all a cup of coffee.'

Ric lit the gas lamp.

'What are you all looking at me for?' said Jock. And then, more urgently, 'What are you all laughing at?'

Fred passed a mirror, and Jock realised that his face was fairly plastered in greasy black grime. Then Ric upturned the enamel plate, and displayed the underside proudly at chest height, like a kitchenware retailer starring in his own cheap television commercial. 'I prepared it earlier by holding it over the candle flame.'

'Okay you win,' Jock conceded happily. 'Who wants a coffee?'

Beatrice

'YOU'RE NOT putting *that* over the mantelpiece.'

'But it's awesome,' Calvin pleaded.

'If it's not bad enough that you kill things for pure entertainment...'

'You're happy enough to *eat* the trout I catch.'

'It's the pleasure you get from catching them that bothers me. Catch-and-release has to be the biggest abomination...'

'What's wrong with catch-and-release? Do you think a fish would prefer to be caught and killed? Do you think this fish...' he pointed to the fragments on the shield '... is happier than the ones I let go?'

Beatrice was Calvin's partner. She was the daughter of devoutly religious parents, with a delightful two-year-old daughter from a previous, disastrous, relationship: Hayley wasn't even born when Beatrice and Calvin got together.

'What is it with Catholics? Sex for procreation not pleasure, gardening for food not pleasure, food for sustenance not pleasure. You seem to hate anyone having fun.'

'That's unfair; I'm not like my parents.'

'Thank God. Someone should tell them that life isn't just an endurance event to test whether or not you're worthy of an afterlife.

Bloody weirdos—probably into self-flagellation too. They're hardly good role models for Hayley…'

'Calvin, stop it.'

'Actually a bit more guilt might not be a bad thing. Perhaps then you'd stop eating all the time.' This, Calvin admitted later, was unfair. Beatrice may have been putting on a little weight, but she was still very attractive, and hardly obese.

'I just think that we should have respect for animals' feelings. Peter Singer thinks we should afford them the same respect that we have for people…'

'He's a bigger weirdo than your mum. Fishing is a natural thing for people to do. So is *enjoying* fishing.'

'You could probably argue that war is natural; doesn't mean we should condone it.'

'Fish don't feel pain, not like we do. They don't reason and don't have emotions and probably aren't self-aware.'

'Sometimes I think that people like you are nothing but animals— *wild* animals.'

'I thought you liked animals. Anyway, you're right: people are becoming more and more like animals. Not wild animals with guts and zest and an affinity with the bush—farm animals, feedlot animals, a bunch of bloody pussies.'

Beatrice was crying now, and Hayley, having been awoken from her afternoon nap, joined right in.

Calvin left the living room and lovingly lifted Hayley from her cot. 'Hey, hey, hey there's nothing to worry about. Dad's here. Come on, we'll go out to the fire with Mum and read *Where the Wild Things Are*. "They rolled their terrible eyes…"'

Spanish inquisition

I WAS in my early twenties when I first made up my mind to travel to a country where I would be obliged to use a language other than English. The country was Chile, the language Spanish. I asked my brother and sister-in-law if they wanted to come with me. No said Chris. Yes said Julie.

Ah, family politics.

In those days there were no adult education courses in Hobart, and no Internet on the planet. I hired some tapes from the State Library. Then I bought a couple of good phrase books and a dictionary. Because Julie and I lived at opposite ends of Tasmania, I mainly studied alone in my living room, though occasionally we practised over the phone.

The good thing about Spanish, I soon discovered, was that since it's Latin-based, most words seem quite logical. Many animals are commonly known by their taxonomic names, or something close to it. Frog is *rana*. Eel, *anguila*. Rat, *rata*. Whale, *ballena*, and so on.

Words that don't make perfect sense are likely to have a built-in mnemonic. For example, the Spanish word for ocean is *mar*, which is conveniently evocative of maritime. Other Spanish words look a little like their English equivalents. *Trucha* (**troo**.char), for trout, springs to mind. And some even sound okay: *salmón* is pronounced sal.**mon**.

Another convenient thing about the language is that it is pretty much perfectly phonetic, so foreigners can pronounce words coherently, including place names like Llanquihue, as soon as they see them. I'll bet no-one's done that on their first visit to Tasmania when they've arrived at Strahan or Liawenee. Or in New Zealand at Rerewhakaaitu or Waikaremoana.

The only confusing thing was the fact that nouns are nominally male or female and have to be preceded by the appropriate definite or indefinite article. There didn't appear to be any logical pattern. Why were frogs and rats feminine? I worried that when in Chile I would forget that dogs, say, were masculine, and automatically emasculate them. Doubtless, if I used *Perra* instead of *Perro*, nobody would have the slightest idea what I was talking about.

I'd never had any interest in foreign languages, much less studied any of them, not even at school. The thing that most surprised me about learning Spanish—it was fun. Often the words themselves were fun. In Spanish the word for a live fish swimming around in the water is *pez*, but the word for a dead fish on your dinner plate is *pescado*, which roughly translates as *used to be a fish once but isn't anymore*. Spanish speakers, I realised, think more of fish than we do, simply because they have two words for the concept rather than our one. Suddenly I understood the restrictions that could be imposed on complex thought simply by limiting vocabulary. No wonder Orwell, in *1984*, placed so much emphasis on the power of the dictionary.

The Chilean dialect is even more fun than European equivalents because it incorporates delightful words and phrases from Quechuan, the language of the Incas. So instead of the Spanish word for baby—*bebé*—most of the locals prefer *guagua*, pronounced *wha-wha* in perfect sympathy with the mewing of a newborn child.

The tapes from the library offered invaluable insights into correct inflection and pronunciation. I quickly learned that there is no Spanish equivalent for the sound of the letter 'g'. In a word like *grande* (big) the 'g' gets minced up in the rolling of the 'r'. In a word like *guanaco* (a sort of wild llama) the 'g' sounds more like a 'wh'.

For correct sentence structure, phrase books proved to be better than tapes. As a bonus, most phrases had been carefully selected to be of practical value: 'What time does the train leave?' 'How much do apples cost?' 'Can I have another beer please?' 'Would you like to come back to my motel room?' That sort of thing. Some phrases, however, were completely baffling. *Es por causa de los impuestos* appeared in three different texts. It translates as 'it is because of the taxes'. Totally useless, except for parody. Julie and I married ourselves by conjuring up situations when you might be able to slip it into a conversation. 'Are you not feeling well?' *Es por causa de los impuestos.* 'You want me to go to your motel room?' *Es por causa de los impuestos.*

It did make me think, though, that it might be good to have an amusing but silly sentence at hand for whenever we couldn't understand what someone was saying to us—a sort of ice breaker. In the end I perfected a line I translated from Monty Python's Hungarian Phrase Book: *yo tengo un aerodeslizador lleno de anguilas*, 'my hovercraft is full of eels'. I loved that word for hovercraft.

Although I had spent a full two months studying Spanish intensively at home, by the time Julie and I boarded our Lan Chile plane in Tahiti, I still hadn't uttered a single word to a native. The hosties raised their eyebrows upon hearing our pidgin civilities, and I could almost hear them thinking 'Alas, more special-needs travellers'. As they directed us to our seats, they insisted upon speaking to us in perfect English. A bit of a let-down really.

A Chilean man sat next to us, at the window, reading the in-flight magazine. '¿Cómo estás?' he asked.

Good god! I understood what he said. It was like magic. The

whole language thing wasn't just a big practical joke after all. My relief was profound. I said excitedly 'Muy bien, gracias'. Very well, thankyou.

He continued speaking in Spanish. 'You are Australian, I can tell. Your accent is just terrible. I imagine that it would be better if I talked to you in English but I do not know anything other than *g'day mate*. Parlez-vous Français?'

That was about the only thing he could have said in French that I had the remotest chance of understanding. 'We will have to talk in Spanish,' I lamented.

'Fair enough.' He was very good humoured. 'Patricio,' he said by way of introduction, offering me his hand.

'Greg,' I returned.

Knots appeared in his brow. 'K-K-Kren?'

'Sorry.' I was apologising on behalf of the 'g' sound. 'Grrreeeg,' I reiterated.

He had another go. 'Wh-wh… Wh-reck?' The effort was so great that his mouth remained distorted long after the words had passed his lips.

'My friends call me La Trucha,' I offered.

'No, no.' He was shaking his head in amusement. 'Trucha is feminine. Your name would have to be… *El Trucho*.' He laughed out loud at his self-created word. And I laughed too, but only because I didn't know that over the next few months I was going to be forced to endure that snippet of comic invention an effing billion times.

He offered me a piece of fine Chilean chocolate, but I politely refused. 'I had a bad allergy a few days ago,' I explained. 'The doctor thought it may have been a reaction to chocolate.'

'What did the allergy do to you?' Patricio asked, politely ignoring the gratuitous bodily harm I'd been inflicting upon his language.

'Fluid retention,' I confided, exaggerating what had happened to my eyes and groin.

'Your allergy to chocolate makes your penis swell up?' He seemed incredulous, but then he added, somewhat wistfully 'I must be allergic to women'. After a good deal more idle chitchat, Patricio pulled two comic books from his briefcase. They were Disney classics by Carl Barks, reprinted in Spanish. 'You can keep them. I got them for Maria, my daughter, but heaven knows you need them more than she does.'

'¿Que?' I said, feeling a bit foolish, like Manuel in *Fawlty Towers*.

'I used comics when I was learning French,' Patricio explained. 'It is a fun thing to do. And there are enough prompts in the pictures to help you guess any words you don't recognise.'

The first comic I looked at was a story about Tío Rico. Uncle *Rich*? Was there no word in Spanish for Scrooge? Perhaps *A Christmas Carol* had never been translated into Spanish. Maybe the English had never been forgiven for the defeat of the Armada, and no writing from England, not even television scripts, could be made to appeal to Spanish-speaking audiences.

The single-word title of my Tío Rico story was unrecognisable to me, so I looked it up in my dictionary. *Lumberjack*.

'What are you laughing at?' Patricio asked.

By now I had convinced myself that a Spanish speaker wouldn't understand Monty Python. 'Yo tengo un aerodeslizador lleno de anguilas,' I said.

He glanced at the title of my comic book. A wave of comprehension washed over his face, and he broke into an animated Spanish rendition of the Pythons' *Lumberjack Song*.

We were high in the air now, and still laughing. The seatbelt sign had been switched off and the hosties were serving alcohol, offering a selection of Chilean and Australian beers. I asked for a beverage brewed in Santiago, one I had already sampled in Tahiti.

'I thought you would want a Fosters, Bruce,' Patricio said, re-enacting yet another Monty Python sketch.

'This is a better beer,' I explained, seriously this time.

'Expensive though,' Patricio lamented.

So I told him how much a similar sized can of Fosters would cost in Australia, and didn't even feel the need to exaggerate.

'That much! Why?'

'Es por causa de los impuestos,' I responded sagely, immediately precipitating an explosion of red wine from Julie's mouth all over the seat in front of her.

Archipelago

THERE WERE two places in Chile I desperately wanted to fish. One was the lakes district around Lago Llanquihue, the other was the stream country in the Chilean pampas, way down south. The cheapest way to travel between the two destinations was by cargo boat from Puerto Montt, through the archipelagos de los Chonos and de la Reina Adélaida, to Puerto Natales.

The ship welcomed economy travellers and was well known among backpackers. The night before we were due to sail, as we wandered about Puerto Montt's delightful quays buying freshly cooked seafoods from various colourful street vendors, Julie and I bumped into several people we had met earlier in our travels, including Janice, who was apparently enjoying a whirlwind tour of South American men, and Liat, an Israeli girl travelling alone. They too, were booked on the cargo ship, and we agreed to meet at the gangway on the morrow.

Next morning, as the four of us queued up beside our ship, we met four Canadians. Each was tall and blonde with bronzed skin, a pigmentation largely bestowed by the glare of the world's best ski fields. Olympic ski fields. They were dressed in identical clothing—black sports pants with blue-and-white Gore-Tex spray jackets. Such clothes, they explained, were gifts from the designer-clothing manufacturers that were sponsoring their effort to be the first people to cycle from Alaska to Tierra del Fuego. Oh, and they had just completed PhDs in physics, chemistry and molecular biology. 'We'll be travelling on the same boat with you,' Adrian, the tallest of the group, noted as he passed seductive glances over each of my female companions.

As they headed off to the end of the queue, Janice elbowed me in the ribs and whispered 'Just look at them, Trout. I can't make up my mind which one to go for—they're like a matching set'.

The cargo boat had no sleeping quarters for its paying passengers. All that was available was a single large room, above deck, which tripled as the kitchen, dining room and recreation area. At one end there were about fifty hard plastic chairs lined up in rows and bolted to the floor like those you might find in a country-hall picture theatre. Except there were no movies on offer. If you wanted to sleep, you simply found a place on the floor.

The good thing was the food. It was cooked for us by obliging all-male staff, and served three times a day for no extra cost above what we paid for the very cheap travel fares. It was invariably plentiful and delicious, and during the whole five days no recipe was served twice. There was also a counter where you could buy alcohol. This, I soon discovered, was how the ship really made its money.

Because of the lack of sleeping areas, drinking games carried on twenty-four hours a day. Adrian showed us a beauty. He got a beer glass, stretched a paper serviette across the rim and down the sides, tight as a drum, and held it in place with a rubber band. In the middle of the tissue he placed a one-peso coin. Then he took a big draw on his cigarette, an unfiltered Camel with enough tar to surface a highway, and burned a large hole in the tissue.

'Did you know that nine out of ten men who've tried Camels prefer women?' said Janice suggestively.

Adrian smiled at her. Winningly. 'Everyone gets a go at burning the serviette,' he explained. 'Your turn ends automatically if your cigarette breaks contact with the tissue. Other than that, you can burn as much as you like. But the person who makes the coin drop has to skol a beer.'

I thought it amazing that Olympians were smoking, but everyone was bored, and the Canadians were out for a good time and seemed determined to live by the adage 'When in Rome…'. I hate to admit it, but despite my first impressions they were genuinely good blokes.

As the game progressed, I became fascinated by how little tissue would hold up the coin. The penultimate burn would invariably leave the coin suspended by just two or three spider-web thin strands.

It was also fascinating how much drunkenness the game engendered.

Our never-ending drinking games were a major source of frustration for the kitchen staff because, after a few days of revelry, a mere wipe of the table and empty of the ashtrays was simply not going to be good enough. What was needed was the proverbial white tornado. They asked us, in polite Spanish, if we would leave the room for 'just an hour or so', but most people were too drunk or tired to be paying much attention.

One cold, grey afternoon, Sergio, the chef, who had been strolling around the deck looking over the side, suddenly ran back into our hovel, gesticulating wildly. '¡Ballenas! ¡Muchos ballenas!' Those of us who could understand Spanish were out of our chairs in a trice. 'Whales!' we relayed to the others.

Everyone raced outside and scoured the water. Close to the ship. Out towards the horizon. Nothing. Perhaps he meant dolphins. We hurried towards the bow. Nothing surfing the wash either. We made our way despondently back to the dining room. The doors were locked. Adrian knocked, and Sergio popped up in one of the door's glass panels, mop in hand, grinning victoriously.

So I had an enforced hour or two strolling around the deck, and this was when I discovered a private little retreat among a load of bagged-up onions, a sort of cave protected from winds where I could lay out a sleeping bag and get a good night's sleep. In fact you could probably squeeze two people in there snugly enough. It was the sort of sanctuary that would be coveted by everyone on board, so I only dared mention it to Julie, Liat and Janice.

I had just set up beds for Julie and myself when Janice approached me coyly and said 'Trout, I know that you found this spot but, well, you and Julie are single and, well, Adrian and I have been gagging for a bit of love-action and…' She was so funny and endearing, that I shrugged my shoulders and gave in. She kissed me with wild gratitude. Really kissed me, on the lips. Adrian was going to be in for the ride of his life.

That evening I sat alone at the bow of the ship, watching shadows of islands drift past in the cold moonlight that was being reflected from glaciers and icecaps. I was hankering for the end of the trip so that I could go and explore the streams of the pampas, and was so lost in thought that I was scarcely aware of the fact that someone had moved in beside me. It was only when I felt a head rest on my shoulder that I bothered to see who was there. The huge whites of those gorgeous eyes were unmistakeable. It was Liat.

'Trout,' she said uneasily, 'sometimes when you are travelling for a long time, you get sort of, you know, lonely.'

My discovery of a private space on board had clearly unleashed a wave of pent up frustration. Liat was aware that Janice and Adrian were snuggled up amongst the onions tonight, but she also knew that the nest would be free tomorrow, if I wanted. I put my arm around her shoulder.

'Trout, this probably sounds a little bold, but I like you, really like you, and trust you, and I really want to make love …' I was becoming somewhat aroused. '… with Adrian.' Then she burst into broken-hearted tears and buried herself into my chest.

Squiggle

THE PLANE trip we took from Punta Arenas back to Santiago started out as one of the most pleasurable I'd ever been on. It was full of excitable primary school kids, and the pilot, taking a course directly over the spine of the Andes, was enthusiastically pointing out the prominent geological features, tilting the wings one way then the other so that everyone on board was assured of good views. On the left were fjords bounded by rock surfaces that had been scraped bare by the rapidly retreating ice sheets; on the right were more durable icefields and glaciers. The pilot named them all, told little anecdotes about the heroics and stupidity of various explorers, and was clearly enjoying himself. He sounded like a sort of Spanish Attenborough—everything he said was accurate, insightful and very entertaining.

Things continued to go well until we approached Volcán Villarrica, which was still smoking dramatically after last year's eruption. The pilot, delighted by the eagerness of the kids, seemed to deviate towards the volcano. Was that allowed? No-one cared—we were being treated to a spectacular view of the crater. And then the plane plummeted.

'Trout, our plane's not plummeting, we just hit an air pocket, that's all.' Julie never did have much tolerance of my fear of flying.

'I've heard stories of plumes of volcanic ash clogging up jet engines…'

'Trout, we're nowhere near the smoke, okay?'

That was quite true, I realised, when I dared look through the window again. The plume was curling to the east, dissipating a hundred kilometres away from our flight path. 'The pilot has stopped his commentary,' I observed.

'The volcano was the last thing worth talking about.'

'The lights aren't working.' That stumped her. All the reading lamps had gone out. So too had the computer screen that had been plotting our course.

I heard one of the children behind me say 'Esto avión es malo', *this plane is bad*, and my palms became even more sweaty than before.

Julie offered no sympathy. 'For goodness sake, take this writing pad and go and play hangman with some of the children.'

I conceded to myself that I needed to do something as a distraction, so I hopped into the aisle in front of us and asked a group of impossibly cute kids if they wanted to play. Too right they did. But things ended up in a farce because they knew so many more Spanish words than I did. So I drew some random marks on a page— a cross, a circle, a wavy line, a couple of straight lines—then traced several copies and said 'This is an Australian game called…' What was the Spanish word for squiggle? I improvised by using the Spanish word for hieroglyphics, '… called Señor Jeroglíficos.' My audience was rapt. 'What happens is that everyone has to try to make a picture out of the, er, hieroglyphics, and when we're all finished we'll vote on who has drawn the best picture and the girl or boy with the most votes wins an Australian coin.' Amid much ooh-ing and aah-ing I displayed a handful of feather-tail gliders, frill-necked lizards, echidnas, lyrebirds and platypuses.

The game continued merrily for a long time, the kids laughing appreciatively every time I did voice impersonations of Bill Steamshovel and Blackboard. 'Hurry up, hurry up,' I grumbled melodramatically at the end of round eleven as everyone was handing in their efforts. 'What's this supposed to be?' I said, holding up a portrait of a bearded gargoyle with a grimace for a mouth and crosses where the eyes should be.

'That's you,' said little Isabella giggling impishly. 'You know, when the flight got bumpy and the lights went out.'

Rage against the machine

WE, MEANING the Parks and Wildlife Service, needed firewood at the Customs House, and, according to Calvin, the best place to get it was 'from that old bastard, Scarface'.

I couldn't raise Scarface on the phone, so I hopped in the car and drove around to his place. It was an undersized ripple-iron house, damp and decaying, perched on a small hill on the outskirts of town. I walked towards the front gate. The property was called *New Haven*, though clearly it was neither new nor a haven. The sign, a pre-routered specimen made from a knotty piece of treated pine, had most likely been bought from a discount store. I supposed it had been a better buy than *Lake View* or *Ponderosa*.

I glanced along the concrete path, which extended fifty metres or so uphill to a door which provided side-on access to a ramshackle lean-to, probably a laundry. There was a wild noise emanating from inside. 'Fark ya, ya farkin farkin *farkin* farker.' My hand rested nervously on the gate latch. Presently there was a wild metallic crash. Followed by more swearing, at higher pitch than before. 'Fark. Fark. Farkin' fark fark fark.' Another crash. A washing machine staggered drunkenly out of the backdoor like some crazed cubist Dalek. A man followed directly behind. He was holding a blockbuster. 'You farkin farker!' he screamed in an even more psychotic pitch, before applying the full force of his anger with a scythe-like sweep of his axe.

The Dalek lurched forward on its jittery casters, and began to move off down the path. Its attempted escape enraged the owner even more. I think he yelled 'You farkin farker!' again, or something like it, but by now his anger had scaled so many octaves that dogs would have been hard-pressed to understand what he was saying. Crash went the axe once more, into the other side this time, and the machine tottered off ever faster. Crash went the axe again.

It was the sort of surreal moment that your brain struggles to cope with, but I eventually summed things up. No doubt about it, there was a lunatic with an axe chasing a washing machine down the hill. Towards me. I did a quick about-face, hopped into my car and drove back to the office.

'No good trying to get any sense out of Scarface today, then,' Calvin agreed. 'You'll have to ring him up tomorrow.'

'What if he recognises me?'

'So what?' Calvin consoled. 'Anyway, I doubt he even knew you were there. When his anger's up, he sort of completely spaces-out.'

Fred agreed. 'I went round to his place once and found him delivering the last rites to his *farkin* lawn mower with a twelve-gauge shotgun.'

'He bought a brand-new chainsaw a couple of weeks ago,' Calvin added, 'and when the *farkin* bastard wouldn't start he doused it with petrol and set fire to the *farkin* thing.'

Eve of destruction

I LIKE people who abuse machines.

One day I went to see if Ric wanted to come fishing up the Gordon with Calvin and me, only to find him firmly ensconced in front of the telly watching video footage of last year's Bathurst motorcycle races. Nothing could persuade him to move.

Calvin and I ended up having one of our best ever trips. The sea trout were up on top, smashing whitebait on a scale I've never seen repeated anywhere. Afterwards we took every opportunity to rib Ric about what he'd missed out on, to shame him about what we were calling his addiction to the idiot box. This was a harsh assessment, really, when you consider that Ric only ever watched telly at Bathurst time. But it was enough to make him decide that he needed to kill his television. It was such a momentous occasion that he invited everyone around for a celebration—quite possibly the world's first bring-an-electrical-appliance-and-method-of-destruction party.

On the allotted Saturday afternoon, Fred rocked up with an old kitchen blender and a blockbuster. Other people came along with infuriatingly cheap-and-worthless power tools that they'd received as Christmas presents from well-meaning family members. There were toasters, too, even a washing machine. We knew things were starting to get out of hand when Calvin carried in a recalcitrant microwave oven and a charge of jelly. And when Scarface arrived with a whole ute-load of knick-knacks and enough armoury to outfit a small African nation, we knew it was time to leave and let the party take care of itself.

Ric and I ended up fishing the Henty River, and we stayed there casting away long after the fish had stopped moving, mainly because Ric was too nervous to go home. Finally, though, his curiosity got the better of him and at about midnight, with more than a little trepidation, we returned to his backyard. There were fragments of plastic and glass all over the place, but the worst seemed to be over. Soon we found ourselves standing with a bunch of mates, men and women, around a half-dead bonfire, drinking too much and telling ribald jokes. Some disposable cigarette lighters were thrown into the flames, someone yelled 'Stand back', and our circle ponderously expanded outwards. After a tense, protracted period of anticipation, the lighters exploded in quick succession. Laughter and censure followed in equal measure, until Fred burst through the circle and sat a beer bottle upright in the hottest coals.

'What ya doin?' one of the more accusatory voices asked.

'It's got an inch or so of petrol in it,' Fred explained enthusiastically.

The liquid bubbled, the circle expanded again, and after a time a jet of flame flew from the neck of the bottle, as glorious as a Roman candle.

Calvin shook his head sadly. 'Pussies,' he lamented, before walking off into the night.

The party was almost ready to disperse, when Calvin returned. He and a mate were lugging an open-topped twelve-gallon drum. 'A sight more petrol in here than in a beer bottle,' Calvin boasted. An inch, in fact.

I left the party immediately, and was half a kilometre away, almost home, when Calvin's device erupted. In the distance I saw a mushroom cloud of flame, and when the sound of the explosion dissipated, I heard laughter and applause.

Empire

'SCARFACE IS a bastard,' I said to Calvin, as we walked up the main street of Queenstown on Tasmania's West Coast. 'Always angry with the world, always picking fights, always just plain nasty to everyone.'

'I know why you hate him. I used to think the same way,' Calvin agreed. 'But I picked him in a fight once—when we were much younger and he insulted my girlfriend—and even though I put up a good show, he ended up beating me. You got to respect him for that. He's not as bad as he seems.'

This was a part of West Coast culture I never understood. Fighting was sometimes used to measure your character, and often as mere recreation, but generally no grudges were held afterwards. Mind you, you didn't *have* to be violent to be respected. Everyone was welcomed into the community as long as they were seen to pull their weight.

Calvin sensed my confusion. 'Scarface has had a tougher life than you know, Trout. Sure he's a bastard. We're all bastards. Given what he went through as a kid, most of us respect him just for surviving. He had this older cousin...'

Calvin stopped abruptly. We had just walked into the Empire Hotel. A circle of onlookers had formed in the middle of the room and inside the circle were two drunken men, yelling at each other, thrusting angry index fingers into one another's chests.

'Who's the other bloke,' I asked Calvin nervously, referring to the one that wasn't Scarface.

'That's him,' Calvin replied contemptuously. 'Scarface's cousin, Three-toe.'

'Three-toe? Chopped his foot with an axe or something did he?' This seemed to me to be a reasonable extrapolation given that the whole extended family seemed to wood-hook in their spare time.

'Nah. He's just a lazy useless prick, that's all. Moves so slowly it's a wonder he isn't covered in moss and algae.'

At that precise moment, as if to confirm Calvin's assessment, Three-toe failed to avoid a sloppy punch from Scarface, and toppled over backwards. Even his fall appeared to occur in slow motion, as if Three-toe's insipid presence had a soporific effect on gravity itself.

Suddenly Scarface was sitting on Three-toe's chest, pinning his arms to the floor with his knees, gripping the front of his shirt with his left fist, and punching his face with his right. Thump!… Thump!… Thump! Three-toe was offering no resistance, was quite possibly dead. Blood was streaming from his broken face. Then, just as Scarface pulled his fist right back and paused, like an archer preparing for a final shot at Olympic gold, the door of the pub swung open. A man rushed in. 'Three-toe! Is Three-toe here? His house is on fire!'

The tension in Scarface's spring-loaded arm instantly dissipated. He lifted his bulk from Three-toe's chest. Then he gripped his opponent's shirt collar with both hands and tried to lift him into a sitting position. 'Three-toe your house is on fire, your house is on fire, you've got to get up!' Scarface gave Three-toe a shake and then said desperately to everyone in the room 'He's fucked. Quick! Let's go get the fire engine before it's too late'.

There was a flurry of people running out of the pub. For a few surreal moments I had the feeling of being an extra in a Keystone Cops skit, and suddenly the barmaid and I were alone in the bar. Well, not quite alone. Three-toe was beginning to twitch and whimper. I didn't really know what to do, but it turned out that the barmaid was also a nurse.

A month or so later, Calvin and I were standing around with Ric and Jock in the same pub when Three-toe edged himself amongst us. Calvin pointedly stopped talking and walked off to the other end of the bar. 'You're looking better, Three-toe,' I said awkwardly.

'Yeah,' he agreed, 'better off than I was a few weeks ago. Don't know what I would of done if Scarface hadn't been round. Pretty much saved me house single-handed, he did. I owe him one. He's a good bloke, is Scarface.'

Later that evening, after Three-toe had drunk himself into oblivion and been propped up, snoring, in a discreet corner, Calvin rejoined us. 'What is it with you and Three-toe?' I asked.

'The bastard's a bigger bastard that you can imagine.' There was hatred in his voice. 'That's probably why Scarface bashed him up— payback for what Three-toe did to The Taxman when he was a kid.'

When I asked what it was that Three-toe did to The Taxman, Calvin intimated that some things were best forgotten 'if you ever can forget them'.

Three months later, I heard that Three-toe was in prison.

Sarah Island

MY DUTIES as a park ranger at Strahan included building boardwalks on Sarah Island, in Macquarie Harbour. I worked with Calvin and Fred for ten days at a time, camping in a small metal garden shed, savouring deprivations similar to those that Jock enjoyed up the Gordon River. We had the advantage of better fishing.

From August until December, migratory sea trout, as well as other wild brown trout that lived year-round in the harbour, could be seen smashing baitfish all about the island, and most were eager to attack lures or flies.

We were totally isolated. No communications equipment worked on Sarah Island. The cruise boats didn't call by. All we had was a fourteen-foot aluminium dinghy with a twenty-five horsepower outboard. This vessel certainly wasn't needed for day-to-day work duties, so I suppose the idea was that if someone was injured, we could transport them thirty kilometres across the oceanic expanse of Macquarie Harbour, all the way back to Strahan. As if.

By day eight or nine of any ten-day stint, our usually laudable work ethic would begin to weary, and then we'd commandeer the boat for recreation. One evening, after we had motored back to our small jetty and unloaded the dinghy, Calvin declared that we had broken our previous record. 'We've got eleven fish from two to five pounds.'

We were still buzzing with excitement as we walked back to camp. 'I guess it's curried trout for tea then,' Fred deduced triumphantly. We drank beer as we cooked, had some red wine with the meal, and for dessert I broke out a bottle of Scotch.

After a long night of jokes and laughter, Fred and I finally extracted ourselves from the campfire and headed off to the shed to find our sleeping bags. Calvin started to follow us inside then stopped and said 'I'd best go and scrape out the frying pan off the end of the jetty or else the possums will keep us awake all night'. Then he headed off into the jet blackness.

When Calvin returned he told us that while he was emptying the frypan, he could hear all these splashes around the shores of the island. 'I couldn't see anything in the dark, hardly knew where I was on the jetty, but I reckon there are some really big trout hammering whitebait right below our camp. I'm going to rig up a fly rod and have a go at them. You blokes going to come along?'

Fred was so incoherently drunk that he didn't offer so much as a grunt by way of reply. Even I felt a bit seedy. 'I think I'll have to take a raincheck,' I said weakly.

'Can I borrow some of your flies?'

'My box of wet flies is on the bench outside the door. I'd go for a luminous Glo-fly. Or a Cork.'

'You're a bunch of pussies,' Calvin chastised jovially as he went to rig up. I could hear him having trouble locating the fishing gear. After an age, I heard him bumble off towards the jetty. Then suddenly he was back, crawling into his sleeping bag.

'I thought you were fishing?'

'I am.'

I switched on a torch. Calvin was sitting up in his bed, a spinning rod in one hand and a stubby of beer in the other.

'Couldn't find your fly rod,' Calvin slurred, 'so I just got one of the trolling rods. Then I couldn't find the lure tin, so I tied on one of your Glo-flies. But the monofilament was way too thick to be able to cast a lightweight fly, so I just put some fish guts on the hook and started bait fishing. But it's pretty cold down there on the jetty so I figured I might as well fish from in here.'

I traced the monofilament with my torchlight. It went from the rod tip, out the door, across ten metres of flat ground beside the dying campfire, and disappeared over the edge of a small cliff. I was about to tell Calvin how dumb I thought he was when the line suddenly went taught.

'I've got one,' he yelled. He was more surprised than I was.

Calvin started reeling-in. I aimed the torch towards the cliff top expecting the line to snap before the fish reached the top. But no. Suddenly there was something big flip-flopping its way across the ground towards the shed.

'Fred, wake up!' Calvin screamed excitedly. But Fred was dead to the world. Calvin wound faster than ever, and the next thing I knew the fish was inside the shed. It was huge. And all over the place.

'Get that bloody great eel off my sleeping bag,' I yelled.

'I'll go and get a knife to… cut its head off with,' Calvin offered drunkenly, staggering out the door, leaving the eel behind, wound right up to the tip-guide, clattering the rod all round the room.

'Where *is* the fishing knife?' Calvin yelled from outside.

'Buggered if I know. Just get anything.'

There was a deafening roar, so loud that Fred woke up. And then Calvin was inside the metal shed chasing the eel about the floor with a chainsaw going full throttle.

'Calvin's gone mad!' I yelled to Fred, who was struggling to make sense of what was going on. Fred couldn't hear what I was saying— none of us could hear much at all for the next few hours actually, except for ringing in our ears—but he got out of there just the same. So did I.

From the safety of the campfire, things seemed less insane, especially once the eel had finally been despatched and the chainsaw switched off. The situation became amusing again when we started cleaning up. Funniest of all was the smell of burning eel flesh emanating from the chainsaw. And the slime on the sleeping bags, and the saw-cuts in the chipboard flooring.

I don't know what time it was when we finally went to sleep, but it was mid-morning before anyone woke up. Fred wandered off to check the mooring while Calvin and I started cooking breakfast. 'Hey,' he shouted angrily from the jetty 'some bastard's gone and scraped out the frypan all over the front seat of the boat'.

Sarah's recovery

THE PARKS and Wildlife warehouse was conveniently located just ten metres or so from the edge of the Strahan wharf. Calvin, Fred and I opened up the supply entrance and were surprised to find someone already hard at work. Calvin's brother, Genghis! (Real name Ian, a bit like Ivan; Ivan the Terrible, a bit like Genghis Khan.) How he got access to our workshop was anyone's guess. I should have confronted him about the breach of security, but there was a more pressing question to be asked. 'Genghis, why have you got Murrell's horn locked in the vice?'

He offered his explanation quite matter-of-factly, as if what he was doing was perfectly reasonable. 'You know that saying, as *stoned as a goat*, it got me thinking.' Then he took a big suck on the fat joint he was holding, put his lips within a centimetre of Murrell's nostrils, and exhaled a dense plume of smoke.

I don't know if you find this as shocking as I did. There were so many contradictions. Although the act itself was probably cruel, Genghis was a truly gentle man who loved animals, especially his goat. And, I have to say, Murrell seemed more relaxed than distressed. I think it was the juxtaposition of so many diametrically opposed emotions that I found hardest to cope with. The normal and the surreal; cruelty and love; humour and horror. The sort of mixed feelings that we have become more inured to since Quentin Tarantino confronted us with *Pulp Fiction*.

I don't know what a more decisive ranger would have done, but I was so overwhelmed that I ended up ignoring the situation. In my defence, I should point out that we had urgent work to do. There was a 'lighter', a sort of flat-tray trailer for a large fishing boat, moored outside, and we needed to have it fully loaded with building materials by mid-afternoon, before the contractor arrived to tow it thirty kilometres down the harbour to Sarah Island.

In addition to premix and cement, we had to transport a stack of concrete-forms—Formatubes. These were huge, heavy cardboard cylinders, four metres long, fifty centimetres in diameter. Later in the week we would set them up vertically on reclaimed land on the western end of the island, chainsaw them off to an appropriate height, fill them with concrete, and hey presto, we'd have a series of piers on which we could place the bearers of a new boardwalk.

We were on the lighter, stacking this unusual cargo, when a cruise boat, just back from a scenic tour of Macquarie Harbour, docked close by. A gaggle of older people, all pleasant folk in nice Sunday clothes, were soon being ushered down the gangway of their ship. Almost immediately, they began congregating on the wharf beside us. I acknowledged their presence with a polite tilt of my head, but kept on working, certain that if I gave them too much encouragement they would keep us talking for ages.

'What are those round tubey things for?' someone said loudly.

Calvin looked up at the group for a few moments, passed me a look of resignation, then turned back and said in hushed tones 'I'm not sure I'm supposed to tell anyone'.

'How come?'

Calvin sat down on the pile of premix and, charming the tourists with his Errol Flynn eyes, proceeded to light up a cigarette. Sensing that they were about to get a special insight into Parks management, the little group shuffled closer and waited respectfully.

'You will be aware that Sarah Island was a notorious penal settlement, a ship-building facility,' Calvin began, 'and that during the height of industry in the late 1820s the vegetation was completely cut down and consequently much of the topsoil eroded away.'

They nodded sagely, proud to have their newly gained expertise in local history so quickly acknowledged.

'What you probably don't know, because it's a top-level secret, is that before the convict era the island was inhabited by wombats. And not just any wombats, I might add, but a species totally unlike any other.'

'What did they look like?' one of the women gushed breathlessly.

Calvin replied so softly that the crowd had to totter even closer in order to hear. 'The long tail was the most prominent feature. It was so kangaroo-like that taxonomists are now wondering whether wombats will have to be reclassified from family Vombatidae to family Macropodidae.'

At this point Fred and I had to turn our backs to the audience lest we give the game away.

'For decades,' Calvin continued, 'zoologists weren't even sure that the species had really existed. There were cursory mentions in some of the Commandant's despatches, but there were no good descriptions, certainly nothing as definitive as a sketch. Which is why no-one knew about the tail. Then, eight years ago, someone from the University came down here and happened to notice some unusual pets grazing on a local bloke's fenced-in front lawn.'

'The Sarah Island wombats!' the ditsy woman deduced out loud.

'Indeed,' Calvin confirmed shrewdly. 'It turned out that this fellow's family had been breeding them, just a few at a time, for generations. The exact origins of the lineage are lost in the mists of time, but the point is we now have a once-in-a-generation chance to bring a completely unique species back from the very brink of extinction. After eight years of carefully managed captive breeding, the original group of two males and two females has grown to six males and ten females. And… can you keep a secret? If word of this gets out it will be more than my job's worth.'

Yes, yes—of course they could keep a secret.

'Well then,' said Calvin conspiratorially, 'we are going to re-introduce the wombat to Sarah Island this very week.'

Two of the group offered a little round of applause, providing sufficient noise to disguise Fred's involuntary snort of laughter.

'But there is a problem,' Calvin continued. 'Although the island has reforested and looks healthy, the soils are desperately thin. Dig down one inch and you're into solid rock. Wombats need burrows to protect themselves from the elements. And they simply won't have joeys if they don't feel secure.'

'So these are prefabricated wombat holes then,' the same dim-witted woman screeched, clapping her hands together with the excitement of it all.

'Last week the Sarah Island Wombat Recovery Program won the World Wildlife Fund's most prestigious conservation award,' Calvin continued. 'Not only that, but the designer of the program is here with us right now.' Calvin flourished his right arm in Fred's direction. 'Ladies and gentlemen—I give you Professor A. Elwin Board.'

Fred turned and gave a small gracious bow. Given that the introduction was so unexpected and outrageous, his acting was commendably convincing, but no-one was watching.

Murrell the goat had just staggered through the middle of Calvin's audience and fallen clean over the edge of the wharf. Then Genghis emerged from the workshop. Realising what had happened, he panicked, stripped down to his underpants, and jumped in after his beloved pet. I have never seen a man more genuinely concerned for the wellbeing of an animal; there is no doubt in my mind that, had it been necessary, he would have administered mouth-to-mouth resuscitation.

For the first time in his life, Calvin had been completely upstaged.

Budgie

AFTER I finished with the Parks and Wildlife Service, I was employed by the Inland Fisheries Commission at the historic trout hatchery known as the Salmon Ponds, on the banks of the Plenty River north of New Norfolk.

Budgie was a volunteer—a mate of a mate—who was on some sort of long-service leave, but wanted, he said, to spend some of his holidays giving something back to society. 'Self-imposed work orders, if you like.' I knew better than that. He was just another trout-obsessed bum who would do almost anything to spend time with the animal he loved best.

I was watching him through the small six-pane window in the south wall of the weatherboard trout hatchery. He was in the Round Pond, staring intently at the business end of a large trout-sized dip net. Another person—a giant tourist with a car-crash face—was studying his every move. 'Please God,' I thought, 'don't ask Budgie what he's doing.'

'What are you doing?' said the tourist.

Budgie stopped. 'This trout…' he said eventually, pointing to a distressed male brook trout with a deformed lower jaw, horribly twisted and locked permanently agape, '… is as ugly as you are, and it needs to be euthanased.'

I noted the tourist's response, the dangerous tightening of muscles in the bare arms and disfigured countenance. It was the aggressive pause of a dull man who feels he has been wronged, but can't quite work out why, or how.

The tourist was Scarface, but Budgie didn't know that—he remained blissfully ignorant of the very real danger he had put himself in.

Scarface's wife, Helen, looked away from her two small children, both blissfully ignorant of the tension between their father and the man with the net. She pierced Budgie with a well aimed look of disgust, tried to anyway, then took her husband by the shoulder. 'Look at little Sammy,' she said lightly, proudly, offering a distraction. 'He's run off to feed the albino trout again.'

The moment of danger passed.

Presently Budgie framed himself in the doorway of the hatchery, blocking out the winter light, cold and grey. He looked ancient, with wispy hair and tessellated skin—a body seemingly inlaid with grime. His neat clothes sat upon him uneasily.

Most dope smokers are open about their habit only when amongst the security of friends. Not Budgie. And it wasn't as if he considered me to be a fellow journeyman or anything. He was full of little acts of defiance; and not so little ones. He'd probably smoke in front of the Commissioner of Police. Little wonder that the building contractors Bram and Graham, who were helping with restoration work, so bitterly distrusted him.

Bush Inn

BEATRICE HAD been visiting Hobart and called in to see me on her way back to Strahan. She was in no real hurry to get back to Calvin, so we decided to have a counter lunch with Bram and Graham.

New Norfolk's Bush Inn is situated on the banks of the River Derwent, at the very head of the estuary. The town itself boasts a population of twenty-five thousand, and also that the pub is the oldest in Australia. If you include as one of the criteria for 'oldest' that the pub must have maintained continual operation, the second claim may even approximate the truth.

Beatrice seemed a little perturbed at the riffraff: log-truckers, people descended from inmates of the once horrific, now abandoned, psychiatric hospital. Unpleasant ghosts that seemed to seep out of a regrettable past. But the building contractors were completely relaxed as they sat on tall square stools at the bar. 'I'll have a burger with side-salad,' said Bram to a barmaid.

Graham, perhaps influenced by his time at Salmon Ponds, ordered farmed Ocean Trout. So did I.

'Can't believe you eat that stuff,' said Beatrice. 'Murder.' She went for chips and salad.

I suddenly wished I'd ordered a vegi burger.

'Did you know that the production of a farmed fish uses seven times its weight in mackerel?' Beatrice said conversationally. I was concerned that she was in danger of becoming as confrontational as Budgie. But I didn't say anything.

'Don't know about that, all I know is that fish is more natural and tastes a whole lot better than ultra-processed tofu,' said Graham defensively.

'Clever argument, that one,' Beatrice shot back.

'Christ, Cocky!' Bram usually called everyone on a building site *cock*. Since Beatrice was a girl, he had feminised the term especially for her. 'These trout are farmed in Macquarie Harbour, and that habitat was totally destroyed by mining operations in the early 1900s, so fish production there is hardly hurting the natural environment, is it?'

'Well they didn't stop farming on the...'

I was sick to death of people arguing. Glancing around the room for a distraction, I noticed a woman sitting at a round table near the window. 'Sammy!' she snapped at one of her kids, the one who was busily transferring a finger-load of snot into his mouth.

It was Scarface's family. Scarface himself was standing on the other side of the room, near a jukebox. He was with another man, of even rougher countenance, and it seemed to me that their conversation was also somewhat heated.

'Shit,' said Graham. 'Is that bloke you're looking at ugly or what.' But then another waitress appeared at the bar with the food, a pretty red-haired hippy chick wearing a red dress of billowing cheesecloth. A large ruby hung from a tasteful necklace and rested prominently against the softness of her low-plunging neckline. 'Thanks,' said Graham leering. 'What's your name?'

I half-expected her to slap him.

'Magenta,' she replied vaguely, before wandering off through the saloon doors to the kitchen out back.

'Imagine being snuggled up in bed with *that*.'

Bram looked at Graham in disgust.

'What would your wife think?' I said jovially.

Graham laughed. 'You can admire a picture without wanting it on your lounge room wall. You can admire women for contradictory reasons too. Magenta there is attractive because she's got red hair. My wife's attractive because she's blonde. Doesn't mean I think one is prettier than the other.'

I was faintly appalled by this analogy. Budgie, I realised, was always more profound. Once he said to me 'You can admire someone for being bold and independent, for knowing what they want for themselves and having the determination to achieve their personal goals. And you can admire someone else for being warm and vulnerable, for sticking with their family and best friends through thick and thin, illness and hardship, even at great personal cost'.

'When you choose a life-partner how do you get the balance just right,' Beatrice wondered out loud.

'Thinking you might've made a mistake with Calvin?' said Graham slyly. Was he making a pass at Beatrice now?

Beatrice went quiet.

'Why don't you try stopping stuffing-up other people's relationships,' said Bram venomously to Graham. 'Take that young girl you're shagging on the side, she's young enough to be your daughter. And what does her new husband think?'

I couldn't tell if Bram was disgusted or jealous.

'They have an open marriage. There are rules though. We're breaking them.'

Bram's tone changed. 'You ever been in love, Graham? I mean really in love?'

Graham's tone changed too. 'There was this girl in primary school, when I was eleven or so… puppy love, they called it, but it was so… My family moved to a new town. They didn't care how I felt. I never really got over it. Still think of her.'

'So you fantasise about an eleven-year-old girl. I reckon that makes you a paedophile.'

Graham took the comment for a conciliatory gesture, and grinned.

I felt for Graham. He, too, knew what it was like for adults to trivialise children's passions. Why should puppy love be somehow less intense than 'real' grown-up love simply because of its brevity? Surely the reverse is more likely to be true? Maybe things only last longer as we get older because we submit to expectations, subdue our passions. I looked back at Scarface's wife. She did it hard. And Scarface himself… Shit! He was now engaged in full-on hand-to-hand combat with the protagonist at the jukebox. They were rolling around on the floor. There was blood everywhere.

'Trout,' Beatrice whispered, 'Scarface has just bitten the other bloke's ear off…'

Bram heard her, but was unmoved.

'… and now he's just spat it out onto the floor!'

Bram casually forked another serve of chips into his mouth and steadfastly refused to look towards the action. 'What did you expect him to do, Cocky? Swallow it?'

Graham nodded casually at Beatrice, silently advising her to follow Bram's lead, to ignore the brawl, not to get herself involved, to pretend everything was perfectly normal, to understand that it was none of our business. Everyone ignored everyone in New Norfolk, I realised. Everyone refused to acknowledge the manual workers, the palsied, the desperately psychotic. And those who were perfectly normal. Like Sammy's mum.

I prodded my trout with a fork, but my appetite had vanished. Which was worse, I wondered, the way Budgie treated Scarface, or the way Bram and Graham treated Scarface? This second option, I had to admit, was exactly the same way I treated Scarface.

By the time we had finished our meal, the combatants had vanished, along with Mum and the kids and the detached ear. No police or staff had intervened. Things had just corrected themselves. I might actually have begun to doubt that the fight had happened at all, but the bloodstain on the floor near the jukebox assured me otherwise.

I realised that Bram and Graham would stay drinking for some hours yet, and invited Beatrice to come back to the Salmon Ponds with me. As we walked out into the foyer, Graham turned to Bram and I heard him say 'That girl's a weird one, isn't she? So's that other friend of Trout's. Cocky and Budgie—a couple of fuckin galahs if you ask me'.

'You don't know nothing,' said Bram, slurring his words. 'Budgies and cockatoos aren't galahs. Well, I s'pose galahs are a type of cockatoo. But budgies aren't. They're all parrots though…'

'Oh shut up,' said Graham.

Muldoon

I MET Muldoon on the Derwent estuary, at Lindisfarne Point, five minutes' walk along a little-used beach. Five minutes from the nearest escape route.

He was large—big-boned, like a Maori. He had dark skin, coloured more with grime than melanin; and a manic Einstein halo of hair, bleached white through some sort of accelerated aging process brought about, I guessed, by hard living or some ancient personal tragedy. His beard, too, was completely white—except for a patch of nicotine-yellow, about a cigarette butt in width, immediately below the centreline of his prominent strawberry nose. It dawned on me that his expansive facial hair was reminiscent of the Furry Freak Brothers, and I began laughing. On the inside, of course.

He was holding an old cane fly rod, a thing even more antiquated than himself. My first thought was that with such equipment he'd be unable to reach the sea trout that were hammering whitebait thirty metres offshore. Then I realised that he was perfectly unaware of the fish. *Then*, after observing him for a minute or so, I realised that he couldn't cast, that he'd probably never fished before in his life.

I panicked. This was the sort of 'harmless' nutter who'd follow you up and down the shore all morning like a hopeful stray. I tried to pretend that we'd not made eye contact, that I was scanning the water and hadn't noticed him.

He strode towards me.

He was shorter than me (sad, but true) and looked up with big rheumy eyes. I swear he was panting. 'You should use one of these,' he gasped by way of introduction, holding forth his fly rod. 'Those graphite things are nothing but crap—no soul.'

His conviction was almost religious. Why was he so keen to preach opinions that he himself had never tested? Suddenly I realised that he had my attention. Suddenly *he* realised that he had my attention. How did I let this happen?

He was a novice with rods, he admitted. What he usually did, for a living, was make bows: long bows, recurve bows, crossbows. He was passionate, obsessed; he scarcely drew breath. And those he did draw were emphysemic. I learned a lot that I didn't need to know. But also some stuff that interested me. Like the archer's paradox, which, it turned out, he'd completely misunderstood.

Within a minute or two he'd decided, entirely by himself, that we were friends, and that I could show him how to cast.

'Alright,' I conceded lamely. 'But never forget this: fishing is about much more than catching the biggest number of fish you can. It's not a mechanical exercise either. No matter how well you learn to cast, it is your feel for the environment, your hunger to explore new territory and to master difficult or unusual conditions, that makes fly fishing a lifelong joy.'

'You're obsessed,' he observed genially. 'A nutter, like me.'

'For the sort of trout fishing we do around here, a nine-foot rod is about the right compromise.'

He glanced dubiously at his seven-foot six-inch museum piece.

'The most obvious thing about a rod is that you use it like a throwing-stick.'

'You mean a *woomera*.'

'But,' I continued, doing my best to ignore him, 'there is another aspect of a rod's action: the flex of the tip. Do you remember flicking rubbers off rulers in the classroom when you were a kid?'

'Spit balls,' he admitted, and despite my worst intentions I smiled.

'Actually, see this?' He plucked a single-tooth plate from his mouth, and the odour almost bowled me over. 'Had it since I was a kid. Me brother accidentally shot an arrow into me front tooth. Lucky we was on a shootin range so he wasn't usin a huntin tip.'

As unlikely as the story seemed, I didn't bother challenging him. I did mention that modern dentists had learned how to construct bridges, but now it was his turn to ignore me. 'Me brother once flicked this very tooth from a ruler at the back of his grade-three class and it landed on the teacher's desk, splonk into her glass of drinkin water.'

'Christ,' I said, forgetting to feign disinterest.

'She wasn't in the room at the time, had gone out for a pee or somethin, and we was able to retrieve it before she come back. Which is how we discovered that her water wasn't water. It was gin, pure gin. And you can stop smirkin, this is a true story. Looking back, and considerin some of the dickheads in my class, she probably would've been better off with somethin stronger: whisky, vodka.'

I realised that I had been staring at his nicotine stain. 'Anyway,' I said quickly, 'you understand, then, that the flick of the ruler tip is enough to propel the rubber, or spit ball, or tooth: you don't need to use the ruler like a woomera.'

I laid fifteen metres of flyline along the beach, and held the rod straight out in front of my body at waist-height, at a right angle to the line. Then I gave the line a short, sharp tug. This caused the rod tip to flex, and when the rod straightened, it picked the line off the sand and sent it flying in the air until it laid out fifteen metres to my right. 'That's called a *haul*,' I explained. 'You'll have noticed that it was a respectable cast, yet I didn't swing the rod at all.'

'It's the same sort of effect that recurve has on a bow,' he observed. 'Here, I'll see if I can do it.'

'You won't be able to do it with that noodle you've got there,' I gloated. 'Think about the ruler and your spit balls: to flick things a long way, quickly and accurately, you need a stiff rod, not a soft one.'

'Actually, if you could design the perfect catapult,' he deduced excitedly, 'it'd have to be very stiff at the butt and less stiff, but not too soft, right at the end.'

At this point I realised that it was the mechanics of rulers, rods and bows that fascinated him, not the finesse of their use, much less the practical benefits they offered to the sportsman. 'And what you'd have then is a graphite rod, not a cane one,' I declared in cruel triumph.

But he didn't recognise my sarcasm, and because of his innocence I continued the lesson. I did a basic cast, using just the 'woomera' action, and repeated it several times in order to highlight the nuances of technique.

'Magic,' he enthused.

'You have to wait until the line has rolled out completely straight behind you before you begin the forward cast,' I cautioned. He watched as the line lifted swiftly and gracefully from the water and unrolled behind me, and he clapped.

'It's all about timing,' I boasted. 'Your turn now.'

His lift from the water was slow and apprehensive. The line took ages to tour through the air, and when it did travel behind him it ran out of oomph before it had time to straighten, much less flex the tip of his rod. 'Use my graphite stick,' I pleaded. 'It's stiffer. It will flick your line from the water quicker and take less time to load up on the back cast.'

But he persisted with his cane beast, and after fifteen minutes or so had actually managed some halfway reasonable casts.

'Now for the tooth-off-a-ruler effect,' I said dramatically. 'At the point I accelerate my line off the water, I'll do a haul, pulling my left hand—the one holding the line—from its position near the handle straight down to my knee. It is a bit counterintuitive but, like I showed you before, it has the effect of flexing the rod tip.' The line sizzled impressively through the air.

Inevitably, when the codger tried to haul, his cane rod proved to be too noodly. Not only was it painfully slow to flex, but since it bent from the very butt, it required enormous energy to fully 'load up'. And then, instead of giving a spritely flick, the tired old thing barely had enough grunt to straighten itself out.

'You need a lighter, stiffer rod,' I insisted impatiently.

He was clearly unimpressed.

'You don't need an expensive stick like I'm using,' I added defensively, 'but you do need something better than you've got. There are some really good intermediate-action rods on the market. They're cheap too.'

'I'm not gunna use that shit.'

'It doesn't have to be shit. Many newcomers make the mistake of thinking that cheaper, slightly soft rods are a silly compromise, but they couldn't be further from the truth. Super-fast rods require split-second timing. If you get your technique slightly wrong, the rod will be flexing forward long before you've completed your back cast, and your line will die mid-air in a tangle of waves and loops. Softer rods are much more forgiving. They also make it easier to play fish without breaking them off. I know there's an attraction, a status, in having the best, but it can be cold comfort—most anglers can never hope to be as good as the equipment they are using. It's like getting your learner's licence and straight away trying to drive a super-bike at top speed: unpleasant and dangerous, likely to result in misery.'

'I'm not going to use *any* graphite shit, fast action or intermediate action, stiff or soft.' He was calm, but firm. He was stroking his cane rod. 'This is a Hardy of England. The reason it's not nine-foot long is that it'd be too heavy. Even at seven-foot six, it probably weighs twice as much as the thing you're using...'

I couldn't believe it: he was justifying his gear even as he was listing more inadequacies.

'...and the reason the guides are so small is that this oiled-silk line is so thin.'

I hadn't really noticed that he had a silk line before—nobody's used them for decades. 'I reckon that's part of the problem,' I offered in a conciliatory tone. 'It's too light to flex your rod. PVC lines are much better: they are heavier, more evenly tapered, require much less maintenance and last longer.'

'This rod's got somethin that rod will never have,' the old man intoned, without rancour. 'It's got history, craftsmanship, devotion. It was hand-built out of living materials. So was the line. You youngsters ...' (it had been a long time since anyone called me that) '... want quick action, instant gratification. You should learn some affection for finesse and history.'

The things he accused me of not wanting were the things I treasure above all else. 'This rod,' I retaliated, 'has something yours doesn't have: the ability to cast a line, the ability to catch fish.'

'Thought you said that fishing's about more than catching fish?' he said softly. Then after a pregnant pause 'Anyway, name's Muldoon'. He offered me his hand.

I reluctantly gave him my hand in return. 'Smith. John Smith.'

Santa sack

I WAS visiting my mate Calvin on the West Coast of Tasmania when his daughter, Hayley, presented him with a wish-list and asked him to post it off to the North Pole.

Dear Santa.
If you can a ford it id really like a new fishing reel. Pleese. My old wun is rusty and wont work properly. If you carnt a ford to give me a new reel becorse all the starving children in africa need cloths, thats alright. a small surprise will be fine
Thanx
Yore bigest fan
Hayley.

Calvin was aghast. 'Daughter, daughter,' he admonished, passing me a sly wink. 'You don't know nothing about how to get ahead in life. Why stop at one measly reel? You need lures too, don't you? And a new polar fleece?'

'That's just greedy...'

'Rubbish,' Calvin interjected. 'Santa's got loads of stuff in his workshop, *loads* of it. I'm going to ask him for a new pair of neoprene waders, a Lamson fly reel, and a new flyline...'

'Dad, you can't do that!' Her voice was filled with disbelief.

'... and a bum bag and some Gink and a holiday to the Top End and a nine-weight Sage fly rod to fish for golden trevally while I'm on the holiday...'

'Dad, no!' Disbelief had turned into alarm. 'Santa won't come to anyone in our family if he thinks we're all greedy and horrible!'

On Christmas Eve, just before bedtime, Hayley went to the Christmas tree and noted reverently, for the hundredth time, how beautiful it was. Underneath, she placed a platter decorated with smoked salmon, King Island blue cheese, chilli olives and water crackers, prepared with Mum's help. Also some white Christmas, made lovingly by Hayley for Santa with no help from anyone. And dubiously, upon the recommendation of her dad, a bottle of Lefroy Irish whiskey. Her note, written in glo-pen with hearts above the I's where dots should be, said sincerely:

Deerest Santa
I know you will be hungry after fliing so far in your slay so I hope you enjoy this food
pleese give the carits to the raindeers
lots of love Hayley
ooooXXXXXX

She had chosen her Santa sack herself: a linen pillowcase from a small camping pillow, originally white but specially tie-dyed in festive reds and greens. Mum laid out one too. And there was a tiny stocking for the family puppy.

Calvin was still in the kitchen preparing platters of cold meat for Christmas breakfast. 'Dad, come and lay out your sack before I go to bed,' Hayley implored.

Next thing, Calvin appeared in the doorway proudly displaying nothing less than a king-sized doona cover.

'Dad, no!'

But Dad did.

An hour after Hayley had gone to bed, she still couldn't sleep She called out for her Mum, and I heard her say groggily 'Pat me Mummy, pat me'.

Next morning, when I went around to share Christmas lunch, Hayley was beside herself with excitement and gratitude, Santa having given her treasures beyond her wildest dreams. Mum had been well rewarded too, with several novels and CDs. Even the dog had a big marrow bone and a packet of liver treats.

'How about Dad?' I asked.

At this Hayley laughed so hard that red cordial snorted out her nose. 'Look, look,' she said excitedly, leading me over to the Christmas tree where the dog was chewing something gross.

'It's a shrivelled-up fish head,' Hayley explained joyously. 'Dad got a maggoty fish head from Santa. Nothing else at all just a fish head! A *fish head!*'

Mathinna

CALVIN WAS visiting me at the Salmon Ponds. There's this great new barmaid at Strahan, he said. Her name's Magenta. She's a really nice hippy chick. A bit weird. She always wears red, makes red jewellery for a living, and she changed her name by deed poll. But she's great fun. Beatrice and her get on like a house on fire. You'll have to meet her.'

'You know, I think I might have met her at the Bush Inn not so long ago,' I said.

'We should go for a fish on the Derwent. That beach at Lindisfarne was great. Remember?'

'Bugger that,' I replied. 'There's this nutter there all the time—Muldoon he calls himself. Mouldy, I call him—but not to his face. Every time I go there, there he is. I feel like I'm being stalked. Tell you what, Lester and I are going to the South Esk. Why don't you come with us?'

Lester is one of my favourite people in the world, a former boilermaker-welder who became a nurse and is now managing

Community Health in northern Tasmania.

The South Esk was a big drive away from home, two hours at least. At 204 kilometres, it's the longest river in Tasmania, but it runs through flat pasture and carries relatively little water. That was the problem. Flows were very low, and even in the fast-water stretches at Avoca and Fingal, the blistering sun had warmed the water to the point where, unusually, the fish were reluctant to rise.

'Best go further upstream into the forested foothills where there's some shade,' I suggested. 'We can camp near the Evercreech Forest Reserve.'

The Evercreech valley is famous for its remarkable forest where the white gums, *Eucalyptus viminalis*, reach ninety metres or more, by far the tallest examples of the species anywhere; bigger in fact than the famous Tall Trees, *Eucalyptus regnans,* in the Styx Valley.

Straight after setting up camp, we drove further up the South Esk valley, through the hamlet of Mathinna. Things remained hot and slow, including the locals themselves, who could be seen leaning over fences, beers in hand, talking to one another, or sitting in the shade of rotting verandahs. Calvin pointed out a grimy bloke whose belly, only partially covered with a dirty blue singlet, overhung his tattered jeans like an apron. He was nattering to a woman with tree-trunk legs and a toothless laugh. 'Mathinner, be damned,' he said. 'Mafatter, more like it.'

'At least they're happy,' Lester chided.

Which was more than could be said for the girl after whom the town was named.

Mathinna's parents were captured by George Augustus Robinson on Tasmania's west coast in 1833. Their daughter was born in a purpose-built Aboriginal settlement on Flinders Island in 1835, yet by 1841 she was living at Government House with Sir John and Lady Jane Franklin. Lady Jane doted on her. There is an iconic portrait, painted by Thomas Bock in 1842, of an angelic girl in a red dress. And some delightful excerpts from letters written to her biological father. Yet in 1843, at eight years of age, the Franklins sent her to an orphan school, and abandoned her completely a short time later when they returned to Europe. She was returned to Flinders Island in 1844. Went back to the orphan school in 1847. Moved on to the Oyster Cove Aboriginal settlement in 1851. Died in 1856, at twenty-one years of age, lost in the void between cultures. She was leaving a white settler's cottage—drunk—and drowned in a puddle.

Hootiner

ALONG THE shore of Lake King William, partway back to camp, amid the thick black mud which accumulates on the flats, I noticed an ancient flint. Not just a flake, a whole tool. I looked at the magnificent trout I'd just killed, its right gill-cover flared around the crook of my left index finger. A short while ago its dorsal fin had been slicing through the skin of the lake in water centimetres deep. It had been hunting snails and water slaters; and I had been hunting it. I visualised my prey roasting on camp coals, could almost taste it.

Tasmanian Aboriginals had a word for fish, *breona*, and I drove through a shack-town by that name on my way here from Deloraine. Breona, north of Miena, which means lake. Great Lake.

Strangely enough, Tasmanian Aboriginals didn't eat fish, none at all; not from rivers and lakes, not even from the coast. Well, they ate abalone and crayfish, but not real fish, not for the last 4000 years anyway. We don't know why. We understand precious little about any of them.

Consider William Lanney. Born 1835, died 1869 aged 34. I can tell you virtually everything else that is known about him in just two paragraphs...

The year of his birth was also the year his family was rounded up at Cape Grim. They were among the last to be taken to the purpose-built 'Aboriginal settlement' on Flinders Island. He spent his whole childhood in Aboriginal settlements, first on Flinders, then at Oyster Cove south of Hobart. Later he became a sailor—his native-keen eyesight proved invaluable for spotting whales. Finally he ended up with the bleak distinction of having outlived all other tribally born men. The colonists called him King Billy. Reverence or mockery, I wonder. In any case, his death, of an undocumented illness, was a slow one. I can't begin to imagine his loneliness.

The night he died, his head was severed and stolen. By people unknown. The authorities then removed his hands and feet to make the rest of the body worthless to other would-be souvenir hunters. He was hastily buried in a Hobart cemetery. And unearthed that very night. By people unknown. His remains have never been recovered.

I learned in primary school that Lake King William was named in honour of William Lanney. But did the King Billy of the north-west coast really have much to do with the land beneath this hydro impoundment on the Central Plateau?

Recently I discovered that the lake was not named after Lanney after all, but for William IV, King of England from 1830 until 1837. Guess who bestowed the name?

In 1842, Governor Sir John Franklin and Lady Jane Franklin embarked on a tour from Hobart past the rural districts of Ouse and Lake St Clair, through the untracked wilds of 'Transylvania', all the way to the west coast. Almost untracked, anyway. With limited time at his disposal, Surveyor Calder had only managed to mark a crude route in preparation. The Franklins took some friends, some convicts as porters, and some police to control the convicts. And it was this group that named 'King William's Mount' and 'King William Plains'.

You do remember Lady Jane, don't you? And her pet, Mathinna?

I was bitterly disappointed to learn the truth about Lake King William. As disappointed as I was when, aged ten, I found out that Triabunna, the town in which I went to school, wasn't named by Aboriginal people, but rather by the Nomenclature Board. Apparently it was an Aboriginal word though, for *native hen*, which, at least, explained the otherwise unaccountable school emblem.

Most Aboriginal placenames in Tasmania are similarly descriptive, and similarly not the actual names of those places used by Indigenous people. Oh well, at least the progressives, people like Ling Roth, tried. They tried all over the place—look at the towns and lakes most familiar to us Central Plateau anglers:

Liawenee (pronounced liar.**wee**.nee), meaning cold water;

Tungatinah (tun.gah.**tee**.nah), light rain;

Waddamana (wad.dah.**mah**.nah), big river;

Liapootah (liar.**poo**.tah), little river;

Wayatinah (way.at.**tee**.nah), rivulet.

Water, it seems, featured prominently in the life of a Tasmanian Aborigine. As it does in mine.

Those of us who like to write, even if we don't write as well as we'd like, take on language as a mistress. We cherish it; try our best to nurture it. I researched Aboriginal language while documenting the nomenclature of the Western Lakes for a trout fishery management plan. I was shocked at how little remains. All we have left are lists of disembodied words without syntax or context, grammar or nuance.

And hardly any of this was recorded prior to the hybridisation of languages which followed colonisation.

The French, led by Marion du Fresne, made contact with natives in 1772, but recorded none of the local languages. They did, however, take an Aborigine's life. Captain Cook, in 1777, proved to be a better diplomat, and his surgeon even jotted down a few words. But it fell to Frenchman Bruni D'Entrecasteaux, in 1792 and 1793, to make the first detailed records, with further contributions by Nicolas Baudin's expedition aboard the *Géographe* and *Naturaliste* in 1802, also in French.

All other language was recorded after first colonial settlements had been established near Hobart in 1803, and Launceston in 1804. *Most* of what we know was documented by George Augustus Robinson, during the period from 1829 to 1834, when he was bringing natives into captivity. Joseph Milligan, who was surgeon-superintendent at the Flinders Island settlement, also recorded a significant amount. But there is precious little else.

The paucity of documented language was exacerbated because mortality on Flinders Island was atrociously high. By 1847, when the settlement was relocated to Oyster Cove, south of Hobart, only about 35 adults and a few children remained.

Because the Aborigines had no written language, what we know was imperfectly recorded in French and English. The spelling in use today is more or less phonetic, and, because notes were often taken in an ad-hoc way, single record-takers were likely to use different spellings for the same word.

The Aboriginal word *hootener* means pademelon, or rufous wallaby, and is almost certainly synonymous with *hootiner*, which means fart. Between the ages of eight and fifteen, I used to shoot and snare pademelons for food. I used to call them stinkies. It seems that I have a lot in common with the first Tasmanians.

How about *Lina* and *Leenher*? The first means crow, the second arsehole. Think of the dark sentiments Tolkien ascribed to ravens in *The Lord of the Rings*, Poe in *The Raven*, Shakespeare in *Macbeth*. Think about what ravens have meant to numerous authors from numerous cultures. We all have a lot in common with the first Tasmanians.

Of course, I accept that I should be careful in my extrapolations. Brian Plomley, who meticulously catalogued most of the words in the historical records, found at least fifteen words for vagina and not one that distinguished bettongs from potoroos. Is this a reflection of the priorities of hunter-gatherers, or the preoccupations of forlorn European sailors?

Another problem arises in that some words appear to be strangely similar to Latin, *lutana* for moon; and *penna* for man, penis and wood being but two examples. This is hardly surprising. The usual thing amongst travellers is to improvise, to instantly adopt any mutually understood word, so that even in a first conversation a sort of lingua franca begins to develop. By all accounts, Tasmanians were exceptionally friendly, so we can assume they tried their best to accommodate. And in so doing, I suppose they assisted in the demise of their vernacular.

I tried, in a children's book I was writing, to take the placenames off sign posts and give them some new life. It seemed like a fun idea at the time: a child who buzzed around incessantly could be called Redpa, which means mosquito; the witch could be Namma, which means, well, witch, and so on. An Anglo-Saxon reviewer at the Tasmanian Writers Centre criticised me harshly: I was not an Indigenous Tasmanian; this was not my language; I was not free to interpret it; did I have no respect? Did I not know that I had to seek permission to write the words *Liawenee, Miena, Triabunna*? Later, when her anger had subsided, she said 'Ciao' and hung up.

I examined the fish. Looked at the lake.

Why do people of mixed blood tend to empathise more with the subjugated part of their ancestry than the bit that's genetically dominant? Why do leftie bleeding-heart fly fishers like myself empathise so much with dying culture? Is it because we understand what is being lost? That we know that with every speck of humanity forsaken, a little bit of each of us dies?

I recalled Budgie speaking desperately of his need to convey what it was that he found important about life: nature and culture. And of the futility of trying. It is hardly surprising. Lots of knowledge can't be written in English. Mathematics, for example. And music. We need, and use, different languages to record such things. What would happen if we were at risk of losing those two languages, completely and utterly? Would we stand idly by and allow it to happen? Do people really believe that alternative languages are merely collections of alternative words?

But if English cannot describe the Tasmanian landscape, nor

describe what it means to have your spirit embedded in this land, what language could do the job? William Lanney's?

I looked towards the south-west, towards the mountains of the King William Range. Immovable, timeless, primal. I have ventured up there many times in the past—to fish remote headwaters—and rested in the shade of the King Billy pine, an endemic tree revered for its grandeur and beauty. Like William Lanney's people, this species was also hounded to the brink of extinction. Craftsmen, me included, simply could not get enough of the sublime rot-resistant timber. Yet on the cold windswept shores of lakes Rufus, George and Richmond, I've found relicts: tough, gnarly, stubborn things that simply will not submit. They are survivors, like the Tasmanians themselves, and the Tasmanians' land.

Yet even the origins of the name 'King Billy pine' are uncertain. In *Forest Trees of Australia*, the CSIRO notes that the name is '... believed to be either after the mountains near where this species occurs or in honour of the "King" of the Tasmanian Aborigines'.

I studied the rippling image of the mountains on the surface of Lake King William. Everything seemed distorted. Can things survive when they have been flooded and subdued? I looked at the trout I'd caught and, notwithstanding the Aborigines' taboo, I felt that fishing had brought me to the cusp of understanding William Lanney's loss. After all, I am a hunter—the land, the water, the wildlife bind me to this world like nothing else.

I used to rejoice whenever my land was protected from desecration by being included in national parks. Such reserves were originally conceived as places for people to commune with wild things. But now, the emphasis is on not interacting with anything. Even here, just outside of the park boundaries, my relationship with the land is shrouded with the uncertainty of economic rationalism, privatisation and litigation. A quick look at the Hydro website casts doubt on the legality of everything, from campfires to camping per se.

When people take my land away, bury it beneath tar and concrete, forbid me access to it, claim that my fishing is barbaric, I feel myself drowning in storms of loneliness and despair. Have I stumbled upon the essence of dispossession? How would William Lanney, his father or grandfather, have felt to stand here beside me at Lake King William? Would they have howled 'Disrespect!' when I titled this story *Hootiner*? I like to think that they would have howled in

laughter. Like Calvin and his daughter Hayley, who would have loved
to have given each of them a Fart Lighting Kit.

I stood there absorbing the mana of millennia, feeling a passion
that I know is being progressively suffocated by modern
technological society. I realised nothing could be taken for granted.
Not forty thousand years of culture, certainly not a few centuries of
fly fishing.

Lord Franklin

As I was walking back to my car, I found myself thinking about Sir
John, the man who named the plains beneath Lake King William then
left Tasmania for the Arctic Circle in search of the fabled Northwest
Passage. He, along with his ship and entire crew, went missing
without trace, lost in the endless Arctic ice. Lady Jane spent all her
fortune and all her years searching for her husband. In vain. Long
after her death, two of Sir John's campsites were discovered. Nothing
more has been found since.

I turned on the car radio. Sinéad O'Connor was singing a
traditional ballad, Lord Franklin. The coincidence was not nearly as
overwhelming as Sinéad's voice. It was filled with Lady Jane's grief.
Suddenly, so was I.

A gutsy Irish singer singing about a gutsy Englishwoman who
one-and-a-half centuries ago visited the Antipodes, adopted and
abandoned a gutsy little Tasmanian girl, and named the lake I'd only
just left. And the name she chose stands testimony to the confusion
surrounding Aboriginal history, my history, the nuances of language
and fate.

Yamame

MARK WAS a physio, a dedicated one. Too dedicated. I first met him through Frances, my long-time partner, who got to know him through her work as an occupational therapist. Lester introduced me to him again soon after that—he had got to know him through his work as a nurse. Danny, a GP friend, introduced me to him yet again. You'd be surprised how many health professionals turn out to be fly fishers. Dedicated ones.

Like the majority of hands-on staff everywhere in every profession, Mark was driven by passion and compassion, not by money, status or power. Although he was bloody good at what he did, he never much liked working in the acute hospital setting. He knew he was helping his patients while they were incapacitated, but what happened when they disappeared back into the community? Without proper follow-up it was possible, even likely, that all the benefits of his work would start to unravel. He also disliked the restrictive, unhelpful, soulless protocols on interacting with patients. The absence of feedback, and perhaps kudos, slowly burned him out. One day, out of the blue, he told me he was going.

'Going where?'

'Doesn't matter. Anywhere I don't have to be a physio.'

'Anywhere' turned out to be Japan. A friend of a friend—a native Japanese landscape painter—invited him to stay for a while on a hallowed property in the rainforested headwaters of the Shinano catchment amid the precipitous mountains behind Niigata. Over the phone, the ever-so-polite artist assured Mark, in staccato English, that he could be easily accommodated in a temporarily unoccupied single-storey building. 'It has three rooms, separated by sliding rice-paper screens. It is decorated with delicate scrolls and flower arrangements, and heated by a fire pot, an earthenware hibachi. The floors are covered in tatami straw matting. There are silk cushions on which to sit and eat. And at night, when it comes time for sleep, you can spread out quilts on the floor.'

Mark was aware that traditional Japanese architecture emphasised harmony with nature. Nonetheless, the exquisite beauty of his little bungalow surprised him. The framing, the wooden posts and beams, had been collected locally decades beforehand and had never been painted. It seemed to him that the trees' souls had been treated so tenderly that they scarcely noticed they had been cut down; they merely rolled over in their sleep and continued living, sleepily sinking new roots into familiar soils and once again submitting themselves to the caresses of mosses and lichens.

On one side of the house a clearwater stream burbled ancient arias. On the other, there was a small temple or shrine. He wondered if it was some sort of family mausoleum, even fancied that he should have learned more Japanese so he could ask his hosts about it. The language barrier, he lamented to himself, was already forcing him to be reclusive. But then, he rationalised, wasn't that the whole point of running away from home in the first place? If it wasn't for the mystery of language and culture, might not this land quickly become as over-familiar as Tasmania or New Zealand? Temperate rainforests all felt pretty much the same after all.

The stream proved to be alive with small iwana, Japanese char, most of which ranged from ten to twelve inches and were happy to scoff dry flies. Rarer and more exciting were the yamame—river-resident cherry salmon. Most of these were from twelve to fourteen inches, a little over one pound, but even the bigger ones in neighbouring streams, some of which weighed up to three pounds, never displayed the sober colours and patterning of mature trout and salmon elsewhere in the world. Instead they clung to their childhood and wore their parr markings with dazzling petulance. Mark wondered if there was a Japanese equivalent to Peter Pan. He hoped there was. If there wasn't, perhaps he himself, along with the yamame, might help fill the void. Here in this ancient, mystical, timeless, sacred place, anything seemed possible.

One day, late in March, he was invited to share a meal with the family in the main house. Here he met Sakura, an impossibly beautiful oriental girl with dark skin that betrayed a liaison between her great, great grandmother and a sailor, a fisherman.

A large percentage of Marks's scant Japanese had been gleaned from fly fishing literature, and in order to open a conversation he noted, imperfectly, that her name reminded him of *sakuramasu*—the migratory strain of the cherry salmon—which would soon be running from the Sea of Japan to spawn in the Shinano.

'The first part of the word *sakuramasu*—sakura, my name—is a celebration of the fact that the salmon, *masu* or *masou*, spawn when the cherry trees bloom.' Sakura's reply was in English. Very accomplished, very cosmopolitan.

Mark wanted his Japanese to impress her as much as her English impressed him, but to his frustration and embarrassment he couldn't even muster up enough words to say 'When will the flowering happen?' He realised, too late, that he was sitting open-mouthed like an imbecile.

'Perhaps you will feel more comfortable if, just for now, you talk in English. No-one will be offended. We can work on improving your Japanese later on.' Her voice was soft and inviting, and she continued chatting in a sing-song manner that relieved him of the immediate need to justify himself. 'The first cherry blossoms have just appeared in Kyushu, the southernmost of Japan's four main islands. Trees growing further north in the colder latitudes flower progressively later. We call this progression the *sakura-zensen*—the cherry-blossom front—but it is more like a welcome zephyr than, what is the English word, a *depression*?'

Mark was still lost for words.

'The *sakura-zensen* will drift slowly northward,' Sakura continued. She seemed to be distracted, as if she was actually watching the advance of the flowers, as if the anticipation itself was a religious experience. 'It will arrive at Niigata in two or three weeks' time, and linger for just one or two days, a week at most if there is no wind or rain. Then it will continue through Hokkaido, the northernmost island, and no more than forty days after it began, it will run out of land and trees and dissolve in the cold desolation of the Sea of Okhotsk.'

Still nothing from Mark.

Sakura broke out of her little trance. 'The *hanami*, or flower viewing, is a time of renewal and hope. But it is brief. If you are too busy, or preoccupied, the opportunity will pass you by.'

'Beautiful sentiments,' Mark managed at last, albeit somewhat clumsily, even though he was talking in English.

She smiled enigmatically.

Midday, two weeks later, as Mark lay sloth-like beneath his quilt, recovering from a night drinking sake with the gardener, there was a gentle tap at the door, and a panel slid open. Through one gummy eye, he fancied he saw Sakura silhouetted in the low spring-time sun, but surely no-one in Japan, least of all a girl he had met just once, would wander unannounced into his bedroom.

'The *sakura-zensen* will arrive tomorrow,' the figure said sweetly.

It was Sakura's voice all right. Mark sat bolt-upright, and used the back of his hand to sweep sweaty hair from his forehead. How slovenly must he seem? He self-consciously wiped the sleep from his eyes, and was both relieved and disappointed to find that the girl had vanished.

He finally found Sakura reading quietly in the main house. She smiled. She did a lot of that. They drove down to the city together, to the park. Hectares of lawn were covered in small picnic blankets, many in soft blue or cherry pink, so tight together that they appeared to be stitched at the seams, snug like a quilt.

'Where are all the people?' Mark asked.

'They will come tomorrow, when the trees blossom.'

'And their blankets won't be stolen overnight? Their carefully selected picnic sites won't be violated, purloined?' They weren't the right words. Were there any right words? Every synonym he could muster seemed too barbaric or absurd, a betrayal of Western expectations, a slander of his culture.

Once again she came to his rescue. 'The Shinto religion does not place overly much importance on the afterlife. In Japan, we strive to achieve perfect harmony in the present. While we are on earth, this life—the one we are living right now—is one to revere and celebrate.'

Mark, who had not yet completely shaken off his depression, thought about the atrocities Japan committed in World War II and wondered how they might fit into Sakura's romantic view of the world. Then he thought of the bombs dropped on Hiroshima and Nagasaki—as he saw it, the two most barbaric acts of terrorism ever committed by anyone anywhere—and decided that the West had no plausible claim to moral superiority. He said nothing.

'Tomorrow the park will be filled with lovers, lovers of all things good in life. Some will marry. The brides will wear white dresses in the Christian style, a good choice I think, because of all the Western traditions your weddings are the most beautiful. Perhaps tomorrow's bridesmaids will wear apricot, in anticipation of the next blossom front not far away.'

'Why marry?' Mark asked. 'It's just one more step towards death.' Straight away he wished he hadn't said it.

She turned her eyes downwards. 'We celebrate death in the

'Buddhist fashion.' There was no way of telling what she meant.

They searched in strained silence for a patch of unclaimed grass. Sakura didn't have a picnic blanket, just a small roll of cherry-coloured tape and four plastic pegs. As they staked out their claim, Mark finally thought of something he could say. 'Your name still reminds me of cherry salmon.' He paused and then added, in exactly the same pidgin he'd used on the night he met her '... which will soon be running from the Sea of Japan to spawn in the Shinano'. She laughed, and kissed him on the cheek.

Later in the evening, Mark led Sakura down to the stream beside his bungalow so he could show her how to catch iwana on dry flies. Instead, they ended up catching several yamame, the first time he had seen more than one taken in a session.

In the morning, they went back to the park. As Sakura had promised, the cherry had blossomed, the pink petals perfect replicas of the parr markings on the salmon they had released the night before. They chatted to neighbours. They sipped sake. They watched lovers get married. That night, Sakura shared Mark's quilt in the house of living poles and rice paper.

Two weeks later, Mark found himself cold and alone in British Colombia.

Minus Thirty

IN BRITISH Columbia's Interior Plateau, Mark stayed a while with an old mate, Murphy. Murphy's hometown was home to just a few hundred people. It was so small that it had no medical staff, not since the local GP died in a car accident, anyway.

For several weeks, Mark stayed with Murphy and his dad. He went to the pub, was invited to parties and evening meals. When people prised his background out of him, they either fished with him, cooked for him, or asked his opinion on medical matters. Sometimes they did all three. Despite some initial reluctance, he found himself doing little physio-type things. He organised a walking frame for Jim the barman's grandfather, and massaged the pain from dear old Jenny Sumallo's back. He could see that the small services he offered had a big impact on people's day-to-day lives. The locals appreciated him. He appreciated being appreciated.

One of the most amazing characters he met was Bela, a seventy-year-old bushman. Every day, Bela went out fly fishing, and he was always eager for Mark to come along. They walked together along well-formed trails through forests of spruce to remote little lakes where they used dry flies to catch cutthroats and stunted bull trout. But Mark reckoned that the best thing was learning how to catch kokanee, a miniaturised lake-resident version of the sockeye salmon. Bela explained how zooplankton like to migrate to the surface and into shallow water at dusk. 'That's when the kokanee come in for the kill. And often enough you find giant rainbows feeding on the kokanee.'

Because Mark was not working officially, just being friendly, he was not bound by the limits of professional physio. He became personally involved with his 'patients' and sometimes offered non-medical help. For example, he and Murphy spent a whole week cleaning up the local cat-lady's putrid tumble-down bungalow. Mark felt compelled to do something for her when, by chance, he discovered that decades beforehand she used to be Bela's lover. He could tell that Bela still had a soft spot for her, but no-one could say why they drifted apart. 'I thought a lot about Sakura and me while we were mopping up cat shit from the bedding,' Mark confided. 'The day I opened a small storeroom door and found a pyramid of unopened milk cartons stacked almost to the ceiling, I wondered in panic where Sakura would be in fifty years' time.'

Considering how much of Bela's life revolved around fly fishing, Mark wondered other things as well. Like how the old man would cope when winter hit and everything froze over.

'I ice fish,' Bela explained.

'Doesn't sound like you at all. You love to stalk your prey, you hate gear.'

'Well, it means I still get outside. Anyway, I make it as simple as possible. No snow mobiles and sled trailers. No collapsible fish hut. No gas barbeques or heaters or motorised augers. Especially no electronic gadgets like fish finders and GPS units. Not even any beer. I take nothing but a short spinning rod, a collapsible three-piece manual auger and some snacks to last me the day. The only luxury is a small collapsible cloth chair.'

Mark never actually went ice fishing with Bela, but the old man talked at length about how it was done. He would drill a hole six or eight inches in diameter. Small was fine for a headwater lake full of stunted cutthroats. But in the kokanee lakes you always had to be ready for 'the biggest rainbow you'll ever hook'. When he was a child, Bela had made the mistake of drilling too small a hole and 'Well, you can guess the rest'. It was clear to Mark that the old man never fully recovered from life's tragedies, not even the small ones.

Mark learned that you needed the ice to be at least four inches thick if you intended to walk out over the water. 'I make sure that the surface is not cracked, nor piled with broken fragments. I auger a hole every hundred feet or so, and if it looks thin I retreat.'

'How do you know where to fish?' Mark asked.

'Beneath the ice, a dull day is the same as dusk. So I drill a hole where the copepods will be, over shallow water or, better still, on the lip where the lake drops away into the deep. I just use a hook, a worm and a piece of split shot. Usually I dangle the bait just two to three feet below surface. Always get a few for the frying pan.'

Mark thought this was a strange comment coming from a bloke who, when fly fishing, released almost all of what he caught.

'Well, you can't rightly let 'em go. As soon as you lift 'em from the water, their skin and eyes snap-freeze.'

Mark was soon to learn that winter days usually stayed at least a few degrees below zero, and nights were much, much colder.

Bela appreciated Mark's company so much that one day he said 'I've got a cabin a few kilometres out of town, you know. I built it when I was a young man and thought that Ruby and me would live forever in the mountains and never grow old'. Ruby was the cat-lady. 'Don't use it much no more. Why don't you hole-up there for a bit? You'd like to do a Canadian winter properly, I reckon.'

The cabin was located at the end of an overgrown four-wheel-drive track that would become impassable once the snows came. It proved to be a single large room with a snug mezzanine at one end. The walls had been lovingly made from forest logs and moss chinking, and were capped with a split-shingle roof. There was no electricity, no electronic gadgets of any kind. A stream, full of rainbow trout, was visible from the single window. The runs were ankle deep, the pools mostly wadeable. The whole thing reminded Mark of a certain bungalow in the hills behind Niigata, and he moved in straight away.

Winter was going to arrive any day now, when he received a

completely unexpected letter. 'Mark. It's Sakura. If you want to see me, I'll be at Vancouver Airport at 9.00 pm on Tuesday October 1.'

On the long, long night-drive from the airport back to the log cabin, the snow began wafting. Mark slept with Sakura on a deer-skin rug in front of a huge open fire. They arose late the following afternoon. After a belated breakfast they went fishing, and managed to hook some freshly run salmon, but by the end of the week winter had hit big time and stream fishing had become almost impossible. They ended up being snow-bound for several months. 'Nothing to do except stoke the wood-fire, read, eat, and shag. All in all, it was the best few months of my life.' Sometimes the temperature got down to minus thirty. Mark said that when it got up to minus fifteen it felt positively warm and he'd find himself outside in a sleeveless shirt chopping firewood.

Early one morning, after a particularly cold night, there was, amazingly, a knock at the door. It was Laird, Bela's neglectful son. 'Dad's fallen into the lake. You'd better come.'

Mark couldn't disguise his alarm. 'How is he? Hypothermic?'

'Stone fuckin' dead.' The voice was unemotional.

'I can't do much for him if he's dead, can I?' Mark retaliated. He suddenly despised the son, and by staring at him he hoped to scald him with his fury. He turned away only when he noticed the torrent of silent tears flowing down his messenger's craggy unshaven cheeks.

'Family need you,' the son eventually managed to croak.

Mark rugged up, kissed Sakura, put on his cross-country skis, and headed off.

'How did he fall in?' Mark asked as he and Laird approached the old man's house.

'A sudden plunge in temperature can make the ice brittle and unsafe.'

'Bela would have known that,' Mark snapped.

Mark was able to reassure the family that Bela was dead long before they found him, that the fact that they didn't know how to give mouth-to-mouth or CPR was, in this case, irrelevant. He made everyone hot drinks, but left as soon as he was sure they would cope without him. Then he went and gave the news to Ruby; and when she broke down, he cried too—uncontrollably—and cradled her in his arms like a baby.

Televised

A FEW months after Ric's bring-an-electrical-appliance-and-method-of-destruction party, all of us were somehow hoodwinked into participating in an eight-ball competition in one of the local pubs. Ric was widely recognised as being the competitor least likely to succeed. But he ended up in the final, possibly by default considering how drunk many of the contestants became while waiting for their turn at the table. And then, Ric's last opponent accidentally potted the black. Despite the fact that Ric's complete contingent of seven balls remained on the table, compared to Genghis' one, he had won. Won a brand-spanking-new colour television.

The wretched thing was promptly hidden away in the garden shed, and no-one in Strahan ever saw it again.

Eventually Ric got transferred from Strahan to Tasmania's north-east, to Fingal in the South Esk valley. One Saturday morning I called in to see if he wanted to fish the nearby Break O'Day River with me, and was surprised to find the house seemingly empty, despite the front door being wide open. I finally discovered Ric hidden away in the spare room, with his telly sitting on its newly opened cardboard packaging, blaring out the latest developments in this year's motorcycle races. He reddened, immediately switched the telly off, and away we went to the river where, as luck would have it, there were worthwhile numbers of trout sipping duns and leaping at spinners.

A few months later he was transferred to Branxholm, north of Fingal, and I called in to see if he wanted to fish the Ringarooma River. This time the telly was perched up on the coffee table in a discrete corner of the living room.

Ric's next transfer took him to Taranna on the Tasman Peninsula. It was Bathurst month again. This time I found my poor addicted friend propped up by pillows in his bedroom with the telly stationed on an over-bed table, apparently stolen from a hospital.

Astrid, Lester's wife, ended up making him a TellyCover. She got a cardboard box and wallpapered the outside with calico. Then, using pastel acrylics, she meticulously reproduced a Leunig cartoon on the front. You know the drawing: the one of a man ignoring a perfect sunrise outside his window in order to show his young son an artificial one on the telly.

Guineapig

CALVIN AND I had taken Sammy, who was six by now, for a fish on a riffly section of the Little Henty River. It rained all day and the water got progressively higher and more treacherous, but Sammy had lots of near misses and we kept thinking that if we stayed just a little bit longer he would eventually nail a fish of his very own. He was so desperate for success that we really didn't have the heart to let him down.

It was late when we drove into Scarface's driveway. The car had barely stopped and Sammy was out, running across the sodden lawn displaying his first-ever fly-caught trout in outstretched arms. 'Dad! Mum! Look!'

Mum, waiting at the door, was just about to voice some praise when Kyle, aged four, appeared by her side wearing a delightful homemade Pokémon suit.

'Well stripe me pink,' said Calvin endearingly. 'It's Chickenpoo.'

'I'm not chicken poo, I'm Pikachu,' pouted Kyle coyly.

'Really? Sorry,' said Calvin.

Suddenly Scarface appeared at the back door. He shuffled Kyle out of his way and confronted Sam, who had just made it to the back landing. 'You didn't feed Dougal today, did you Sam?'

Sammy looked at his fish; the moment of magic evaporated. All he could muster was a crestfallen 'Sorry, Dad. I forgot'.

'You forgot?'

Sammy said nothing.

'Well you can go out to the back paddock right now and pick it some grass.'

'It's pitch black dark. It's pouring with rain.' There was fear in his voice.

'You should have thought about that earlier in the day, shouldn't you. It's time you learned to take your responsibilities seriously young man.'

I offered Sammy a torch, but Scarface insisted that doing it in the dark was part of the punishment.

'We'll be off then,' said Calvin who knew too well that when nothing helpful could be done it was best to do nothing at all. 'See you Sammy. Bye Helen. Toodle-pop Chickenpoo.'

I would have liked to have offered Sammy a supportive 'chin up' before we climbed back into the car, but he was too far away for me to be able to say anything secretly, and anyway, he had completely withdrawn into himself.

Sammy fed his guineapig religiously after that. Every day we would see him out picking grass.

A few weeks later, Calvin called round to see if I wanted to fish Lake Margaret with him. He was driving his brother's flat-tray. 'All I've got to do, before we go, is pick up a load of firewood for Beatrice from Scarface's place.'

We drove up the driveway into the paddock behind the back fence, and figured that in order to get as close as possible to the woodpile, we should move the hutch. When we lifted it up, Dougal rolled out of the bed box. He was nothing more than a lump of gooey leather and partially exposed bones.

Scarface, we realised, was leaning at us over the back fence. 'You've found Dougal then. I wouldn't feel too bad about it if I were you— he's been that way for over two months. Died of starvation I'd guess. I trust you won't let Sam know that we know his little secret, will you?'

Magic

THE TAXMAN'S drowning at the mouth of the Henty devastated the whole community. A fundraiser was held for his young family, especially Lucy, his little girl with Asperger's. It took the form of a mini carnival.

Scarface, perhaps subconsciously aware of how much the world hated him, locked himself in stocks on the main street near a bunch of marquees, some of which were selling preserves and cakes, others housing chance-games like Crown-and-Anchor. In front of him, on a trestle table, were piles of rotten tomatoes from his neglected garden, and for five dollars you could buy three pieces of fruit and throw them at him. He finished the day with $750, making him the biggest money raiser by far even if, as Calvin suggested, he probably pilfered some of the takings for a few slabs of beer.

Calvin didn't make as much money, but he was far and away the best entertainer of the lot.

One of the key events was a variety night in the community hall. Anyone could perform—all you had to do was pay a registration fee. Almost everyone in the whole town turned up, and all *they* had to do was pay an entrance fee. It was quite an earner, really.

The first act was a bunch of high-school kids doing energetic covers of Sex Pistols songs. They received thunderous applause. Next was a melodramatic pantomime from the grade twos, Lucy's class, and because no-one could figure out whether to laugh or cry, most ended up doing both.

And next was a solo performance by Calvin. He walked onto the stage in a magician's suit, and approached a small table laid out with a black velvet tablecloth that draped all the way to the floor.

'Ladies and gentlemen, boys and girls, tonight a special treat—the most miraculous magic ever performed. This is not, I repeat, *not* an illusion. But first I need a member of the audience to volunteer a personal item, preferably something extremely valuable. A watch? Jewellery?'

No-one dared breathe.

'Don't be shy now, it will be returned at the end of the show.' Calvin scanned the room looking for a victim, and ignoring several friends who were by now waving various trinkets in his direction, he settled his gaze on Ric who was determinedly proffering nothing whatsoever. 'Ah, we have a willing volunteer at last,' he announced. 'What is your name, sir?'

'It's Ric,' shouted Hayley innocently, and everyone laughed.

'Mr Ric,' Calvin continued, 'what do you have to offer me, sir?'

Ric squirmed. 'Ah… er… nothing… sorry.'

'Boo!' hissed several people simultaneously, still primed from the pantomime.

'Come now, Mr Ric sir, what's that bulge in the pocket of your jacket? It wouldn't be a brand-new Lamson fly reel would it? One you bought this very day for yourself, just like one Santa refused to give me for Christmas because I was a terribly naughty boy?'

'Er…' said Ric pathetically, and there was more laughter.

Calvin turned his attention to the front row. 'Miss Hayley, if you would be so kind, could you please collect the Lamson fly reel from Mr Ric?'

So Hayley, cute and innocent as a fairy, floated off through the crowd and asked Ric ever so politely for his spanking new treasure. The audience roared its appreciation.

'Thankyou, Miss Hayley. You may sit back down now.' Calvin held the reel aloft, first to the left then the right. He tilted it melodramatically, this way then the other, so that it reflected light, and with his free hand he flourished a silk scarf from his breast pocket. 'One piece of precious... er... jewellery; and one scarf—silk, you will notice, so as not to damage the lustrous finish of watches, jewellery and other, er, items.'

More tittering.

'Behold as I tenderly wrap the jewellery in the scarf.'

After the package had been gently placed on the table, Calvin reached down and, from behind the trailing tablecloth, produced a tiny tack hammer, which he held forth between his index finger and thumb, and then threw unceremoniously over his shoulder.

Silence now, borne in equal measure of confusion and anticipation.

Calvin reached down once more, and brought forth a standard twenty-eight-ounce claw hammer, which he also promptly threw over his shoulder. It landed with a dramatic crash on a strategically placed pile of old crockery, creating a noise which Calvin masterfully ignored. In the next instant he was holding aloft an eight-pound sledgehammer.

The crowd erupted with clapping and foot stomping.

After some time, when everyone quietened down, Calvin held the hammer high above his head, paused, and brought it down with a mighty tooth-loosening blow.

The reel, still completely encased in the scarf, now lay on the floor in a sort of no-man's land atop a crumpled pile of black velvet between two halves of table. There was a collective 'Oooh'. And then Calvin set to work on the package, belting it ever more flamboyantly, resembling nothing so much as a member of The Who abusing a guitar.

Finally it was over, and as we all wiped the tears from our eyes, Calvin called Ric up onto the stage and passed over the sorry bundle. It resembled an impotent old beanbag. Even from the back row we could hear the grind and tinkle of metal fragments. No-one was in any doubt that this was not an illusion.

'Sir, your reel,' Calvin said unapologetically before exiting stage left. Quickly.

Exposed

Beatrice could hear gentle splashes and drips—Calvin and their daughter Hayley, now aged eight, were having a bath together. She walked quietly to the open doorway. The darkness was broken by the sudden flash of a zippo lighter and a jet of blue flame. Next came Calvin and Hayley's laughter. Raucous, full-on, unbridled.

'What *are* you doing!' Beatrice's voice was so overwhelming that it absorbed all other sound, leaving the whole house in menacing silence.

Calvin still wore a grin, but it was lopsided. He couldn't comprehend anyone being angry at something so hilarious.

Hayley couldn't comprehend the danger either. 'Do another one Dad, show Mum.'

'Show me what, exactly?'

'Lighting a far...' Calvin realised he was entering enemy territory and faltered. He tried to secret the syringe beneath the water, then realised the futility.

'That's disgusting.'

'It's only a little fun...'

'It's child abuse, that's what it is.'

'I'm sorry,' he offered as sincerely as was possible when there was no sincerity in his heart.

It wasn't the answer she expected. 'Don't you dare subject Hayley to this sort of filth again.'

Calvin opened his mouth to defend himself and thought better of it.

'Remember, she's not yours.' Now the silence was total. Unbearable. 'I didn't mean that,' she said with faltering sincerity.

A void had opened. Black and empty.

Tomato sauce

CALVIN WAS in the Accident and Emergency section of the local hospital, looking more sheepish than distressed now that the worst of it was over and he knew everything was going to be alright. His brother, Genghis, had gotten completely drunk in a friend's lounge room and Calvin, thinking it would be a fun thing to do, stripped him naked, smashed a beer glass on the floor, and smothered him with tomato sauce. When Genghis woke up and realised he was bleeding to death, he panicked and ran for help, straight to the people who were still outside milling around the barbecue. Unfortunately for him, the lounge room and the backyard were separated by a glass door. Suddenly he was flat on his back again, surrounded by broken glass again, covered in blood again. Real blood.

Now he was being patched up, and Calvin was, somewhat belatedly, being reprimanded. 'The trouble with you is that you drink too much,' said Beatrice angrily. 'You always get overexcited and don't know how to act responsibly.'

'The trouble with you,' Calvin retaliated, 'is that you don't drink enough. You need to learn how to loosen up a bit.'

Bear necessities

IT WAS very early in the morning, before the first influx of visitors was likely to arrive at the Salmon Ponds, and I was using a large dip net to extract old, ailing fish from a concrete fish race. Mark walked into view and said brightly 'Hey Trout, watcha doin?' I had no idea he had returned from Canada.

'Tourists complain to the minister if they see a fish's final struggle across the finish line. Apparently it's cruel for animals to die naturally,' I said.

'Now, there's a take on the animal liberationists' usual dogma,' Mark noted jovially.

'When did you get back? I'll make us a cuppy. Actually, I'd best finish this job first.' It was so cold and icy that if I moved back inside beside the fire I'd be in danger of settling in for the rest of the day.

While I worked, Mark sat on the bank of the pond telling me about his adventures in British Columbia. Apparently his time in Bela's cabin was notable for more than sex, books, food and wine. Just before the big snows arrived, salmon started to appear.

'First on the scene were sockeye salmon. Then came the rainbow trout. They were either giant gerrards from the lakes a hundred kilometres away or steelhead from the ocean yet another couple of hundred kilometres downstream—there was no way of telling which. In any case, they were there to feast on the freshly laid salmon eggs. And not long after the rainbows arrived, black bears started coming out of the forests—mothers with cubs.'

Mark was becoming quite animated now. He had sunk to his knees and was stalking on all fours along the edge of the concrete race, the one in which I was still dip-netting for sick and dying trout. 'The mothers would flip fish out onto the banks with their paws,' Mark declared, suddenly doing just that, tossing a fungus-riddled trout onto the bank. Then he stood up, leaving the trout flip-flopping pathetically on the grass. 'At first, the bears found it hard work,' he continued, as the first tourist of the day gingerly toed the distressed fish back into the water, where it promptly died. 'As soon as a bear entered the water, the fish would scatter upstream. Or down. But after a week or so, the river began to get clogged with fish, not just sockeyes and rainbows either—kokanee and coho too. Soon there were so many fish that they couldn't easily escape the bears. There were huge bottlenecks at the heads and tails of all the pools. Now the mum bears encouraged their children to catch food for themselves, and the cubs found they could do it easily.'

When I asked, Mark confessed that he'd cast a fly to the fish while they were spawning. 'But anything I hooked was so hemmed in that it was no more able to move than a sardine in a can. So, I only did it once.'

'Except that other time, the morning after Sakura arrived,' I reminded him.

He did his best to ignore me. 'The last fish to appear on the scene were the chinook salmon, and almost instantly, the brown bears appeared. These mammals were huge—the blacks took one look and bolted for the hills—and they needed a huge dose of protein and fat to tide them through the torpor of the coming winter. They couldn't really be bothered with the trout or lesser salmon; they were mainly interested in the huge nutrient-rich chinooks. By now the stream was so packed with salmon that even in the glides hundreds of fish crowded together in impenetrable masses. Each brown bear would wade out and examine the flush of spawning salmon as if it was a smorgasbord. Sockeye, nah. Rainbow trout, no. Kokanee, you've got to be kidding. Then it would locate a chinook salmon and grin ferociously. No pussying about with paws now. The bear would plunge its head straight into water and emerge with a writhing ten- or fifteen-kilo fish held sideways in its jaws.'

Mark emphasised this last point by plunging his own head into the water and managing to almost bite a trout. The tourist, fearing for Mark's sanity, scuttled out of sight.

'Finally the trout and salmon, weakened by bear-bite, exertion and metabolic decay; scarred from bustling about amongst themselves; would get covered in fungus and begin to waste away. This happened to all the salmon, every one, and half of the trout too. By now the nutrient value of the fish had greatly diminished, but catching them was never easier, and the browns bears became less protective. The black bears rejoined the fray. Bald eagles too—great flocks, hundreds and hundreds.'

'You seem an awful lot happier now than when you left,' I observed.

He agreed. 'In Japan I realised that I needed to fish more than I'd been doing in Tasmania. In British Columbia I realised that I still wanted to be a physio. Then I felt ready to come home. I'm not going to work in a hospital anymore though. It'll be community work where I can monitor people's progress and ensure that they get the best ongoing support that my profession has to offer.'

'Do you still think fishing will keep you young like Peter Pan?' I asked, expecting a witty or frivolous reply, not a silence that seemed to go on forever.

'I don't suppose fly fishing stops anyone from dying,' Mark said eventually. 'But one thing I learned from Bela is that it's possible to live so well that dying becomes a small price to pay for the privilege of ever being born.'

False casting

BEATRICE CALLED in to see me at the Salmon Ponds, and after a while she asked me what fly casting felt like. I think she was trying hard to understand Calvin. I collected my fly gear from the house, and went to the workshop. One by one I put half a dozen old wet flies in the bench vice, and twisted off the bends of the hooks. Then I went back out to the main lawn and demonstrated the basics of casting, much as I had done with Mouldy Muldoon. Budgie, the cantankerous volunteer hatchery worker, who had been trimming the boxthorn hedges, stopped to watch before moving in beside us for a closer view. He was clearly impressed—Beatrice was a natural. When it came time to go inside, I invited Budgie in for a few nibbles and drinks. I left the rod leaning against the hedge as we walked through the front gate. My two friends sat side by side on the lounge and chatted enthusiastically. If I didn't know better I'd have suspected they were infatuated with each other.

It took a few hours, but inevitably Beatrice suggested we go for a moonlight walk around the grounds. The air was surprisingly warm and still. Fish were rising noisily in the races and pools, making condescending sucking sounds. Budgie walked back to the hedge and returned with the fly rod. 'You should have a cast in one of the ponds,' he suggested to Beatrice. 'You can't really get the timing right if you're not lifting the line from the water.'

'Won't the fish grab the fly?'

'Yep,' said Budgie. 'You might even have one on for a second or two. But Trout's broken the hook off. Remember?'

'It would still be cruel, wouldn't it?'

'The trout won't give a damn. Even wild fish usually just carry on feeding when you use hookless flies.'

'I would sort of like to know what it was like to feel a fish on the line,' Beatrice admitted uncertainly. 'You sure it won't worry the fish?'

'Of course not.'

'Trout?' she said, seeking my confirmation. But before I could answer she seemed to make up her own mind. 'No, I can't Budgie. The whole idea is barbaric.'

'Look it's not as if you are going to catch a fish or anything.'
Budgie was becoming annoyed, tending towards sarcasm. 'It's not as
if you are going to do anything sinful, interact with nature or
anything.' Now he was being brutal. 'You've thrown javelin haven't
you?' He sounded softer now, trying his hardest to exercise patience.

'Yes,' Beatrice agreed suspiciously.

'You didn't feel you were spearing an animal at the time, did you?
And after the event, you weren't corrupted, didn't suddenly feel an
urgent need to go off and impale wallabies? And so what if you did?'

'I accept that some things are natural for some people in some
cultures. But fly fishing isn't necessary for our survival. And trout
aren't natural, they don't even belong in Tasmania.'

'Are you saying that it's unnatural for one species to aid the
distribution of another? That a lizard is illegitimate if it hitches a
ride on a coconut raft? That a seed puked up by a currawong has no
right to grow?'

'All that is fine. It's when people intentionally shift species all over
the globe that it's morally wrong.'

'So people are something separate from nature then? Not of this
world? What a pious pretentious piece of postmodern claptrap. Pah!
You greenies are just the same as all the other religious
fundamentalists.'

Beatrice was not one to wither. 'You are a greenie, I know you are.
So is Trout.' She was offering a sign of kinship, looking for a
truthful route to peace.

'But I'm not the sort of greenie that would try to stop anyone
from interacting with nature,' Budgie said angrily. 'In my mind,
people and the natural world are not separate things. People should
never be removed from nature, not mentally or physically, not
through ignorance and especially not through bureaucratic
intervention. I have never been able to accept all that religious
claptrap about …'

'What claptrap?' Beatrice demanded.

'That humanity is inherently bad, tainted with some sort of
original sin. That we are a blight in the Garden of Eden, That we are
something apart from nature. That we should feel dirty about our
pagan desires. That self-denial and abstinence are good. Virginity,
pure. Guilt, essential. That people who do not convert to this
doctrine are infidels. And that the infidels will lead humanity unto

Armageddon. That the end of humanity will be a good thing.' He was in full rant by now, but he was forced to pause for breath. Very briefly. 'And I fail to see that suppressing your passion, submitting to authority, embracing denial or guilt, somehow makes you a better person. Or society a better place. Leave that stupid view of the world to nutters like Jonathan Swift. They might despair about our bestiality, aspire to some sort of imagined perfection. Not me. I celebrate our primitive passions. I actually think they lie at the heart of what it is to be human at all.'

Although Budgie was being cringingly rude, his speech was so succinct and heartfelt that I felt like applauding. I didn't though; diplomacy was paramount.

'Surely you accept that we need laws, rules and morals,' Beatrice implored. She seemed to be looking for reasons to keep liking Budgie. 'You don't support anarchy do you?'

'Well,' replied Budgie, 'I'm no great fan of rigid structure, myriad do's and don'ts, security, safety, contrived experiences, zoning, timetables, any of the sorts of things beloved of religious leaders and government agencies. It's all shorthand for suppression of the human soul.'

'I was only saying I didn't want to fish,' Beatrice said softly, trying desperately to put things back into perspective.

'It's the way you dismiss it as *only fishing* that's getting me riled,' Budgie elaborated, softer now. 'Fishing is my attachment to nature, the world. It is the cement that binds me to my best friends. The same cement that permits me to be human to everyone else.'

'Sounds like you are as religious as me,' said Beatrice, attempting a giggle.

'Like hell,' said Budgie. 'Trout, you're an atheist too, support me.'

I didn't want to become a part of the argument. In any case, I doubted that I was an atheist. 'I think I'm more of an agnostic,' I said

'Agnostic?' Budgie fumed. 'That's no position at all. It's just an excuse for not knowing how to think.'

I wondered, then, if Budgie's atheism was his tool for avoiding the need to consider alternative truths. He seemed to be as protective of his own beliefs as Beatrice was of hers. Perhaps that was why they radiated such obvious chemistry.

Rats of Maria

THE NIGHT that Beatrice stayed over at the Salmon Ponds, water rats or platypuses, probably both, got into the rearing troughs and indulged themselves in an eating frenzy. Next morning, thousands of fry and dozens of fingerlings were missing. Then we discovered brown rats in our bins of trout-food pellets. We spent several hours doing our best to vermin-proof everything before retiring to the caretaker's cottage for morning tea.

'Bloody vermin,' said Budgie. 'I stayed in the Sir John Falls camp once. Saw enough rats there to last me a lifetime...'

'You think the rats are bad at Sir John Falls?' I interrupted. 'Let me tell you a thing or two about rats.'

In the aftermath of the Great Depression, my dad's family acquired a lease on Maria Island. They farmed sheep mainly, and a few cattle. Wheat was cut by hand with a scythe, and stacked in stooks—shoulder-high bundles, leant against one another like wigwam frames. The little acreage of flat pasture had originally been a dense tea-tree swamp, and it too had been cleared by hand. The water was drained via a series of narrow hand-dug gutters which led straight to a small tidal inlet. These channels were waist-high and about the width of a duck.

Whenever my father and his teenage brothers were hungry, they used to lay a line of wheat from the estuary up into one of the gutters, and then wait on top of the bank, their frozen faces peering silently over the edge. Eventually a duck or ten would waddle up the grain trail, and the lads would jump them. The birds would panic, of course, but the walls of the gutter prevented them from opening their wings and flying off.

'So that's what your ancestors ate then—ducks,' said Beatrice condescendingly. 'Living flesh.'

'And spuds,' I added enthusiastically. Distraction was always the best policy when Calvin's wife was starting to get all evangelical about God or the environment.

Potatoes were dug in the autumn and buried in a pit of dry soil under the cover of an old barn, where they wouldn't rot or go green. One year the rats were in plague proportions, and as the cold of winter approached, they began raiding the spuds. The boys tried setting the dogs onto them, but the rats just retreated to the gutters. In fact, the drains proved to be a veritable haven for vermin. It seems that they either bred there or used them as highways in and out of the wild. So the brothers hatched a plan. They emptied a forty-four-gallon drum of diesel into the main drain, and allowed the trickle of water in the bottom to disperse the fuel all the way from the barn to the estuary. Then they struck a match. There was a squealing and scrambling, and presently dozens of fireball rodents emerged from the trenches, like platoons of suicidal soldiers. The rats faced fierce resistance from the enemy—half a dozen teenage lads armed with mattocks, brooms and rakes—but had the advantage of numbers and madness. They raced across no-man's land and sought refuge in the first shelter available, the stooks of hay.

'And that was it,' I concluded, allowing disbelief to dissolve into laughter. 'A whole harvest—a whole year's worth of blood, sweat and toil—up in smoke.'

Budgie found the story so funny that his laughter had become a choking cough. Even Beatrice was chuckling, though she must have been aghast at the idea of setting fire to animals, even if they were only rats. Perhaps she had satisfied herself that they were introduced rats—black rats or brown rats—not native swamp rats.

Budgie's house

BEATRICE WAS mildly surprised when Budgie invited us to dinner at his place. That was just the first of several surprises. 'In fact you'd best stay the night. I've got spare rooms, spare beds.'

Why would Budgie have a spare bed? He didn't have any friends, nor even acquaintances that might conceivably want to stay in his company for a moment longer than absolutely necessary.

When we pulled up at his place in Hobart, he met us at the front gate and led us into his backyard. The back door opened directly into a modest kitchen-dining area, from which an open doorway ushered us into a similarly small lounge room.

The warmth was radiant, and became hotter as we entered the

lounge. 'A wood heater,' Budgie pre-empted proudly, knowing that Beatrice was opposed to them.

I studied the flames, ghosting yellow and orange behind a large glass door. Electric heaters had been installed on various walls, but it was clear that they hadn't been used in years, probably not since Budgie had bought the place.

To be truthful, it wasn't just the heaters that were in need of a good dusting. The windowsills were festooned with a potpourri of mummified houseflies, damsel-flies and beetles. And the rest of the house was in careless disarray. Books lay everywhere. Real paper ones. On windowsills, tables, mantle pieces, coffee tables. Many were opened. The house wasn't smelly or musty; it just oozed of quirky neglect. Little things were ignored because the owner was preoccupied with other things. The only items that might remotely be described as unhealthy were several half-drunk cups of tea, one decorated with furry globules of grey mould, another whose contents had completely evaporated leaving behind a ring of scum, now flaking from the sides.

I also noticed that the plasterboard walls were adorned with fly fishing memorabilia. It seemed to be an intensely private collection. Beatrice paused at what she first took to be a framed painting but which on closer inspection proved to be an actual artificial fly protected behind a small square of non-reflective glass. The background had been signed in exquisite copperplate. 'With deepest love, Lai.'

She stared harder at the fly itself. It was a small, sparsely dubbed black thing of no discernable merit. 'What sort of animal is this supposed to represent?' she said in mock horror.

'Flies don't actually have to imitate any specific insect,' Budgie replied, matter-of-fact. 'That's a black nymph. It's a fly I designed. I originally called it the Maiden Fly because it only had a few hairs. I even had a bead-head version which I called the Maidenhead. But when a magazine editor from New Zealand asked me to write about my favourite flies, I figured I'd have to give it a new name. Lai suggested the Naked Nymph. A more witty name than the original, I do believe.'

'Hence her signature?'

'Well actually there's more to the story than that. That fly was created and framed by Lai just after she read the article. She tied it from her own pubes.'

Budgie was chuckling, and Beatrice began to laugh with him.

'What's a nymph?'

Budgie raised an eyebrow.

'Not a girl. I mean, you know, a fly-type nymph.'

'Where have you been? Though I suppose its not unusual anymore for people to have only a political interest in nature, not a practical understanding, nor a passion fostered of physical involvement. Many insects—mayflies, stoneflies, caddis-flies, damsel-flies, dragonflies—lay their eggs on water, and upon hatching, the young are especially adapted to live some or most of their lives underwater. This is the nymph stage, something like the caterpillar stage in butterflies. Trout eat nymphs.'

'So it *is* an imitation?'

'Not really.' He picked up a book, one of several lying higgledy-piggledy on the mantelpiece of a boarded-up fireplace in the kitchen: *The Truth About Trout*, by Robert Sloane. 'This book was written way back in 1983,' Budgie began. 'Now, there is a whole fly-fishing culture built on the assumption that trout are selective and only eat whatever is available in profusion at any particular time, and for a century or more before the publication of this book and, indeed, ever since, many anglers devoted themselves to *matching the hatch*—in creating perfect imitations. Rob, though, noted that large nondescript flies often worked better than "perfect" imitations. He wrote that, *in nature, it is the role of the predator to select the weak from the strong, the recognisably abnormal mutants from the normal population, the different from the usual*. You see, trout are like people. They find glitz bigger and better than real life. They actually prefer artificial things to natural ones. It is self-deception, to be sure. There is a sting in the tail.'

'I don't like contrived or manufactured things any more than you do,' Beatrice offered defensively.

But Budgie wasn't listening. 'Nor do flies have to represent insects at all. Trout eat, among other things, fish. Look at these.'

Protected under glass in another intricate wooden frame were a series of flies tied to look like various fish. Beatrice read their names: *Lamprey. Whitebait. Golden galaxias. Redfin perch. Jollytail.* They were exquisite creations that were clearly not the clumsy labours of lower-class barbarians.

Budgie knew what Beatrice was thinking. 'Jane Gardner, writing in

FlyLife, once noted that fly-tying reminded her of *ladies who used to make lace with little wooden spools and silver hooks.* She could think of nothing else that inspired *such intricacy, such silken thread detail, in men.*'

'Tell me about this then,' said Beatrice, seeing some enormous flies adorning a windowsill, like sea shells in a child's old-time picture book. From a time when kids were legally allowed to comb beaches for natural treasures.

'Trout are happy to eat mammals and birds,' Budgie lectured enthusiastically. 'That one is a duckling I used on Lake Titicaca in Bolivia. That one,' pointing to a thing that closely resembled a grey toilet brush, 'is a vole I used in Mongolia to catch taimen, a giant salmonid, the largest in the world, which looks rather like an elongated brown trout, except that most of them weigh five to fifty kilos.'

'This one is cute,' Beatrice enthused.

It was a very realistic looking mouse fly. These are used a lot in New Zealand, and shortly you will learn some astounding things about them.

All Tied up

BEATRICE WAS intrigued with my collection of wet flies, which I'd just retrieved from the boot of my car and was displaying on Budgie's table. 'These don't look much like frogs.'

'Don't have to—function, function, function, that's the key. Simplicity is important too. I don't like wasting too much time tying flies. I'd much prefer to be outside fishing.'

'I guess it's cheaper to tie your own.'

'Probably not.'

'Then why don't you just buy what you need?'

I was about to explain how difficult it is to find exactly what you want. The wet flies in the local tackle shop might superficially look the same as the ones you tie yourself, but on closer inspection there's always something wrong. Perhaps the hook is excessively heavy and prone to snag on weeds. Or the fly is overdressed so that the gape is too narrow to hook fish properly. Then you go to the dry flies and the workmanship is so poor that you just know the hackles will unfurl the instant the first fish is hooked. Not only is that an infuriating waste of an expensive fly, but being forced to tie on a new fly means that you'll probably find yourself wasting critical moments at the height of the hatch. You sigh. In all likelihood the emergers will be no better—they'll probably have synthetic posts and won't be as visible or easy to keep clean as ones which feature white calf tail. And so on and so forth. But I didn't get the chance to say anything at all.

'Most of the flies you see in tackle shops these days are bulk orders from India and China,' Budgie opined. 'They are tied in sweatshops by kids for a pittance. You know what free trade is? Legalised slavery, that's what. You buy in, you become part of the system.'

Beatrice was onto Budgie by now. 'How about that fly vice of yours. It's made in India.'

'Well I can't afford anything more expensive, can I? I'm not happy about it. The point is I *try* not to over consume.' Budgie probably had a point there—other than books and fishing memorabilia, his house was excruciatingly Spartan. But I couldn't help noticing that, like Beatrice, he thought that committing little sins was okay, provided you felt guilty about it.

'And I try, within my means, to do the right thing,' he continued. 'At least the inequities of life bother me.'

'You remind me a bit of Spike Milligan,' Beatrice suggested. 'Once, on the radio, an interviewer suggested to him that his manic-depressive disorder, or whatever it was that he had, might be part and parcel of his creativity. Spike was outraged. Clinical depression, he insisted angrily, was a drain on creativity and nothing more. But I think he might have been missing the point. I think what the interviewer was trying to say was that if you are intelligent and well read—if you have insight and compassion—you are bound to be depressed. I don't think she was suggesting that depression was a cause of compassionate creativity, merely that it might be a symptom. Spike suffered because he cared.'

'Which is more than most people can honestly say,' concluded Budgie. 'I mean, people want to think they care, but they hardly ever do, not really. Here in Tassie, whenever pollsters ask people whether or not they support logging in oldgrowth forests, seventy to eighty per cent always say no. Yet pro-forestry governments always get elected. If people care at all, they don't care much—certainly not enough to change the way they vote. That's where us passionate fly fishers are different. The environment is part of our day-to-day lives; it defines us, is part of our body and mind. I do care enough to change my vote.'

'Liar, liar pants on fire,' said Beatrice. 'I bet you've always voted left of centre.' She was enjoying herself.

Budgie was too. 'Well voting is just a farce anyway. I mean Newspoll can sample two thousand people and predict with absolute certainty any election result. Why bother going through the fuss of an election at all, I say. There's never ever been an election in any electorate in Australia decided by one vote. My vote has never made one iota of difference. Democracy is just a very clever method of crowd control, something designed to make people think they contribute to governance. In real life it's as corrupt as any other bureaucratic consultative process.'

'You're speaking crap Budgie, losing your touch,' Beatrice challenged. 'When it comes to climate change, or commercially tied flies, you say we should all consume less, that ordinary people can make a difference, that making a big difference starts by convincing lots of individuals to make miniscule changes in their own lives.'

'Well, I suspect the best anyone can do is to not vote. You never agree with a politician on all issues. Usually you're forced to pick a line of best fit, to vote for someone who is least bad. And then the bastards that stumble over the line claim to have a mandate for everything, including stuff they never mentioned at all while campaigning. Actually, now I think of it, it'd be best to always vote the incumbents out, to let them know that you hate their guts.'

'I reckon, Budgie, that it'd be fairer if you got to vote for each minister.' Beatrice was being serious. 'Imagine if you got to pick the Minister for Education, Minister for Environment, Minister for Finance, Minister for Defence. Each party would have to put someone up who actually had experience in the field, and we'd get to have a say on all the big issues.'

'Not bad,' Budgie admitted. 'Totally impractical of course, but that makes me like your idea even more. Especially if all of Australia had a Hare-Clarke system. Proportional voting should be compulsory in all democracies. I mean, if you can command just a bare majority, why should you have complete dominance. Actually democracy itself is against the natural order…'

'What?' That was my contribution.

'Look, suppose you have three kids. Each weekend you fish somewhere, either for the trout in the high country or for saltwater species on the coast. Now suppose two of your kids are fanatical trout fishers and one is a fanatical surf-rodder, and you take a vote. In a democracy you would always go inland, never to the coast. No-one believes that would be a fair or proper outcome…'

'I've got a bottle of whisky in the boot,' I said.

Wing

WHAT MOST intrigued me in Budgie's house was a large oil painting of a red spinner wing, also signed, exquisitely, by Lai. There were no long brush strokes, just thousands of carefully placed dots, though you didn't notice this until you were up close, which was where I was when Budgie said 'Lai always thought that renaissance paintings were all the better for the way the oils crazed over centuries. She reckoned that they matured like good wine. So, in the picture you're looking at, she used her brush to sweep up her oils in order to manufacture fault lines. And you'll notice that they weren't done in any ad hoc way. The lines she created define the actual veins of the wing'.

'I love the impressionist thing too,' I said. 'You know, the way it's built up with spots of contrasting colours so that from a distance the oils seem to vibrate and shimmer. The 3-D effect is bloody stunning.'

'It draws you in, doesn't it.' Budgie was becoming nostalgic, sentimental even. 'At times, when I look deep into that single wing, I see great swirling clouds of spinners dancing in the evening sun, light refracting in rainbow colours from their transparent wings, like multicoloured scarves shed during a frenzy of pagan pirouettes.'

I was a bit embarrassed by his poetry. 'I guess that was the whole point of the painting,' I offered self-consciously.

'Lai felt that mayflies are like the gypsies of romantic literature. She savoured the notion that they live life on the edge, their homes nowhere and everywhere, dancing to the freedoms and harshness of nature, determined never to suffer the imprisonment of security, their immortality buried within their furious commitment to the next generation.'

There were tears tracking down his face.

San Juan

BUDGIE AND I were walking along the banks of the lower Macquarie River looking for rising trout. There weren't any. So Budgie used his foot to rouse some grasshoppers out of the tussocks. No sooner had they settled upon the currents, than a large fish rose up and started engulfing them. Budgie cast to it, landed it and set it free. 'Hope you don't think that's cheating,' he said, clearly unconcerned about what I thought.

'We've all done a little unscrupulous berleying,' I laughed.

On warm days at Dee Lagoon, gum beetles take to the air and fall thick and fast on the lake surface. Currents—in wind-lanes, off points, in back-eddies—herd the beetles together, and because beetles don't much like being drowned, they begin to crawl out onto each other's backs. Soon you end up with enormous blankets of the things. Overnight these living rafts drift onshore. One cold morning when the beetles weren't flying about and landing on the water and there wasn't much of a rise, I gathered up a nine-litre bucket of gum beetles and sprinkled them over a bay. Within minutes, every fish within cooee was up and feeding. 'Boy did I have fun,' I bragged to Budgie.

He chuckled appreciatively. 'I spent some time in New Mexico. They have a fishery there, the San Juan River. The authorities became alarmed about something they called shuffling, which was just scuffing the freestone while you were wading and then fishing in the silt trail. It was reasonably effective. Leeches and scud and all manner of mini-beasts would be dislodged, and trout would move into the plume to feed. There's nothing anglers hate more than other anglers catching fish, so in 1986 the Fish and Game Department made shuffling illegal.'

'You outgrow berleying,' I said. 'Or you don't,' I added pointedly.

'Can't see why it bothers anyone either way, other than what you said about anglers hating other anglers catching fish.' Then I told him how I once transferred a bunch of big surplus-display rainbows from the Salmon Ponds into the Craigbourne Dam, how the fisheries officers themselves complained to the Commissioner about anglers catching them. It was slaughter, they frothed. They just couldn't accept that the only reason for me putting the fish into the lake was for them to be caught.

And Budgie told me about some research Lai did on the San Juan. 'She found that shuffling had no measurable effect on the fish or the overall quality of fishing. The main spawning areas were unaffected, while bug counts and fish growth suggested that any impact on the ecology was infinitesimal. But the Department tried to prosecute people anyway. The defence lawyers pointed out that shuffling was difficult to define. Any angler wading anywhere made a silt trail of some sort, and just standing in the water made a velocity shelter that trout actively sought for feeding stations. The judges threw the cases out and said that in order to be taken seriously fisheries officers would have to observe the shuffler for a full twenty minutes and be able to demonstrate that the offender was actually kicking up the stream bed and placing flies directly into the plume.'

I expressed hope that the ruling was a fitting end to the story.

'Not at all. All of a sudden, the agency was considering banning traditional down-and-across wet-fly fishing altogether. They even talked about installing video surveillance networks. Lai decided that doing research was useless. What was the point when the people that made the laws ignored the results of your work? She was also aghast that all this over-regulation, this Orwellian oppression, came from the left, from her side of politics. It was the beginning of her depression, I think.'

Négligé

MAGENTA, THE barmaid I first met at New Norfolk, fell in lust with Zongo, a Parks and Wildlife ranger, the instant she moved to the West Coast. The first daytrip they enjoyed together was to the Henty River, where Zongo happened to catch his first ever ten-pound brown trout. He was so excited that he decided he'd get The Taxman to mount it. Unfortunately, as he was seeing Magenta to her front door, her cat slunk into his car and mutilated his trophy beyond repair.

It was a shaky start for a relationship, and even when they finally went on an overnight bushwalk together, Magenta confessed forlornly that there had been precious little romance. What was wrong with Zongo, she wondered. Was he shy? Gay? Did the fault lie with her? Was she defective? Well, she told me resolutely, the frustration and wondering wasn't going to go on for any longer. She was going to invite him around for a meal, and seduce him.

I reminded her that she couldn't cook.

'I sorted that one out ages ago,' she said. 'What you do is, you get the boy home and put a bunch of finely chopped onions in a frypan with a little spicy oil, and then you put the frypan on a gentle heat…'

'Go on like that for much longer and you'll have me convinced you're a qualified chef,' I interrupted.

'Onions smell divine, so by this stage your partner truly believes you're a gourmet. Then, if you act quickly enough, you can race him off to the bedroom before he ever learns the truth.'

'Probably okay for a one-night stand,' I conceded. 'But I'll bet deceit isn't in the grand plan for Zongo.' I danced a goad around the room:

Magenta and Zongo sitting in a tree
K.I.S.S.I.N.G
first comes love, then comes marriage
then comes a baby in a baby's carriage

She smiled with exaggerated outrage.

***

Magenta bought an ever-so-sexy négligé, and spent the rest of the week fussing. She bought scented candles, a luxurious fireside rug, lots of gastronome nibble-food: cold-smoked salmon, blue cheese, stuffed olives, a bottle of cabernet—what the heck—two bottles of cabernet.

The cat, apparently, was disgusted with her—on the first day of her preparations, he farted in her arms, then promptly fled through the front door, never to return.

Zongo arrived on Saturday night, on time, with a posy of flowers. (On creative impulse, five minute's walk from Magenta's back door, he'd pinched them from the graveyard.)

Magenta, flustered, was still trying to light the effing bastard bloody fire when she noticed Zongo framed in the doorway.

'Want a hand?' he offered sympathetically.

She tried to laugh off her embarrassment. 'You can light my fire anytime.' It came out all nerdy.

He scrunched new newspaper and rearranged the kindling. She poured wine and prepared some water crackers.

'Thought you were going to cook onions.'

She was completely lost for words.

'Calvin told me. He also said I was a moron and that if I stuffed this evening up he was going to set off the world's biggest oxyacetylene bomb right in my bedroom.'

'How did Calvin know?… Bloody Trout—I'll kill him…'

'I don't intend to stuff the evening up,' Zongo interrupted.

An hour or so later, Magenta said 'Just wait here a minute, Zongo. I'm going to go and slip into something more comfortable'. That also came out all nerdy, but by this stage it didn't matter.

She walked into her bedroom, undressed, and stared at herself approvingly in the mirror. Then she opened the wardrobe. The cat, the one that had by now been missing for several days, had pulled the négligé from the coat hanger and was curled up fast asleep. She looked harder. The négligé had been totally shredded. The cat was leaking. The cat was totally dead.

Magenta wanted to cry. But she ended up laughing out loud. Zongo appeared at her side, and sensing that whatever was going on inside the wardrobe was no laughing matter, he reassuringly slipped his hand around her naked waist. She gestured into the coffin. 'I bought it specially for tonight.'

He stared. Hard. 'Look, I know you know that I hated that flatulent animal, especially after what it did to my trophy Henty trout, but …'

She cuffed him playfully. 'Not the effing cat. The thing the cat's up and died on.'

A pause. 'Oh.'

Zongo shovelled the cat into a cardboard box and took it out into the dry, dry paddock. Magenta, still naked, walked beside him with a crowbar. 'There's no way you're going to shovel a hole into this rock-hard clay.'

It was, by necessity, a shallow grave. They piled dry clods back over the cat's body, but failed to disguise the incriminating mound. They were overcome by the sort of panic they assumed might be felt by a cheated lover after a spur-of-the-moment murder—they had to get rid of the evidence. But how? Finally, desperately, Zongo decided to tamp the grave down by jumping on it.

The cat did one last spectacular fart of defiance.

Opinionated

I HAD taken Budgie from the Salmon Ponds to fish for sea trout in the Henty River, and afterwards we had driven to Strahan to see Calvin and Beatrice. After dinner, when Budgie began expounding contrary views on just about everything the rest of us cared to talk about, Beatrice, exasperated, accused him of being opinionated.

'Would you prefer that I had no opinions? Like half of the people in the world.'

'Half the people in the world have no opinions?'

'Well, that's pretty much exactly how many people of below-average intelligence there are.'

Beatrice wasn't to be sidetracked. 'An opinionated person, Budgie, is someone who won't listen to other ideas.'

'Rubbish!'

Beatrice smiled like a victor.

'An opinionated person, Beatrice, is someone who refuses to consider new facts or new ways of looking at existing facts. Don't confuse them with people like me. I'm merely abrasive and arrogant.' Everyone ignored Budgie's melodramatic pride, except Beatrice, so he moved to ramp up her interest. 'Take evolution versus creationism, for instance. It's a subject on which, over many decades, I've kept myself well read. I've considered all the facts and viewpoints, and I've reached conclusions. If someone says creationism should be taught in science classes, they're going to have to have a strong new argument to keep my attention. I'm not going to pretend to be interested in rhetoric, especially not if the person I'm talking to has thought less about the topic than I have.'

Beatrice was incensed. 'I thought you liked broadmindedness, thought you were against censorship. Why shouldn't kids be exposed to viewpoints different from your own?'

'Look, I've got no argument against you teaching creationism in religious study, mythology, fairy tales...'

Beatrice reddened and shifted confrontationally.

'... or history or even philosophy. It's just that creationism isn't science. In fact, Christian science is an oxymoron. You may as well argue that darning should be taught in mechanics.'

'You're just playing devil's advocate again, aren't you?' Beatrice said hopefully.

'What do you think philosophy is?' Budgie demanded.

Beatrice refused to be intimidated. 'I guess,' she said thoughtfully, 'it's the art of pure reasoning, of developing ideas using information that's already available.'

'And it differs from science in that it requires no experimental proofs,' Budgie expounded.

'So? Aristotle himself abhorred experiments. You told me that. You said he thought they adulterated the beauty of pure thought.' Beatrice was enjoying herself.

'He was a bloody idiot. But I'll agree with you on one thing—most great scientists were, are, philosophers.'

Beatrice responded thoughtfully. 'Well, whatever you say about the world's great thinkers being philosophers, the discipline is now considered to be wishy-washy. In our brave new outcomes-driven world, there's been a move away from philosophy. If it's not science, its not legitimate, or at least not respectable.'

Budgie was, amazingly, sympathetic. 'It's worse than that,' he said softly. 'If it's not *applied* science, it's considered wishy-washy.'

Somehow the chemistry between Budgie and Beatrice had become blatant. I looked at Calvin and shifted uncomfortably in my seat. Budgie noticed, and he shifted tack.

'The reason philosophy is considered wishy-washy is that it's now more commonly associated with moral or religious thinking, mainly because ideas in this field are rarely measurable or easily subjected to experimental proofs.'

'Why are you so protective of science?' Beatrice asked, clearly hurt. 'Is science your religion?'

'The scientific method is reasonable. You observe. You see a pattern. You devise an experiment to test if that pattern holds true in other situations. You draw conclusions. You subject your work to peer review. If it's not replicable, it carries no weight. And it is a hallmark of good science that it not only explains existing facts but can predict future events. That's why fly fishing can, to some degree, be compared to science. It's also why evolution is more valid than creationism.'

'Evolution is just a theory.'

'All science is theory—that's the point,' Budgie thundered. 'But evolution is a theory only in the same sense that *the Earth is not flat* is a theory, or *trout eat insects* is a theory. Explain this to me: in what way is creationism science?'

Beatrice paused to gather her argument, forgetting that Budgie, like nature, abhorred a vacuum. 'Anyway,' he exploded, 'you were wrong about science being my religion. Fly fishing is my religion.'

'You just said fly fishing was science.'

Budgie, briefly, was lost for words.

'You boys and your fishing,' Beatrice continued. 'You're so preoccupied with little stuff. How about big issues: climate change, starvation, war? You think you're a leftie, but you have no social conscience whatsoever, at least not in any practical sense.'

'Little stuff is what makes life worthwhile.' It was Budgie's turn to be defensive. 'It's as essential as any of the basics. Do you think life would be worth living if you were locked in a cage with nothing but shelter, food, water and clothing? To ask me to forsake fishing is to ask me to commit suicide. Everyone has something little that fills their soul … '

'You're being illogical, emotional.'

'I'm being perfectly logical—it's my primary tool for justifying the illogical. Most of the things I care about are illogical. Same with you. Religion is entirely illogical. In the battle of hearts and minds, it is far more important to win hearts. It doesn't matter how much sense there is to an argument if no-one cares. To sneer that something is an emotional argument entirely misses the point. The fact that a topic arouses emotions is the only thing that makes the topic worthy of attention at all.'

'What the hell are you trying to say?'

Budgie faltered.

Beatrice pressed her advantage. 'Why spend money on space travel when you could use the money to prevent so much misery in Africa?'

'For the same reason that you spend money on trivials like …' Budgie was up from his chair, dancing around, displaying various knickknacks in the manner of a dollar-store proprietor starring in his own locally produced advertisement '… like CDs… shampoo… coffee… incense… ugg boots…'

'Budgie, stop it,' Beatrice pleaded, totally exhausted.

'Anyway, the space program has given us unexpected things like weather satellites, and the number of lives it saves through the accurate mapping of cyclones and hurricanes has justified the money spent on the space program many times over.'

'Budgie, why does everything have to become an argument?'

'Let me tell you something,' he said. 'The only thing my mother ever appreciated was hardship.' He too was beginning to sound exhausted.

The room, I noticed, had become silent.

Budgie passed a hard look at Beatrice. 'I don't think hardship is cool or good. I'm not into hair shirts or self flagellation.' It sounded like an accusation.

'What *are* you into?' said Beatrice. This, too, sounded like an accusation.

He paused, but not for dramatic effect. He seemed genuinely contrite. 'I realised long ago that passion is the only thing I care about, the only thing I admire.'

Beatrice blushed.

Budgie, embarrassed, turned away. All of a sudden, he realised that he was facing the rest of us, and it was as if an enchantment had been broken. 'Beatrice admires passion too.' He sounded angry now, like a cornered quoll. 'That's why she loves me.'

Beatrice blushed an even deeper shade of red.

Budgie stormed out of the door.

Calvin kicked a hole in the plaster wall near the heater.

Documentary

ON THE drive back from Strahan to Hobart I said to Budgie 'Why don't you write something about your fishing experiences? All the stories you've told me are eminently publishable'.

'Everyone *writes* about fishing, so I wouldn't want to do that.'

Clearly he had a mind to do something else. I waited in silence for him to elaborate.

'I had an idea for a movie, a documentary,' he admitted coyly. 'Got the idea from your original concept for *Frog Call*, actually. The way you said that the essence of fly fishing was linked to the way trout feed on various mini-beasts, and the way you could pick an animal of prominence for each month of the year.'

He had shed his morbidity like a shuck. 'Tell me more,' I encouraged.

'Well it'd be a trout-fishing documentary without any anglers whatsoever. An Attenborough-quality production depicting the most spectacular things we fly fishers watch trout do. It would include the best of the Tasmanian stuff: footage of spawners grubbing in the gravel after eggs, estuary fish wrestling with lampreys, sea trout seining up whitebait on the sand flats of the Henty, brown trout tailing in the shallows after frogs, rainbows filter-feeding for daphnia and copepods like basking sharks, fish at Little Pine Lagoon clomping down duns. But I'd go further. I'd track down New Zealand leviathans sprinting about after mice, taimen eating voles, Titicaca rainbows eating ducklings, cutthroats eating October caddis. By covering the world, every fly fisher on the planet would be enthralled and inspired. So too would all the people who liked *The Blue Planet* and *Wolves of the Sea*.'

'I'm inspired,' I said. I genuinely was. 'So when are you going to give the idea some legs?'

'Don't have photography skills.'

'Budgie, stop being so bloody negative. You have the *knowledge*. You know where and when the events happen, you have enough broad experience to be able to put everything in context. You know all the guides and experts. All you have to do is make a proposal and find a producer. Let them organise the technical stuff. You need only concentrate on the text, the format and the recruitment of local expertise.'

Lampreys

IT WAS interesting that Budgie should mention that trout eat lampreys.

In late June, juvenile lampreys, about six or seven centimetres long, migrate en masse from headwater tributaries out towards the oceans. Trout and many other fish species can be seen tormenting schools of the critters on the water surface. Such trout are easy to fool; all you need to do is to strip a big wet-fly past them. Young lampreys that survive being eaten by sea trout and other oceanic fish go on to become lethal oceanic parasites of sea trout and other oceanic fish. They use their mouths to latch onto the sides of any decent-sized prey, and suck them dry. You might suppose this to be poetic justice.

Lampreys spend several years at sea, abandoning consecutive fishy hosts as they die, and then head home. By the time they re-enter the estuaries, they are forty to seventy-five centimetres long, but by now they no longer feed nor pose any threat to trout. They migrate into freshwater streams, spawn and die. I don't normally notice their upstream migration, but beginning in early August, I do notice post-spawned lampreys in the lower parts of tributary creeks, totally exhausted, bumbling down shallow currents, becoming ever more bruised and gaunt.

Guess who eats them now?

On several occasions I've watched a big estuary trout writhing around on a shingly spit, grappling with a half-living lamprey. Such trout often have trouble swallowing such a huge mouthful, and after numerous attempts they usually puke the whole thing back up. It is at this point, when they are circling around trying to decide whether or not they should have another go, that they are inclined to opt for something altogether less difficult—like a big wet Woolly Bugger.

Dead lampreys, especially long-dead ones, are more easily consumed than live ones. I had one large trout vomit five putrid corpses as soon as it was grassed. The smell was almost enough to make me contribute my own stomach contents.

So there you have it: trout grow big by eating small lampreys, middle-sized lampreys grow big by eating large trout, and trout grow bigger still by eating full-grown lampreys. What do you make of that?

Lake Beatrice

ALTHOUGH ITS wild rainbows and brown trout don't rise particularly well in late autumn, Calvin decided to walk, alone, to Lake Beatrice. He chose the destination for sentimental reasons, because of the placename. He and Beatrice had been together for almost nine years, and he knew if he couldn't work out some honest way of celebrating their anniversary it would be the ruin of him. He needed to work out how.

He had walked at night, first along the mostly empty bed of Lake Burbury, which was abnormally low because of the drought, then up the little stream which connected Lake Beatrice to the now-exposed King River. And because it was night, because he couldn't distinguish dry boulders from wet ones, he'd been forced to wade rather than rock-hop. The walk normally took an hour or so. Five hours later, after midnight, there was still no sign of the lake. It was raining, the stream was rising. He was cold and tired, but everything was hemmed-in with rainforested cliffs and there was no room to set up a sleeping bag, let alone a tent. He found himself growing ever more weary, and that's probably why he slipped and fell into the rapid. Somehow he managed to cast off his pack, but he lost his torch in the process.

He supposed he would survive, that sometime later in the night he would make his way back out to the road and crawl into the warmth and security of his panel-van bed. Alone. It would be less lonely than sleeping with Beatrice.

He lamented the growing gulf between the two of them at night, the way he often found himself clinging to the cliff-face at the far side of their bed, staring into the abyss. He recalled the occasions he had crawled out from under their doona, pulled a spare mattress from the camping room and slept on the lounge-room floor, just so he could feel less desperate.

She never mentioned those times, never said anything at all, not in the morning, nor in the days and months that followed. Yet always the next night she instigated sex. Silent love. Not overly enthusiastic or inventive, just desperately real.

It bothered him that she was more interested in him if he ignored her. Such a destructive paradox. Now, on the riverbank in the pissing rain, he swore at the injustice of it all, and stamped his foot. He slipped awkwardly on the slimy shingle, and his big toe slammed hard against a partially submerged boulder. He scarcely noticed the pain. It was lost in the turmoil. There must have been a time, he reasoned, when she used to flirt with him. There *must* have been.

These days, if he flattered her, she more or less ignored it. If he didn't flatter her, she ignored that too. If he said 'I love you', she might occasionally say 'Me too'. But never of her own free will had she looked at him with smiling eyes and whispered *I love you*. Surely it was such a simple thing, such a natural thing, to tell your best friends that you love them. A nourishing thing, gentle like drops of summer rain. A rain that stops things from wilting, feeds sparkling streams, fills empty basins. *Nine years* without her once being able to bring herself to say 'I love you'. Was it unreasonable for him to want, to need, his lover to declare her love? What did it mean that she couldn't say such simple words?

He had tried to talk about it, but it had been such a difficult topic to discuss. He felt like he was pleading. Which, he supposed, he was. And what value is a declaration of love that has to be extracted by force? She listened well, cried sometimes, said little, made love afterwards, the best love. And life continued on as before, *exactly* as before, as if there had been no conversation at all.

How many times, he wondered bitterly, can you declare your love to someone who can't reaffirm that love? How many times can you flirt with someone who doesn't respond, not in any way?

The backpack had washed away into the blackness. There was nothing to do except pick his way back down the stream. At least five more hours of drudgery, if hypothermia didn't get to him first, if the freezing water didn't become a flood.

Maybe the reason Beatrice didn't understand his need to be reassured was that she never had any cause to doubt that she was loved. Because for years he couldn't stop telling her he loved her. Not when she emerged naked from the shower, not when they did cryptic crosswords in bed together, not when they watched Hayley opening her Santa sack.

Eventually, miraculously, he staggered onto the buttongrass flats fringing the empty flood-basin. The night was just as dark outside the gorge as in. 'My, how time flies when you're having fun,' he thought wryly. In truth it was becoming hard to think anything at all. His teeth were chattering, his joints stiff. He staggered off across the plains, and was soon trudging through black silt, treacherous like quicksand.

A year or so ago, the thought occurred to him that maybe he only ever professed his love in order to get a response, and all of a sudden being affectionate seemed too much like begging, so he stopped altogether. And felt empty. As bleak as the Burbury flood plains, black and boggy, cold and barren. Defiled.

Once, he implied that he wanted to leave her. He didn't really want to though. There were no women as sexy, competent, laid back, intelligent, electric. He also had too much invested in their relationship, the balm of history. So why did he say it? To get a reaction, he supposed. He hoped that she would lash out, cry, profess love, profess hate, do something—anything—passionate. She just went quiet, and was as unfathomable as ever.

Despite all this, he knew she loved him. So why was it so important for him to hear her say it? Was it her problem, or his? It hardly mattered. The point was, how could he bring himself on this coming anniversary to celebrate something she couldn't even bear to name?

Suddenly he was falling. Then he wasn't. He looked up. He had slipped off a high embankment into the old bed of the King River. Was he hurt? He was so cold he couldn't tell if any bones were broken or tendons torn. But if he was okay, the sandy esplanades along the bed of the King would afford an easy route back to the car. The clouds, he noticed, had completely dissipated. He was looking at the stars. It occurred to him that his relationship with Beatrice was like the universe itself. Finely balanced, expanding against the pull of its own gravity, a force almost exactly sufficient to result in a cataclysmic contraction. His thoughts revolved like planets around stars, his self-confidence swirled in galaxies of confusion. Emotions threatened to explode like supernovae.

Once more, life seemed too difficult to contemplate. It would be easier if he just slipped himself into the cold inky waters of the King. It wouldn't take long for the suffering to subside, not in the condition he was in. How seriously did he want to die? Not at all, he decided. Not yet, or else he would already be dead.

Easter bunny

HELEN, SCARFACE'S wife, was heavily pregnant when she had an unexpected bleed and was admitted to the Royal Hobart Hospital. Suddenly, for the first time ever, Scarface found himself fully responsible for looking after two kids under the age of five. It was just a few days before Christmas. He hit the drink.

At daybreak on Christmas morning, Sammy and Kyle woke up excitedly only to find Dad slumped over the lounge surrounded by empty beer cans. Their Christmas stockings were hanging limp from the mantelpiece. 'Dad,' Sammy said, bewildered, 'why hasn't Santa come?'

Scarface, barely awake, tried to roll over and go back to sleep. But the kids kept pestering him. When they finally burst into tears, he sat up groggily and said 'How the fuck would I know what happened to Santa, eh? For all I know he could've had a fuckin car accident or something'.

To give Scarface credit, he felt a good deal of remorse when he'd sobered up. He even invited Calvin and his family around for what turned out to be a pretty good Christmas dinner.

Kyle said to Beatrice 'We thought Santa hadn't come, but in the middle of the day Dad found our presents in the woodshed'.

'Yeah,' Sammy added. 'Dad reckons he can't fit down the chimney anymore now that we have a wood heater. The flue's too small. Next year we'll have to make sure we leave the back door unlocked.'

A few months later, Calvin bumped into Scarface in the pub and said 'I hope you've fixed up the kids' Easter eggs'.

'Too right I have,' Scarface enthused. After closing time, he even made a point of taking Calvin to the car and proudly showing them off. Two small no-brand eggs, one each for Sammy and Kyle. Nothing for Janet, his new baby.

Calvin came around to my place in a state of moral outrage. 'It's not as if the old bastard has no money at all—he was able to afford a bottle of Black Label whisky for himself.'

It all came to a head a few days later when Scarface won the pub's Easter lottery. First prize was a hamper full of Easter eggs, many of which were made of exquisite Belgian chocolate. Scarface turned to everyone at the bar and said drunkenly 'Person who offers me the most money can have em. Starting price is twenty dollars ninety-five'. That was the price of a box of beer. But nobody was prepared to rip Scarface off, not while he was so drunk, anyway.

That night, Calvin invited me around to his place where Beatrice was sharing a gin and tonic with Magenta. 'He'll keep trying to sell that hamper,' he said. 'It's up to us—we're going to have do something to make sure his kids get a decent Easter.'

In the wee hours of the morning, the three of us—Calvin, Magenta and I, not Beatrice—snuck around to Scarface's place and, quiet as a mouse in the pitch black dark, Calvin used a coat-hanger to jemmy open Scarface's car door. The next morning, we sifted through the hamper and picked out a fair quantity of the best eggs and bunnies for Sammy and Kyle. Calvin sold the rest of the goodies off to his mates, who were allowed in on the joke, and used the money to buy Helen some Easter gifts of her very own—a couple of novels and a fancy blouse that we all knew she had been coveting. He even bought a brightly coloured plush toy for Janet, the baby.

Very early on Easter Sunday, Calvin donned a crude Easter Bunny suit and secretly crept into Scarface's house. Conveniently enough, the back door had been left unlocked. 'Didn't need the disguise,' he said to Magenta and me when he made it back to the getaway car. 'Everyone stayed dead to the world.'

Scarface came round to Calvin's place a few days later. 'Family life's been pretty good lately,' he conceded. 'Kids've been well behaved. Helen's been downright horny. Can't be absolutely sure who to thank for what happened on Easter morning, but I thought you might like this.'

In his hand was a bottle of Black Label whisky.

Keas

WE'D SCOURED the township of Arthur's Pass. Nothing.

Climbed Cons Track to the top of Mount Cassidy. Nothing.

Scrambled up Avalanche Peak with fully laden packs and ventured more than a kilometre along a narrow, precipitous razorback. Still nothing.

・ *Artificial* ・

'This parrot has ceased to exist,' I said in an effort to lift Frances' spirits.

I had been living with Frances, a girl I met on Tasmania's West Coast, for a few years by now, and as soon as we found out that she was pregnant we celebrated by having a holiday on New Zealand's South Island.

'Do you think we will we be able to find the scree slope?' She was referring to the one leading down to the hut at the head of the Crow River valley.

The mist was settling around us—as grey and dense as a woollen duffle coat, but a whole lot less warm. 'More chance of finding the bloody parrot,' I conceded. There was nothing to do really except abort our tramp and retrace our steps all the way back downhill to the township. So near and yet so far from one of the main backcountry destinations we'd earmarked to fish on this all-too-brief trip.

'I could go on…' Frances offered. She was passing her hand over her belly, caressing our unborn baby.

'We'd be mad if we tried to go on.' Now I was being responsible, doing my best to hide my profound disappointment. But it turned out to be the right decision. Things became so foggy that every step was fraught with danger. We scarcely got off the ridge before nightfall.

That night we stayed in a cramped, musty cabin at Arthur's Pass, the only accommodation available on short notice. Frances pored over a map looking for an alternative walking destination, one that still filled our primary objectives—backcountry, good fishing, a chance of finding keas—but which wouldn't be so bloody steep.

The kea is an iconic bird. The world's only alpine parrot. The only carnivorous parrot. The most cheeky parrot. Actually, that bit about being carnivorous is not so much truth as notorious legend, largely perpetrated by disgruntled sheep farmers. Yes, keas have been filmed landing on the backs of sheep and burrowing their beaks through the thick wool and skin to reach the fat surrounding the kidneys, but they prefer carrion, and the bulk of their diet comprises berries, nectar, leaves and roots. The bit about being cheeky is spot-on, though. They pluck the rubber off your boots, rip open backpacks and—for this they deserve thunderous applause—shred vinyl rooftops on seventies car models. They are rarer than they used to be, the parrots as well as the cars, but Arthur's Pass was supposed to be a hotspot.

'How about this?'

Frances had found a tramping track on the eastern edge of the Arthur's Pass National Park that extended up the Andrews Stream valley, continued over a very low saddle into the Casey Stream and went on to a substantial hut near the confluence of the Poulter River. From here we could walk along the edge of the Poulter's wide freestone bed until we arrived at the Minchin Stream, and from there another couple of kilometres through rainforest would get us to Lake Minchin. The whole trip was probably just twenty-five kilometres, and pretty flat, especially once we left the Andrews valley, so it was doable in a day. Not only that but I looked up Lake Minchin in one of my guidebooks and the author said it contained trophy browns. As for the keas, well, being alpine birds, we had effectively scratched them from our itinerary the moment we'd consummated our hate-affair with precipitous mountains. What the heck, they weren't the most important thing in the world.

We started off early the next morning, and almost went straight back home. Although the beginning of the track didn't look particularly steep on the map, we had forgotten to account for the sheer scale of the New Zealand landscape. Frances rechecked the cartography. In order for the contours to be reproduced without them all blending into one thick line, the vertical interval was one hundred metres. One hundred metres! No wonder we were climbing up and down, up and down, up and down without crossing any lines at all.

Luckily, after the first couple of kilometres, the track improved and our spirits lifted. Even so, by the time we got to the halfway point, Casey Hut, it was early afternoon and we were in need of a rest. The shelter was a substantial thing, lined inside with dressed timber and fitted out with a wood heater, stainless-steel sinks and sixteen well-made bunk beds. We ate inside because outside the sandflies drove us crazy, especially if we stood still or sat down.

I was just about to take a bite of my sandwich when we heard someone throw a stone onto the corrugated iron roof. Just what we needed—hoons in the bush. The missile clattered down into the gutter. Then we heard someone hitting the roof with a stick. Dok, dok, dok, dok, dok … Another clatter. Another dok, dok, dok.

We raced outside. There was no-one to be seen.

'Look up there,' said Frances.

On the ridge-cap, seven keas in a rowdy line were jostling each other like children waiting impatiently for a turn on a piece of playground equipment. The one in front gave a little jump, landed on his bum, and slid all the way down to the gutter, whereupon he picked himself up, clawed his way a couple of metres along the edge of the gutter, and then used his long beak to dok, dok, dok his way back up to the ridge, rejoining his mates at the end of the line. Before he was all the way to the top, the next parrot was already halfway down the slide. The whole game was astoundingly ordered, as if the birds were aware of the possibility that a school teacher or playground monitor might be surreptitiously observing them.

Our lunch lasted half an hour or more. The parrots were still playing when we left.

The rest of the walk was very flat and easy, but it was almost dark by the time we got to Minchin. The lake proved to be a crater in the middle of a freestone streambed. It banked up to the sides of the forested valley, but a vast sand-and-shingle flat extended from the northern shore. The lakeshore was choked with weed, but three-quarters of a flyline offshore the water plunged into seemingly bottomless depths. The lip was alive with rising fish, some so big that their slurping rises gurgled like the last swirl of bathwater down a plughole.

I couldn't land the first few fish I hooked. Couldn't even slow them down. They steamrolled off into the depths, stripping off the flyline and backing all the way to the arbor knot. But we soon landed a number of smaller fish, all rainbows from half a kilo to about one-and-a-half kilos. The bigger fish we landed were old, so it seemed strange that we were hooking so many that were even larger and stronger. It wasn't until the next morning, when polaroiding from a rock slip, that we realised that the big fish were eels—giant things as long as your leg and just as thick. The other thing we saw, circling and squawking about the open-tops high above, were keas. Like ravens, Frances suggested. More like currawongs, I thought.

Bar the incessant sandflies, Minchin was idyllic and we stayed several nights. Then we decided to walk out slowly over two days, which really is the sensible thing to do, especially now that I know that there is superb fishing en route in the Poulter itself. This decision gave me time to fish Minchin on the morning of our departure, and because the trout were rising so well, we left rather later than was strictly prudent. Still, we got back to the Casey Hut in good time and decided to see how much further we could get before dusk. That ended up being the head of the Surprise Stream.

The surprise, we quickly discovered, was the sandflies. They swarmed in clouds as thick as the fog on Avalanche Peak, obscuring visibility to the point where my outstretched hand seemed dark and fuzzy. In fact, when I brought my hand close to my eyes it still seemed dark and fuzzy. It was so completely covered in carnivorous insects that it looked as if I was wearing a woolly black glove. Which is what I should have been wearing for protection, but wasn't.

After three nights in the bush, Frances decided that despite the insects she needed a wash before bed. She stripped quickly and waded knee-deep into the creek, dancing, flapping her arms. I flourished two towels about her like a magician performing some sort of vanishing act. No such luck—nothing vanished at all. Things appeared though—dozens upon dozens of bloody sores, all over Frances' body, like beads of red sweat.

Luckily we'd set up our tent before starting this little exercise, but just crawling inside the zippered insect-screen allowed sufficient time for hundreds of sandflies to infiltrate our sanctuary. We pressed them against the inner skin of the tent five at a time, three at a time, one at a time, until finally there were none left. None left inside, that is. Outside there was an incessant hum as platoons of the damned things became trapped between the outer and inner skins. The sound didn't stop until after dark. Only then was I was able to unzip the door and cook some food in the vestibule. So it was well after midnight before we lay down to sleep.

It seemed like I had just drifted off, when the tent fell down around us. I imagined that it had collapsed under a tonnage of sandflies, but the fabric which blanketed us felt as sheer as silk. Everything was dead silent. It was completely dark. There was not a breath of wind.

'What's going on?' Frances asked sleepily.

I had visions of a lunatic stalking trampers in the bush, the sort of psychopath that might get his thrills by tormenting his victims before finally raping and murdering them, so I said nothing, just scrambled about until I found the zipper, then wormed my way outside. There was a flurry of air. Followed by a series of victorious screeches—loud *kee-ah*s which rang in my ears long after the birds themselves had flown away.

By this stage, Frances had managed to find her way outside too, and we inspected the damage. There wasn't any. Not to speak of. All the keas had done was systematically pull every tent peg from the ground. After that, they had been quite content to revel in the pandemonium they'd caused.

Frances looked above her. Only the faintest hint of dawn had crept into the valley. 'At least it's too early for the sandflies,' she said.

Unfortunately, I had become aware of an ominous background hum even as the words were leaving her lips.

Dry fry

WALKING ALONG a swampy tussock-flat flanking the Poulter riverbed, about halfway between the Minchin Stream confluence and the Casey Hut, we were startled by a loud rush, a sound akin to a huge flock of ducks landing on water. Except there were no ducks. Nor any water, as far as I could tell.

'A Haast eagle?' Frances joked, referring to the extinct raptor, twice as big as a wedge-tail, that once preyed upon moa until the moa was hunted to oblivion by the Maoris three or four hundred years ago. The rush of adrenalin we'd just received accentuated the feeling of dread I'd long associated with Haast eagles. Imagine the horror of having your child carried off between blood-drenched talons, higher and higher, over the mountain tops, out of sight.

'Look!' Frances had wandered off into the tussocks. I could barely hear her above renewed rushing sounds, now coming in waves. I ran to her side, and found myself standing beside a narrow swamp, maybe twenty metres long, barely ankle deep. It was crammed full of fish. Tiny fish. Quinnat salmon fry. Countless millions of them.

With every movement we made, the salmon panicked and boiled the water, but there was nowhere for them to go. They were packed in tight like salted anchovies. The sun beat down, the water was tepid, the outflow gutter bone dry.

The fish would die today or tomorrow if we didn't do something.

The only container I had was a billycan. I could fit in no more than a couple of hundred at a time, and since the Poulter River was half a kilometre away, across an exposed bed of blistering-hot shingle, the futility of attempting any rescue quickly became obvious.

We walked on. There were many more weedy tarns filled with many more distressed fish. Sometimes we saw a heron or two gorging themselves. Mostly only rapacious wolf spiders. The great majority of the fish were simply going to decay into the same fetid slime that had already corrupted the shallower puddles through which we tramped. Kilometre after kilometre.

Laughing Dog

I WAS once employed as the summer ranger for the Western Lakes, a wilderness area on Tasmania's Central Plateau. The most important part of my work was simply to wave the flag for the Parks and Wildlife Service. Actually, the flag was not so much waved as worn— on one shoulder of the staid khaki shirts. It featured a head-and-neck profile of a wide-mouthed Tasmanian devil, a mascot affectionately known by field staff as 'the laughing dog'. Some rangers' dogs continued to laugh brightly right through the summer. Perhaps they were amused by their owners' spotlessly clean uniforms, the impossibly crisp creases, the way everything stayed spruce enough to impress the most patriotic of scout masters. I can't begin to imagine how anyone could maintain such impeccable laundry while living out of a backpack in the wilderness. Or why anyone would bother trying. My own shirts crumpled quickly, and soon became grimy and tattered. After the first day of hard walking, my dog didn't laugh so much as sweat and pant.

My first few two-week stints were to areas so remote that the only eyes that set sight on the cloth devil were those of wallabies and actual devils. My new assignment, thankfully, was to be in a more fashionable destination.

The picturesque Pine River valley is well sheltered from the prevailing westerly weather, and there are several idyllic campsites amid clumps of stunted sub-alpine trees. Moreover, the main lakes constitute an angler's paradise, Lake Antimony being noted for its wade-polaroiding, and Silver Lake for its unrivalled dun hatches. I was satisfied that the campsites received enough use to justify the inventories I was required to undertake. And I was quite excited by the prospect of actually talking to an angler or two. Perhaps I might even complete enough user surveys for the information to be statistically valid.

On the day I set out from the Liawenee ranger station for my assignment, an ugly low-pressure system settled in over the plateau. At the last minute, I was instructed to camp at Christys Creek, on an elevated moor which was exposed to the very worst of the weather, six long kilometres east of where I was to carry out my day-to-day tasks.

The track from Lake Ada past Talinah Lagoon and Christys Creek to Talleh Lagoons and Lake Fanny was originally an old stock route (it is clearly marked on an anonymous roll plan dated 1849). For a while, in the 1960s and early 1970s, it was infrequently used by four-wheel-drive vehicles, and a group of anglers even forged a crude extension from Talleh Lagoons to Lake Antimony, where they built a small hut. But since 1978 it has been managed as a walking track. It remains quite well defined as far as Christys Creek, where it forks and, for a kilometre or so, exists as two more-or-less parallel tracks. Then it reconverges and becomes more overgrown, and by the time you reach Talleh Lagoons it can be quite difficult to trace, particularly in fog or snow.

I set up camp on the north braid of the track, near the banks of a good mayfly lagoon, one of the best waters in the Christys chain— but not before I satisfied myself that my bright tent was visible to passers-by, even if they were using the other braid.

Each morning I walked for two or three hours to the Pine valley— head-first into the weather—and at the end of each day I had to walk back again. This really didn't leave much time for campsite inventories. Nor did it leave much time to talk to anglers, though in lieu of the weather, I knew that wasn't going to matter at all—people would surely be as scarce as thylacines.

On day six, as I approached the main campsite at Silver Lake, I was surprised to see a tent. I squinted into the rain. There was someone at home, someone to talk to. Stripe me pink, it was Magenta!

'I needed some time out to contemplate life, the universe and

Zongo,' she said despondently.

I felt slightly guilty feeling so upbeat when she was clearly on a bit of a downer. 'You're the first person I've seen in days,' I explained.

'Reckon you'll find anyone else?' She was smiling at the weather; the question was clearly supposed to be rhetorical.

'Frances plans to walk out to Christys with our son tonight.'

'That's brave of her. Tom's, what, six months old?'

'Five, but Frances' brother and his girlfriend will probably walk out with her, to keep her company and help carry baby supplies.'

We retreated out of the weather into Magenta's snug nest. She made me a cuppy, then another. I kept saying that I had work to do, but found myself becoming less and less motivated.

'Bugger the work,' Magenta recommended. 'No-one should be expected to work in this weather. Anyway, the department shouldn't send people out here alone for days on end with no communication equipment. You'd only have to twist your ankle or something and you'd be as good as dead. I'd like to see how the Service would explain that to the local tabloids. It's absurd. The only reason you get the surveys done at all is because you put in twelve- and fourteen-hour days. If you put in the requisite eight hours, you'd scarcely have time to walk the round trip from Christys. Face it, your job is untenable, you owe no-one nothing. Just have another cuppa and relax.'

During the course of the last few weeks I had rationalised all that Magenta had said over and over again, but hearing her saying it out loud, of her own accord, lifted a huge weight from my conscience. That afternoon, not evening, I walked back to camp with a spring in my step. Perhaps Frances would arrive early. I made up my mind that if the weather was better tomorrow, I wouldn't work at all. We'd just sit and talk and drink cuppies. And, weather permitting, maybe catch a riser or two.

Halfway home, the rain stopped. And the wind. Suddenly, everything was eerily silent. The air quickly thickened into a dense fog, and proceeded to get thicker. I almost missed the fork in the track, and didn't see my tent until I was upon it. There was no-one there. It was just possible that my family was camped somewhere not too far away. More likely, they took the south braid of the track, got sick of looking for me, and went home. It was drizzling again. I crawled despondently into my sodden tent and cooked a meal.

By early evening I was convinced Frances wasn't going to find me. I thought about going for a fish, but I could hardly see the lake, let alone spot tailers or risers, not that there was much likelihood of finding either. I sat in the tent, half-heartedly reading the final chapters of my third paperback. This was the last book I had with me. What would I do when it ran out of words? My thoughts turned mutinous. Bloody Parks and Wildlife Service.

'Hey Trout, you in there?' It was Magenta. She unzipped the tent and poked her head inside. 'The weather's got to me. I'm going home.'

'Want to stay the night?' I asked hopefully.

She peered back into the sleet and mizzle. 'Nah,' she said apologetically. 'I just want to get out of here. The climate's doing nothing to cheer me up. I'll make us a cuppa before I head off though.'

We sat huddled in the tent. The Trangia boiled water in the vestibule. Steam condensed thickly on the inside of the tent fly. When the tea was finally poured, I found it more soothing just to hold the warm cup in my cold hands. 'I'd offer you some nibbles,' I said, 'but things have been so wet and boring that I ate ten days' worth of bickies in two sittings.'

'I've got some cakes,' Magenta replied cheerfully, pulling her sodden pack halfway into the tent. After a bit of rummaging around she withdrew a bag of Anzacs. Then she found what she was looking for: some rock cakes. 'Here, have one of these,' she offered.

'Would it be alright if I had an Anzac instead?'

'Well you could, Trout,' she said dubiously, 'but you might not like them very much.'

'Why not?'

'Well, ah, you see...'

'They're *hash* bickies, aren't they?'

'Well, yes. Particularly good ones, if I say so myself. A novice like you wouldn't be able to handle much. Just a nibble might be alright, but a whole bickie would probably have you right off your face. Any more than that... well, I'd hate to think.'

So we sat there huddled up together eating rock cakes, talking about the bush and Zongo, and fishing and Zongo. We ridiculed and bemoaned bureaucratic idiots who'd send you out into the bush in weather like this to a place where no practical work could be done.

We talked more about Zongo. And finally we realised that the drizzly tattoo on the tent had completely faded away. Magenta pushed her head outside. The air had cleared to the point where you could almost see the other side of the lake. 'I'd best be off,' she said. 'It's as good a time as ever, and if I don't leave soon I won't get back to the car before dark.'

She stuffed her gear back into her pack, gave me an affectionate peck, and headed off down the track. I watched her until she rounded a distant boulder, and kept watching until the boulder itself was swallowed up in the creeping greyness.

It was just after dark when I finished the last of my reading material. I felt lonelier than ever, bored and trapped. I hated being where I was. Because I hadn't done enough exercise to feel like sleeping, I made myself yet another cuppy. That was when I noticed that Magenta had overlooked packing her bickies. The Anzacs, not the rock cakes.

The bickies sat there, poisonous in the candlelight, glowing like an apple in the Garden of Eden. I pushed them away. I hid them under the sleeping bag. I put them out in the vestibule. I put them inside the pack out in the vestibule. But the temptation that radiated from them responded to my unfriendly behaviour by mutating into something uncontainable.

'Bugger it!' I eventually declared out loud. 'I'm bored and hungry.' Just one little bit couldn't hurt, surely.

I had one little bit. Then another.

By leaving a piece, by not eating an entire biscuit, I tried to convince myself that I'd only eaten half of one. And then, admitting that I was just deluding myself, I scoffed the bit that was left. The guilt, I decided, was worth it.

I lay down. Things were feeling decidedly warm and fuzzy. If only the bureaucrats could see me now. I pressed my cheek snugly against my shoulder and laughed out loud. The dog laughed right back.

What I really needed was a wee. That would mean getting out of my warm tent and going into the rain. Absurd. The dog and I giggled at the thought. Giggling felt good—I mean the physical act, the vibration of my lips.

The torch failed to penetrate the mist. Awesome. I staggered forth, like Mawson, I imagined, and pissed against a boulder. Hilarious! Then I found it impossible to see or remember where the tent was.

It couldn't be more than ten metres away, but in this fog it might just as well have been kilometres. I was scared now. If I died, at least that would teach the bastards. I laughed again, felt good again. I wandered slowly in all directions, ever so cautiously. Was this what it was like on Mt Everest, in the death zone, where the very act of putting one foot in front of the other was exhausting and obscenely dangerous?

All of a sudden, miraculously, I was back at the tent. I crawled inside and savoured the warmth and security. I snuggled into my sleeping bag. The world, although a little unsteady, was secure and beautiful. I drifted off to sleep with snapshots of life's most wonderful events kaleidoscoping through my head.

I don't know what time it was when I woke up. All I know is that it was pitch black and that I had the munchies. Big time. I turned on the torch. I could have killed for some lollies or potato chips or… what was this? A bag of Anzacs? Where the hell did they come from? I certainly didn't pack them in. How weird. But then again, how opportune. I took one out. Hmm… it tasted *gooood*. I figured I'd better have another one. These biscuits were, in fact, the tastiest, most more-ish things I'd ever eaten anytime, anywhere.

I lay back down, sated and, for a short while, perfectly content. Then the world began to spin, slowly at first, then as fast as a neutron star. I felt myself falling, found myself flailing. I held on to a bundle of clothes—the one that doubled as my pillow—like a lifesaver. I remember vomiting. I remember believing I was going to die.

Throughout it all, the bad and still badder, the dog just wouldn't stop laughing.

Tanglefoot

NOTHOFAGUS IS Latin for 'new beech', differentiating Gondwanan trees from the similar-looking *Fagus* (beech) of the northern hemisphere. Living varieties of the genus are found in south-eastern Australia, New Zealand, New Guinea, New Caledonia, Chile and Argentina, while fossil species turn up in Antarctica.

In Tasmania, the dominant rainforest tree *Nothofagus cunninghamii* is known locally as myrtle, the more 'correct' name, 'myrtle beech', having been totally eschewed. It features strongly in my life. It produces magnificent hardwood, especially for joinery. It also provides spectacular prehistoric habitat on some of my favourite streams, the Weld and Hellyer rivers being but two examples. It even persists on sheltered slopes and gullies in the high plains, forming dainty clusters of welcome shade and moisture.

The other Tasmanian representative of the genus, *Nothofagus gunnii*, is a small, shrubby, sub-alpine tree which happens to be the only native deciduous tree in Tasmania, and the only native deciduous cold-climate tree in all of Australia. It sprawls in entanglements over high-country hillsides and provides a magnificent spectacle in autumn—Anzac Day, April 25, being set aside by a great many anglers and bushwalkers for annual pilgrimages to places as revered as Lake Dove and the Mt Field lakes.

When I was younger, *Nothofagus gunnii* was widely known as tanglefoot, an affectionate reference to how dismissive it is of our desire for convenient access. You might know it from the glorious photos that have appeared in wilderness calendars dating back to the 1970s and 80s. If so, you will be aware that botanically literate photographers, reliant upon mainland sales, have almost universally captioned the relevant images with the contrived and rather dull name 'deciduous beech'. Thus tanglefoot has gone the way of the Aboriginal languages. The only good news, linguistically speaking, is that for some obscure reason the other common name, 'fagus', is now at least as popular as 'deciduous beech'. Many of my botanical mates loudly object that they are not *Fagus*, they are *Nothofagus*, conveniently overlooking the fact that nor are they 'deciduous beech' but rather deciduous new-beech.

Mouse

IN NEW Zealand, there are five species of *Nothofagus*. Here too, prosaic names such as silver beech, mountain beech and red beech have largely replaced local names like tawhai, tawhairauriki and tawhairraunui, but if the nomenclature has become boring, the trees themselves remain magnificent and inspirational. Every four to seven years they undergo mass seeding, creating an oversupply of forest food which, in turn, triggers high fertility and survival among mice, resulting, within the space of a few weeks, in veritable plagues.

The mice are most active at night, but in good years there's a constant flurry of activity even during the day. Local lore has it that the seeds ferment on the trees and the mice eat themselves into a drunken stupor. In any case, the rodents scurry along branches overhanging the water, and rain down into rivers and lakes. Trout quickly learn that a splash means a solid lump of protein with minimal fuss. They will sprint from metres away, often straight across a big current, to intercept a mouse. They fairly streak along, creating huge wakes and splashes.

Locals tie giant mouse-imitation flies. But actually, anything that makes a splash or wake will do. I've even resorted to gluing a whole wine cork to a fly hook, to good effect I might add. Perhaps it's the alcohol again.

Many anglers are besotted by the fact that fish gain an awful lot of weight during mouse plagues. David Tasker, writing in *FlyLife* magazine, noted that although fish of sixty-five centimetres in length usually scale-in at seven to eight pounds, in a mouse year they often hit the magic ten-pound mark. But for me, such statistics are trivial. It is the feeding display itself that enthrals. Indeed, no-one who sees it, not even people who have no affinity with trout fishing, can escape its drama.

Do you think that the experience should be considered invalid, or somehow less enchanting, because it is a tale of two feral animals in native bushland?

As much as I love remote places, I've learned not to overplay the importance of 'virgin' wilderness. In truth, I've never really understood this obsession people have with virgins—I've always thought it a bit creepy, actually, something best left to the occult.

Anyway, when you overplay the purity thing, someone inevitably points out that there is no longer any square centimetre on the planet uninfluenced by humanity. No matter where we are, we are surrounded by climate change, radio waves and atmospheric pollution, and everything is affected by changes in ocean currents and the redistribution of species. You could also argue that the human legacy in New Zealand dates back not just two hundred years, or even a thousand years, but back further still, into primal eternity.

Clearly it is not virginity that makes wild places important, any more than virginity makes people important. So what, I wonder, is important?

Bucket

THERE WAS a mouse plague on the North Island when I called in to see one of the local fishing guides, someone I didn't know. It was a self-introduction recommended by a mutual friend, and the guide wasn't expecting me. I found him in the shed behind his house, staring into a plastic garbage bin, totally absorbed. I announced my arrival with a self-conscious 'Hello'.

'Be damned,' he said incredulously without lifting his gaze. 'Come and look at this.'

I stared into the bucket. It was half full of water. There was a mouse swimming around the perimeter, like a trout in a circular rearing pond. It was so exhausted it looked like it should have been covered in cottonwool fungus.

'He's been swimming like that for a full day-and-a-half now. How much longer do you reckon he can hold out?'

Ouse

I WAS driving with Calvin from Hobart back to Strahan. We had already commented upon some of the more ostentatious entranceways to various rural properties—ridiculous stone or brick edifices that contained more materials and labour than many people could afford to incorporate into the family home—when, on our approach to the rural township of Ouse, I noticed a huge gantry straddling a driveway. On top was a life-sized fallow deer—a snow-white stag with massive golden antlers.

'How long has that been there?' I said, gobsmacked.

'I didn't notice it last week,' Calvin admitted. 'Do you reckon it's made of fibreglass?'

'Well, I suppose we'll know soon enough.' It seemed such an obvious target for larrikinism: 'Hey boys let's go and bag ourselves a deer. I hear that a huge white stag has been seen loitering around on the edge of town. Do you think we should use a .303 or the elephant gun?'

'If I lived in this town, I'd have its arse stuffed with jelly in no time,' Calvin confessed.

But, miraculously, it was still in one piece when we drove back to Hobart a week later. In fact, it's still there now, years later. So far as I'm aware, no-one has ever attempted to violate it in any way. There's not been a single piece of witty graffiti, not one effigy of a New Zealander performing an unnatural act. Nothing.

What, I ask, has the world come to? Sometimes I despair for the youth of today.

Fallows

DURING THE last decade or so, Tasmania's fallow deer population has grown exponentially, with herds burgeoning all the way from Great Lake across the Midlands to eastern destinations like Lake Leake and Tooms Lake.

Tooms Lake is set in dry eucalypt woodland, a haunting remnant of what much of eastern Australia used to be like in the late 1800s. It doesn't take too much imagination to invoke the atmosphere created by Rolf Boldrewood in *Robbery Under Arms*, and subconsciously at least, you are always on the alert for something out of the ordinary.

Danny, a doctor friend of mine, was discussing this very thing with a mate of his as they were driving home from a Tooms fishing trip. A hint of moonlight, perhaps nothing more than Starlight, faintly illuminated the narrow gravel road and made the trees stand out like silhouettes. Branches reached threateningly across the road, as if beckoning travellers to 'Stand! Bail up!'

'Banjo Patterson country, this is,' suggested Danny.

'Nah. It's too real. It's more like Henry Lawson country. You can feel the deprivations that early settlers would have endured, sense the desperate isolation… Did you hear that?'

'What?'

'That sound. Outside.'

Danny strained to hear what his friend heard. It was a sort of menacing rattling noise. 'Perhaps something's stuck under the car. Could be a twig or something wedged in the muffler bracket and dragging along the road,' he suggested hopefully.

They pulled over to the side of the road, and just as Danny began to open the door, something roared past them, inducing a rush of adrenalin. It took some time to work out what had happened.

'A bloody motorcycle without its headlights on,' Danny deduced at last.

'He must have been riding in our slipstream for the last kilometre or so,' his mate agreed. 'That would account for the strange sound anyway.'

'How far do you think he can go with no headlights before he has an accident?' Danny wondered.

It turned out to be precisely ten kilometres. The motorcycle rounded a corner and slammed smack-bang into the middle of a fallow deer. Its rider had no idea how lucky he was that a medical doctor was on the scene within minutes. Given the extent of his injuries, he had no coherent idea of anything much.

Roadkill

OBSESSIVE FLY fishers, like me, are wont to fish from first light until after dark, which means we often find ourselves driving to and from remote places at night. Marsupials are similarly nocturnal, and they too tend to congregate along roads.

Road verges are relatively wet, not just because runoff collects in gutters, but also because water spraying from the wheels of passing vehicles drifts and irrigates wide esplanades. The apparent good health of roadside tree plantings, such as those in Tasmania's Midlands, often gives a false impression that climate change isn't as bad as people say. But if you get out of your car and wander fifty or a hundred metres away—another thing fly fishers are prone to do— you too often find the ground decidedly dry and sick. The esplanades are uncommonly green, and this is why they are such an attraction to marsupials, which in the height of summer often find they have nowhere else to graze.

Brushtail possums, pademelons and Bennett's wallabies are the things most frequently illuminated by headlights, though bettongs and bandicoots—as well as introduced rabbits and hares—are common enough. Happily, forester kangaroos, one of Australia's two largest marsupials (the other being the red kangaroo) are also more abundant than they used to be. So too are fallow deer. Last year I had to stop on the Barren Plains Road, on the way to Shannon Lagoon, while hundreds of does and fawns crossed the road in front of the car in a manner reminiscent of antelope on the Serengeti. It was hardly an inconvenience—more a privilege. Does and fawns may not be native, but they are delightful, and the stags, when you chance to see them, are truly majestic. Well, most are. Recently, between Bothwell and the Steppes, a fully antlered animal fleeted across the road directly in front of us and, most unusually, failed to clear a fence. We watched as it flailed about astride the top wire, its scrotum firmly appended to the barbs. Eventually, with some reservations about how big and violent it was, Frances, Jane, Tom and I decided that we would have to at least try to help it. But upon seeing such a team of nervous amateurs, it panicked and literally tore itself free.

There is a scene in the film *The Sound of One Hand Clapping,* where the father, driving at night with his estranged daughter in the passenger seat, repeatedly runs over wallabies. He isn't trying to hit the animals, nor does he veer to miss them. You don't see the carnage. All you hear is a *thwock,* followed by more obstinate driving, a little later another *thwock,* and another, and the silence in between like an unbridgeable gulf. Blurred are the boundaries between insensitivity, belligerence, inevitability and hopelessness.

My own father never seemed to be callous—at least he gave a cursory swerve wherever possible—but to my disappointment he never went back to check whether any of the many animals he hit needed to be put out of their misery. I resolved from an early age that I would learn how to drive properly. Alas, what I actually learned was that it is impossible not to run over wildlife. Some nights marsupials line the roads in their countless dozens, like guards of honour. It is generally supposed that they run in front of your car because they get dazzled by the headlights. Ha! More likely they are simply full of high spirits. Like adolescent humans, they seem to have a heightened sense of their own invincibility and are easily influenced by peer pressure—'Go on, run now!'

Wallabies don't only hop out in front of you—they are just as likely to race headlong into the side doors. On one memorable occasion, a huge Bennett's wallaby jumped off an embankment smack onto the car bonnet, which promptly crimped, unclipped itself, caught the wind and folded back towards me, smashing the windscreen as it went. Finally the hood broke from its hinges and tumbled over the roof, barely missing the car following behind.

You might think it improbable when I tell you that the wallaby escaped unscathed. But it's often the case—when you go back, the victim is nowhere to be seen. If you do find it—if it is crippled and bloody and barely alive—what then? Do you ignore the fact that, despite its pain and suffering, it clearly doesn't want to be 'put out of its misery'? Do you promptly stomp your heel on its head in full gruesome sight of genteel visitors or delicate young children? And what about the joeys, pink bung-eyed embryos with no hope of survival? It's hardly surprising that many people simply can't bring themselves to return to the scene of the crime.

Unfortunately, driving more slowly is only a partial solution. For many years we have lived a few kilometres up a bush valley on a winding gravel road where it is nigh on impossible to exceed forty kilometres an hour. Yet we run over almost as many animals here as we do on highland roads where we travel twice that speed. Even if we drove slower than forty, which would be impractical, it might not help all that much. We once saw a wallaby, a hundred metres or more away, bounding straight down the middle of the road towards us. Frances slowed down, and eventually stopped. The wallaby's response was to speed up. It came on so fast that when it hit the car, it died as assuredly as a certain spring salmon in the Little Qualicum River (which you will hear about soon enough).

Overkill

A FRIEND of mine told me of the revulsion he felt on his first fishing trip to Tasmania when he saw the carnage on our roads. Tasmanian drivers, he felt, must be unnaturally reckless and barbaric. Then, to his horror, he promptly proceeded to plough straight into a pademelon. He backed back. The wallaby was still alive. He cradled the limp thing in his arms. There was no obvious bleeding or broken bones, and after a time he fancied that he could feel its strength returning. After cleaning the gravel from its mouth, he placed it back on the road verge. It was dazed, but after fifteen minutes of tender loving encouragement, it seemed to recover its faculties. Finally, it glanced over its shoulder, as if to offer sincere thanks, and hopped away across the road—straight into an oncoming four-wheel drive.

Grave robbers

IN A strictly biological sense, the carnage on our roads probably doesn't matter. Wallabies have lots of joeys in their lifetime, so the population is mostly limited by environmental factors such as availability of food. In fact, despite the roadkill, there may be more marsupials in Tasmania now than ever before. Brushtail possums, for example, have taken advantage of unnatural pastures to the extent that in many areas they are literally in plague proportions. Not only are the exotic grasses lush, permitting more animals to survive per hectare than would normally be the case, but they don't contain the fertility suppressants that occur in natural foods such as eucalypt leaves. But the news is not all good. In times of drought, armies of possums are forced to retreat, first back to lush road verges, then into remnant stands of forest where they cause devastation.

Whether or not roadkill represents an environmental tragedy, I've never met anyone in Tasmania who enjoys running over wildlife. Still, given that roadkill is inevitable, the question arises: what should we do with it?

Marsupial fur is extremely good for dubbing flies, and many fly tiers scour roadkill for fibres of unusual texture or colour. But there is only so much you can use. Lester gave me a few tufts of fur from a pure-gold brushtail (very rare) and although I've used it to tie hundreds of whitebait flies, I fear I still have several lifetimes of fur left over.

Calvin has taken a more novel approach. He has stretched an old wire bed-base across a narrow creek at precisely the point where it enters a substantial broadwater, and kept it fully laden with broken possums and wallabies. The proliferating maggots drip into the current and are washed into the pool, and the edges of the current have become the prime feeding grounds for the very biggest of fish. These leviathans defend their perpetual banquet with such savagery that nothing is safe, not small trout, not moderately big ones. Nor big Black Matukas.

I too have long adopted a pragmatic approach, taking anything I hit back to the kitchen table.

Strangely enough, it is the quantity rather than the quality of roadkill that remains the main topic for discussion amongst visitors and the local media. But the wonder is that you don't see even more roadkill than you do. It's not as if it rots away particularly quickly. If, one morning in the outback, you hit a red kangaroo, it is malodorous by afternoon and completely rotten within a few days. Not so in Tasmania.

A large wombat was once killed at the foot of our driveway and after a day or two Frances convinced me that it should be removed before it got really sordid. As I approached, I saw its belly vibrating and thumping in the manner of a heavily pregnant woman's midriff. Then, in a moment eerily akin to the scene in *Alien*, Halla, my daughter's Jack Russell, then a small puppy, burst from its anus. She was messy but, mercifully after two days, the carcass hadn't yet begun to pong. Honestly, in winter Tasmanian roadkill has a half-life that would put uranium to shame. I know this because Halla, having grown bigger, now drags roadkill up onto the front lawn, and from our verandah we are treated to front-row viewing of its decay.

The Devil you know

YOU NOW know what happens to roadkill when Calvin or me or Halla are about, but what about all the rest of it? Some councils, embarrassed by what the carnage does to our 'clean, green' image, employ people to scour the roads at dawn and shovel last night's carcasses onto box trailers. They think that tourists won't be up and about yet. They don't think about the nocturnal habits of fly fishers. What happens to carcasses thus collected, we wonder? I doubt they give them to Calvin for his wire bed. My guess is that they hate him for his propensity to secretly emblazon their modern-day death carts with giant stickers promoting one or other of the local meat-pie companies.

Another reason that roadkill disappears is that Tasmania is well populated with scavengers. Crows, for example, which you see picking and probing at carcasses from one end of the state to the other. Crow feathers are highly valued by fly tiers because they make good beetle backs, and some of my mates have jokingly tried to run crows over. I say 'jokingly' because everyone knows it is impossible. They are aware of everything around them and always manage to hop away at the last minute, often with 'just one more' entrail hanging from their beaks.

Quolls, too, are efficient scavengers, and despite their small size, they can literally run off dragging a full-grown pademelon. But they are not as cautious as crows, and often end up as fodder for fellow quolls.

A scavenger we see a lot less of these days is the Tasmanian devil. Populations of these fantastic animals have always been prone to booms and busts. When I was a child they were so rare that my dad, as one of his save-the-kids-from-getting-bored-in-the-car games, used to offer a two-bob bit to anyone who saw one walking along the road. Even a dead one was good for a shilling.

Devil numbers built up in the 1970s and 80s, and for a while it was nothing to see them scouring the road verges during a night-drive through the Central Highlands. While farmers used to hate devils, thinking them killers of lambs, fly fishers seem to have universally appreciated them, demonstrating tolerance, even pride, when they found that their fly rods had been chewed to bits overnight. 'Teach me for not cleaning the fish blood off the handle, won't it?'

In recent years, devils have developed a grotesque facial tumour disease which, it seems, is a contagious cancer transferred from one animal to another during fights—a behaviour for which devils are renowned. The contagious cancer theory was at first difficult to support. Devils, like a surprising number of other mammals, most famously cheetahs, have in the distant past dwindled to just a few survivors. This means that they do not possess much in the way of genetic diversity, and *this* means that it is relatively hard to distinguish between the DNA of one individual and that of any other. Eventually, though, researchers did find one animal whose DNA was quite distinctive, and since her cancer cells were not similarly distinctive, the matter seems to have been settled.

We now believe that devil facial tumour disease originated in one animal in the north-east of the state. We know that it has spread rapidly, and that in many areas it has resulted in ninety per cent mortality. What caused the original mutation? Depending on which barrow you have to push, you might blame 1080 poison, pesticides, feral animals, rabbit calicivirus or any number of other nasties, but the truth is we just don't know. We should be doing a damned lot more than we are to find out. Isn't the thought of a contagious cancer scary enough to warrant a major investigation?

In addition to wider considerations about human health, the environmental ramifications of devil facial tumour disease are almost too gruesome to countenance. You see, the reason Tasmania has so much roadkill is that we have so much wildlife, and the reason we have so much more wildlife than mainland Australia is that we don't have foxes. And in all probability the reason we don't have foxes is that we do have Tasmanian devils.

Historically there have been several attempts by hunting clubs to establish foxes in Tasmania, some well documented, many not documented at all. And everyone pretty much agrees that the odd fox has been slipping into the State's ports for years—Melbourne's Webb Dock has been home to upwards of sixteen foxes per square kilometre, and reliable witnesses in Burnie have seen at least one stowaway leap from a shipping container. Despite the ease at which the species has managed to establish rampant populations in temperate habitats all over the world, foxes released in Tasmania have failed to survive or procreate. The only plausible explanation is that devils dig up their dens and eat their young.

In recent years, foxes have again found their way into Tasmania. Some have arrived in shipping containers from Victoria. Some have been deliberately introduced by locals, perhaps as revenge for some perceived injustice inflicted upon them by the National Parks and Wildlife Service. If they establish, you won't see so much roadkill in Tasmania, and that will be far more tragic than seeing so much of it.

Are foxes likely to reach critical mass and then prove impossible to control, as they have elsewhere in Australia? Despite years of massive baiting, trapping and spotlighting programs, the government-funded Fox Task Force has not captured a single fox. A couple of carcasses have been turned in by members of the public, but there is always a sneaking suspicion that these are plants, either by people out for a lark, or by environmentalists worried that, in the absence of hard evidence, funds will dry up and foxes will become established after all.

I quizzed one reliable source on this matter and he insisted that the evidence was overwhelming: so much circumstantial 'proof', so many sightings. I don't doubt his sincerity. Mind you, in the past he has been dismissive of exactly the same sort of evidence in favour of the continued existence of thylacines. 'Clusters of sightings are just what you expect because people are easily influenced by media and prone to hysteria. Consider all the people who claim to have seen Elvis or been abducted by aliens.'

As for me, I just don't know what to believe. But if foxes do establish, it is likely that animals such as native hens, pademelons, bettongs and bandicoots will become extinct in the wild, as has already happened on the mainland. These creatures are so much a part of what is unique about Tasmanian fishing that I can't bring myself to imagine my world without them.

Nappy

WHEN TOM was a baby, he used to spend one day every week at childcare. Cotton nappies, much in favour amongst the environmentally conscious parents who dominated this particular facility, were stored in open-fronted pigeonholes. I was continually dazzled, and bemused, by the spanking-white bundles of softness—rows upon rows of them—that surrounded Tom's abrasive grey pretenders (his nappies, not his carers). His nappies, you see, were treated somewhat differently than those of his mates. Frances and I would take him bushwalking for days on end, and so as not to pollute the drinking water in the streams and lakes, we simply sealed his nappies in plastic shopping bags and carried them out to be properly washed at home. Unfortunately, on the way home we might call in to, say, Lester's place and end up staying for a day or two, and the forgotten nappy bags frequently ended up stewing in the car. In summer, conditions in the boot must have been oven-like. When we finally got home, the nappies would get a quick hosing and then a thorough wash in cold water and detergent. We figured that this process, regrettable as it often was, had to be healthier than impregnating nappies with bleaches, antibacterials, fabric softeners and other harsh chemicals. My grandma used to say that children needed to play in grime in order to grow up strong. Ideally, she stressed, they should consume a pound of dirt a year. Perhaps we took her advice too much to heart—we certainly noticed the odd double-take from Tom's carers.

One day when I called in to pick Tom up, I was met by the director and ushered into the front office, where I was given a comfy chair, a soothing cup of tea, and some tender advice. 'You know, if you ever find yourself caught between a rock and a hard place, if you are ever really hard up, there are government assistance programs you might be able to access.' Guessing it was something to do with the state of the nappies, I didn't think much about it. But that evening, Tom told us that his class had been discussing 'the five food groups', and when people were given the opportunity to talk about what they had eaten yesterday, Tom had proudly boasted 'Roadkill!' Presumably, the staff had visions of Frances and I scouring the roads looking for not-too-rancid carcasses. Perhaps they would have found the truth no less shocking.

New Holland

TROUT CONSUME a whole menagerie of mini-beasts, many of which are even weirder than the things in Budgie's fly collection. In addition to fish, birds and mammals, they are also partial to amphibians.

When promoting my previous book *Frog Call*, the thing most radio presenters got me to explain to their listeners was why a book that is inherently about fly fishing would feature a frog on the front cover and in the title. I answered this question more than a dozen times, so by the end my answer had become quite polished...

Frogs are green and precious. They are revered by fly fishers because trout forage for them in extremely shallow water along the marshy edges of lakes and rivers, displaying dorsal fins and tails like marauding sharks. But frogs also have an uncanny ability to connect with people of all walks of life. The front cover went through several drafts, and the one I originally liked featured nothing much more than the eye. New Holland's marketing people insisted that a less cryptic image would be better. Their message was simple—if the cover is obviously a frog, people will be disinclined to pass the work over. People love frogs—frogs are saleable.

The other thing about frogs is that they are in serious decline. This is a worldwide phenomenon, and a pretty scary one. The problems frogs face are not well understood, but probably have something to do with infection by exotic fungi, ozone depletion, chemical pollution, global warming and large-scale habitat destruction. So what is our response? We make it illegal for children to wander around in swamps gathering tadpoles, to kill passion for the natural world before it has even been conceived.

The question I wanted readers of *Frog Call* to ask themselves was this: what can we do to help people involve themselves so intimately with the natural world that animals and plants become more spiritually important than the promise of material wealth?

Dulverton

As a kid I used to use frogs for trout bait. I agree, it's strange that someone who loves frogs so much could kill them, but I'll unhappily confess to all manner of hypocrisies.

Many of my friends would push a hook up through the frog's bottom lip, out through the top of the head, cast it out and let it swim around until it was engulfed by a trout. The whole concept gave me the eebies. I'd grab hold of the frog's back feet and flick its head against a rock, killing it stone dead in an instant. Then I'd stick a hook through its head, cast it out onto the water, and slowly retrieve it. I soon found that I preferred active fishing to the more passive variety. Anyway, my frogs didn't crawl out of the water onto strapweed or, indeed, scuttle up the bank.

When a trout grabbed the bait, I'd release the bail-arm of my spinning reel. The trout would usually run, stop and swallow its meal, and when it moved off again I'd set the hook. The method was so effective that I soon stopped prospecting and began aggressively looking for rising and tailing trout. My catch rate improved dramatically; so too did my enjoyment of fishing. I didn't realise it at the time, but I was well on my way to becoming a fly fisher.

In my mid-teens I used to fish Lake Dulverton, near Oatlands, before land mismanagement and climate change reduced it to a claypan. In those days it was stocked with wild brown trout salvaged from the spawning run at Great Lake. These weighed three pounds when transferred, which was about as big as they could be expected to grow in their home water. But in Dulverton the high productivity of the shallow weedy lagoon, combined with a general absence of fishy competitors, resulted in a new burst of growth. Within a year the new transfers would average five pounds, while those that survived two years (and plenty did) would attain an optimum size of seven to nine pounds. They provided very exciting fishing.

One energetic six-pounder swallowed my dead frog right down into its gut. Since there were other fish tailing at the time, I didn't waste time retrieving my bait; it was quicker to snip off the line and fix up a new rig.

It was several hours before I got around to cleaning my catch. The instant I split open the fish's stomach, the frog hopped out onto the kitchen table. Then it sat up and looked me square in the eye. Despite having had its head bashed against a rock and hook threaded through its lips, it seemed as healthy as Jonah. So I gently removed the hook and placed it back in my aquarium of live bait. It began eating mealworms the very next day.

Two weeks later, I was back on the shores of Dulverton. The first frog I extracted from my bait can just happened to be Jonah himself. I tried to bring myself to thread him on the hook, and failed. It's a common enough story, I suppose. I've heard deer hunters in New Zealand talk about similar events. You know: tracking an animal for weeks on end, finally cornering it, the look of pitiful resignation in the animal's eye, and the curious inability to pull the trigger. I ended up releasing every frog I had right there and then, and never again used another one as bait.

But I did end up finding out that imitation frogs—frog flies, if that's not an oxymoron—were every bit as effective as the real thing. All you had to do was use something of appropriate colour that was bulky enough to make a splash or wake but not so heavy that it would sink too quickly and get snagged on shallow weeds. Rabbit fur, deer hair and cork proved good enough. If presented with just enough splash, you could even get a trout to race around from the other side of a semi-submerged log or tussock.

Nugetena

THE STRANGEST frogger I ever saw was at Lake Nugetena, in the Western Lakes. The day was damp and drizzly and, because of the stillness, very foggy. But it was impossible not to notice this trout. It lay at the head of a weedy bay, and it was big—five pounds or more. Moreover, it was sitting in just an inch or two of water, and was almost completely exposed. It seemed to be using a low sphagnum bank as a pillow. Then it lifted its head up onto the bank and gently plucked off a frog. The rest of its body did not move one iota. In the next fifteen minutes or so it ended up taking four more frogs. The trout couldn't see its prey, but knew exactly when a frog had hopped within reach, and snipped each one at the critical moment without fuss. Was it hearing or feeling the vibrations as they hopped on the moss? Could it build some sort of mental picture of its prey's movement, in the same way that a bat locates food with sonar?

Arachnophilia

IN SPRING it's not just frogs that feature prominently in a trout's diet. When writing *Frog Call*, I ummed and ahed about having a whole chapter devoted to spiders. Now that I think about it, perhaps the book should have been called *Spider Song* and featured a huntsman on the front cover. Then again, I doubt the publishers would have stood for it.

***

We hadn't travelled far out of Lester's driveway when, in response to the first sunbeams of dawn, I flicked down the car's sun visor. A huntsman spider plopped onto my crotch, precipitating a sort of constricted star jump which involved a rather melodramatic release of the steering wheel and, simultaneously, an involuntary plunge of the right foot on the brake pedal. The car veered wildly to the left and stalled in a flooded—fortunately shallow—roadside gutter.

Lester was asplutter with laughter. 'You should have seen the look on your face!'

How embarrassing. Huntsmen are *not* Sydney funnel-webs, which we all know (proudly, if not accurately) are the most poisonous arachnids in the whole wide world. Nor are huntsmen anything like redbacks which, of course, are far nastier than the black widows of America and the katipos of New Zealand (even though these three species are virtually identical). Huntsmen, it has to be admitted, are completely harmless. Well, they have a powerful bite if grossly mishandled, but I wasn't about to lose any future claim to manliness by trying that on as an excuse.

'You're still just as scared of spiders as you were when you were a baby, aren't you?' Lester goaded relentlessly.

I wound down the window. Then I gently picked up the spider, a hundred millimetres across the legs, and cast him into the wild. 'I'm not scared of spiders. I released this one with my own bare hands, didn't I?'

'He would have been safer if you left him in the car. He'll probably get carried away in that flooded gutter and end up being eaten by one of those Meander River trout that we'll be soon be stalking.'

Hmmm. Good point, actually.

Yesterday the Meander had broken its banks, and now the water was at a perfect level, spilling just ten or twenty metres into the pasture. The fish wouldn't be able to disperse over whole paddocks; they would be concentrated in very shallow water adjacent to the main river channel, where they'd be forced to expose their dorsals and tails—or at least make bow-waves and ripples—as they fossicked around looking for goodies delivered by the floodwaters.

There would be no frogs—it hadn't been wet enough for long enough. There might be worms, but that was more likely to happen in a day or two's time, when, in fear of drowning, they would begin a mass exodus from their holes. No, the most likely items on the menu would be arthropods, like spiders. Lots and lots of spiders. Indeed, my old zoology textbook claims that one hectare of ungrazed paddock may support as many as five million of the blighters, a figure that won't surprise anyone familiar with riverside ecology.

One of the most fascinating spiders we see along the banks of the Meander (and elsewhere) is a large black thing with an outsized abdomen which is often horribly disfigured with fuzzy baubles. The instant you touch these cancerous pimples, usually from a cowardly distance with a slender stick, an army of spiderlings scatters all over the place, in a manner rather reminiscent of the enthusiastic contestants in Monty Python's 'hundred-metre sprint for people with absolutely no sense of direction'. Hang around quietly for long enough, and you will see Mum school-bussing around the immediate surrounds collecting her children who, despite their chaotic exuberance, all manage to clamber back aboard in the end.

Of course, not all spiderlings stay on their mother's back. Some (usually orb-weaving spiders, never the black ones just mentioned) engage in a practice known as ballooning. They climb to the top of pin rushes and fence posts where they tilt their abdomens skywards and begin extruding silk. The breeze pulls the lengthening thread until finally the force is so great that the baby spiders are plucked from their vantages and carried skywards. Sometimes they fall to earth almost straight away, but other times they are carried for hundreds of kilometres, sailing on the wind like miniature kites being pulled backwards. At times I have seen the air filled with thousands of such fairyland wanderers.

Garry Larson, another spider lover, once did a cartoon with the caption, 'MORE FACTS OF NATURE: As part of nature's way to help the spread of species throughout its ecological niche, bison often utilize a behavior naturalists have described as "ballooning."' It featured bison gliding over the prairies attached to brightly coloured helium balloons and... well, I'm sure you get the picture.

Just as impressive as the ballooners are the nurseryweb spiders. Although these creatures look like common wolf spiders, they like to lie in wait on the water's edge with their front legs resting on the surface, alert to any vibrations. Then they dart out over the water and, if necessary, dive down to snatch insects, tadpoles and even small fish (including trout fry). Their nests—fist-sized purses of densely woven silk—are usually constructed on the tips of reeds and other waist-high plants, and they can be so prolific that upon entering a paddock you can get the feeling of being in a poppy field. On occasion, when there have been too few risers, I've been tempted to tear apart a bunch of nursery webs and sprinkle the contents onto the currents. But up close, the nests seem too eerie to violate, much like the cobwebs that festooned Miss Havisham's abandoned wedding breakfast in Dickens' *Great Expectations*.

Most spider webs are enchanting. The intricate lacework of the adult orb-weaving spiders always reminds me of the curtains in my childhood nursery. And the funnels of house spiders are enticingly like dangerous portals to new worlds, à la *The Time Tunnel*, which I used to watch on telly when I was a toddler. But my favourites are the refined doilies which, collectively, often cover entire paddocks, but are invariably overlooked until the time when, on a cold autumn morning, they are gloriously highlighted with dew or frost.

Some of the rural creeks I fish—tributaries of the South Esk and parts of the Coal River—are only a metre or so wide. Here, spiders often spin invisible webs from one side to the other. You only notice such handiwork when, after a splendid once-only chance of a cast, your flyline ends up levitating a metre or so above the water. This can be incredibly frustrating, but your spirits are restored the instant a spider rushes out, captures your artificial fly and begins wrapping it up in a cocoon.

There are so many spiders on the pasture flanking our riverbanks and lakeshores, that it wouldn't surprise me if 'five million per hectare' was an outlandish underestimate. Honestly (ish), I reckon I've seen that many spiders crammed into the gut of a single large trout.

But the fact that spiders are eaten by trout is not the only reason fly fishers are grateful to them. Spider silk is a liquid protein, fibroin, which is extruded through a cluster of conical spigots, or *spinnerets*. It hardens not so much on exposure to air, but more by polymerisation through the process of being drawn out, most commonly by the spider walking or abseiling away from the attached end of the line. Science has mimicked this method of making thread, and thus enabled the manufacture of the monofilaments and fluorocarbons that we fly fishers rely on for leaders and tippets. If zoologists and chemists had not found spiders so interesting, we'd still be using horsehair or catgut, and much of the fishing we treasure today would be impossible. Furthermore, the protein itself has a tensile strength that puts steel to shame, and the basic chemical structure has been replicated to create gel-spun super lines, which have extraordinary breaking-strains and almost zero stretch.

In Volume Two of *The Complete Far Side,* Larson noted parallels between spiders and his father, an avid angler. He was especially taken by the analogy between fishing lines and spider silk, and concluded that his dad was really just a big arachnid.

I suspect that all fly fishers are just big spiders. So, to paraphrase Larson, if you run into us, please don't squish us.

Huntsman

THE STORY Lester invoked about me being scared of spiders when I was a kid was a family favourite, but it was wrong. Wrong, wrong, wrong.

At the time, I was a baby alone in a big empty room in a wooden cot encircled by a neck-high balustrade. I was at the stage when I could stand but not walk. So young, in fact, that my memories of the incident are an intriguing collage of pictures, sounds and smells;

tapestries of superfine detail. I can recall the exact patterns in the lacework curtains, all the intricacies of the wood grain in the ply dado, all the detail of the elaborate brass doorknob, the subtle differences in people-smells. I can even recall the melodious burble of talk. The sounds are so well recorded that I can delve in and identify words that I didn't understand at the time, though this is dangerous territory because with age it becomes more difficult to discern the original memory from the reconstructed ones.

There are other memories too, like the way I loved the large wooden beads on the cot's built-in abacus because they were exactly the same as one another except that they came in different exciting colours (mostly big, bold and primary). Yet the thing that most fascinated me was the rather drab world of mini-beasts. I knew by heart every cobweb of every big black house-spider. I watched, fascinated, as mason wasps helicoptered baby spiders past my cot and entombed them in clay crypts within the timber cornice.

One morning I awoke to find a mason wasp trapped in a house-spider's web. Fortunately for the wasp, the house spider didn't appear to be at home. Unfortunately for the wasp, the gigantic huntsman patrolling the walls had no qualms about stealing other spiders' food. He raced forward, grabbed the wasp in his fangs, and found himself partly entangled in the web. Soon he was flailing madly, then he freed all but one foot which remained firmly attached to the end of a stretchy thread. No amount of frantic tugging seemed to ease his plight.

I found the experience truly amazing, and desperately needed to share it. I shouted for Mum and Dad, but with my sister and brothers already up and making their own demands, I knew my parents wouldn't be quick to respond.

Time was running out—the huntsman had escaped by now and was racing off with his prize. Soon he would be gone, and no-one would know what I had seen.

Then it hit me—the shocking realisation that there was a *word* for 'spider'.

I have a perfectly preserved recollection of that moment. A memory about words completely devoid of words; a picture-construction in which nouns, verbs and objects are overlaid and fused together in a single entity, devoid of time.

I remember grappling with too many vitally important

happenings: the spider about to run away before anyone could bear witness, the enormity of the whole 'words' thing, the struggle to work out or vocalise the word for spider, a terrible sense of abandonment. In the end, I burst into tears. Hysterical ones apparently, because the next instant my parents burst into the room. Having found me screaming at a huge spider, Mum tried to reassure me that Dad would soon *kill* the horrid thing. I didn't understand the words she said, but I understood what was going to happen. I cried louder and tried to hide under my bunny blanket.

That is the last time I remember viewing the world without the constraints and prescriptions of grammatical structure.

Interesting, or even poignant, you might think. 'Supplanted memories,' Lester insists knowledgably. 'No-one can remember things that happened when they were one year old.'

No point arguing that one—not even my psychology teachers ever bothered to hear me out.

Fly skinking

SHORTLY AFTER my daughter Jane's second birthday, she walked into the house holding a bluetongue, her two pudgy hands tight round its belly, its head upright looking straight ahead, bewildered. Despite everything, the lizard seemed to appreciate her warmth and instantly lapped food from her finger: fruit yoghurt, mashed strawberries, canned dog food.

Eight years later, we built our new house. Bluetongues proved to be relatively scarce on this particular bush property, so on the first sunny day in early spring she resorted to hunting smaller skinks. This was a hard task amongst the rocks and scrub, all the more so because of the enthusiasm of Jane's faithful Jack Russell skink-hound, Halla. Eventually I showed Jane how to make a skinking rod out of a bush pole and a fixed length of fine monofilament. 'We'll attach a small bait with a slip knot,' I said. 'You don't want a hook.'

As a kid, I used to use live caddis-flies for skinking. But on this spring day the air was biting cold and insects of any sort were scarce. 'Finding bait is harder than catching skinks,' Jane protested truthfully, petulantly.

Next day I returned from the local pet shop with a tub of commercially grown mealworms; the same pet shop I bought my first aquarium from when I was my daughter's age. 'Watch me,' I said as I dangled a mealy in front of a sun-drenched metallic skink. It came forward with staccato movements, like some miniature dinosaur from a low-budget horror flick.

'He's got it,' Jane yelled ecstatically, restraining her eager puppy. 'Lift him, lift him up.'

'You've got to wait till they choke it down out of sight.'

When I eventually did lift the rod, Jane raced the bucket underneath, and a couple of shakes later the lizard dropped into captivity.

'We can keep some in my old aquarium if you want,' I suggested. 'They'll even have babies in summer.'

'Can I catch a skink now?'

'I'll just show you how to keep the line from tangling up on the grass... There you go—put the bucket under him.'

'Can I have a go now?'

'You've got to move carefully, no sudden movements, no passing shadows. Watch me now...'

'Dad this is my game, not yours.'

Metallic skinks are easy to catch, as are velvet-skinned ocellated skinks, and by dusk Jane and I had quite a bucketful. Somehow I managed to convince her to release all but the six biggest, the ones that would be the easiest to care for. Looking in awe at what was left, she said 'What'll we feed them?'

'Mealworms, of course. Until the weather warms up anyway. Then you can collect small insects from under the porch light like I used to.'

'Won't they fly away when we put them in the tank?'

'Not if you pull one wing off.'

'Ew... I think I'll just use mealies.'

'I'm not going to keep buying mealworms. You'll have to breed your own.'

'Cool.'

Scouring the drier parts of our property Jane eventually found some beautifully patterned skinks that were larger than most others. But whenever one grabbed a mealworm, the skink instantly retreated

into its burrow and proved impossible to pull out. Several days and
dozens of mealworms later, Jane finally returned triumphant. 'Look
at this! Look at this!'

'So that's what you've been doing up on the hill all this time. You
should have told me. I could have helped.'

'That's why I didn't tell you.'

Jane asked me what sort of lizard it was, and I didn't know. So she
bought herself a handbook and declared her trophy to be a White's
skink, 'one of 18 lizard species found in Tasmania'.

Quite early on, Jane decided that her Holy Grail was the she-oak
skink, a large but slender lizard which slithers like a snake, beautifully
patterned, grand and rare. She caught one within a year, a fantastic
specimen over thirty centimetres long—the equivalent in Tasmania
of catching a ten-pound wild brook trout.

What next, now that the ultimate goal had been achieved so early?
An appreciation of the finer details of her sport proved to be Jane's
salvation. Despite enormous natural variation in the colour of
metallic skinks, she eventually concluded that some of the ones she
caught and reared must be a different species altogether. 'An eastern
three-lined skink!' she declared, thrusting a small lizard into my face.

'How can you be sure?' I asked dubiously.

'Red under the chin gives the males away in the breeding season,
but since it's spring I've had to look at the frontoparietal shields.'

Strewth.

Soon Jane was busy planning trips to exotic places. 'Come on Dad,
if you take me to the Waterhouse lakes you can fish for trout in
Blackmans Lagoon while I fish for Bougainville's skinks in the dunes.
It's an amazing animal. In Tasmania it's a live-bearer, but the same
species on the mainland lays eggs.'

'Sounds impossible,' I said sceptically.

'They have a neat trick,' Jane explained. 'They just hold their eggs
inside their body until they hatch.'

Like other Tasmanian wetlands, the marshes at Blackmans Lagoon
are frequented by big black tiger snakes. As soon as we reached the
water's edge, I found one lying perfectly still, in wait. Suddenly there
was a blur of movement—and then naught but an empty space where
a frog used to be. 'Awesome,' said Jane.

'Watch this then.' I broke the hook off a Mrs Simpson and tickled
it right past the snake's nose. The fly was taken immediately, and

swallowed right down, just like a lizard eating a mealworm, only much faster. I had to reel the snake several metres across the marsh before it finally let go.

Later in the day there was an unexpected smut hatch, so I returned to the car to get my dry-fly box. What was this? Almost all of my midge flies were missing. And *what was this*? An incriminating pile of twisted-off barbs.

'Size 22 Midges are fantastic for skinks,' Jane declared enthusiastically when I tracked her down. 'Mind you, dead drift is useless. You have to twitch them...' She was grinning mischievously, provocatively. Like a reptile.

Who swallowed a fly

THERE WAS a massive midge hatch going on at the Pump Pond, and I disturbed a dense cloud of the noisy buggers as I brushed past an overhanging tea-tree. Some of them disappeared down the back of my throat, others got trapped behind my glasses. When I finally stopped coughing and spluttering, I was relieved to find that my tears had at least flushed the midges from my eyes. But, just as I was beginning to savour the return to normality, I became aware of an ominous buzzing in my left ear. After five minutes it became quite apparent that trying to ignore the sound just wasn't going to work— the noise was driving me insane.

What was it they had taught us twenty years ago on that basic first-aid course? Was it to pour warm cooking oil into the ear? An unlikely course of action to recommend, surely—I had visions of a Shakespearian poisoning. But then, I suppose the oil would goo-up the insect's wings and at least stop the incessant buzzing. It might even flush the bloody thing out.

In the absence of oil, I ended up plonking my head in the lake and manoeuvring it this way and that until my ear cavity was sloshing about like a three-quarters-empty hipflask. I waited. Yes... Yes! The noise had stopped. I could still feel the pitiful thing scratching around, but at least it was silent.

The trout were rising spectacularly by now, so of course I kept fishing. Many hours later, well after dark, as I walked back to the car I realised that the insect was becoming ever more active. In fact, it was starting to drive me nuts again.

As soon as I walked into the living room, before I had even said hello, I was begging Frances to pour some oil in my ear.

'I'm not sure I'd be happy doing that,' Frances replied. 'Too much like the *juice of cursed hebona* thing. You know, the way Hamlet's father was killed.' She insisted on making a call to Accident and Emergency.

'I'm not going into Accident and Emergency. For heaven's sake, you work in the hospital, you know how understaffed it is in there. All that would happen is that we'd wait all night in a cold cavernous waiting room amid...'

'Pull yourself together. It's just a phone call.'

Frances explained the situation to the triage nurse.

'I am prohibited from advising you on how to perform medical procedures at home.'

'I only want to know if oil is okay. Okay?' Frances was sounding mildly agitated now.

'Look, I'll tell you this much: if you came in here, the first thing we'd do is switch off all the lights in the observation room and shine a torch in your partner's ear. Thirty per cent of the time the insect will be attracted to the light and crawl out of its own accord.'

Frances thanked the nurse and switched the lights out. The kids, already awakened by my overt crabbiness, got out of bed and circled around as though they were watching a live performance of 'Play School'.

'Stop wriggling,' Frances pleaded. 'I can't see a thing... Wait a second, yes I can. No, it's retreated back inside your head. No, it's coming out again. It's got *green* eyes. It looks a bit bigger than a midge. Actually, it's bloody huge.'

'Can I have a look?' said Tom with macabre enthusiasm.

'Me too,' added Jane.

'I asked first.'

'Arrrgh!' I shouted in frustration, and everyone went quiet while Frances got back to work with the torch.

I vaguely remembered a story told to a newspaper by an Australian who had been imprisoned in one of Thailand's most notorious gaols. His cellmate went mad—slowly at first, then in a rush. It turned out that cockroach maggots had eaten their way through his ear drum into his brain. I squirmed. Did Frances have any idea how hard it was to be still when there were insects in your head?

'Be still,' Frances implored once more. 'Quick Tom, get some tweezers.'

But before Tom had returned from the bathroom, the thing had crawled right out onto my cheek.

'Awesome!' Jane exclaimed.

'A spider,' Tom added in conclusion. 'A big green one.'

'Did you stick it in there to eat the fly?' said Frances winking at Tom.

'See if there's a bird, and a cat, and a dog,' said Jane.

'I s'pose we can assume there's no horse,' said Tom with melodramatic disappointment, before toddling off back to bed.

Smell

MICK, MY next-door neighbour, a friend and fellow angler, wasn't much fun on the flight from Melbourne to Hamilton, New Zealand. He was preoccupied with his new compact digital camera—reading the instruction booklet, tinkering with all the electronic buttons, taking pot shots at whatever was close at hand. My ear hole, the drinks trolley, the hostie's gorgeous bottom.

'Did you know,' I said, 'that when Magenta went to Malaysia she didn't take a camera with her? She took a tape recorder instead. She sampled the haggling that went on in the crowded markets, the roar of waves on the beach, the whooping of orang-utans in the jungle, the crying of a newborn baby, the snoring of her very temporary travelling partner. She reckons that snippets of sound trigger the memory much more effectively than photos ever will.'

Mick stopped tinkering and looked at me. 'Could be something in that,' he agreed. 'I mean, I know how good smell is for memory. That chemical tang that some glues have always takes me back to my father's workshop, and I'm right there with him again, binding guides onto split-cane rods. Whenever I smell fresh lawn clippings, I'm suddenly down at the creek at the bottom of the school oval, catching jollytails with a worm skewered on a bent pin.' He looked wistful.

I was reminded of my time in Chile. Whenever I was in the bush, even when I wasn't fishing, I felt extraordinarily happy, as if I was on some sort of high. But after a few days in a big city like Santiago I got homesick, sometimes overwhelmingly so. During one such depression, I chanced to walk into a side street that passed through a grove of Tasmanian blue gums. The smell of eucalyptus oil was instantly soothing. I found a shop that served fine coffee—al fresco, on a quaint wooden table beneath the shade of the very biggest tree—and I stayed there all day. 'It was such a balm that I've actually stopped making disparaging jokes about aromatherapy,' I said.

From Hamilton we drove straight to Rotorua, the geothermal centre with city parks and roadside drains that spew out misty clouds of rotten-egg gas. Inevitably Mick said something like 'Trout, you need to go to the toilet with a good book', and of course I batted-off his fart jokes with schoolboy humour of my very own.

This was the genesis of what turned out to be a sort of olfactory tour of the North Island. We noticed aromas like never before. The insipid fragrance of tourist shops, the scent of women, the smell of hot bitumen, the musk of wild pigs, the pine in the plantations.

When travelling at night between Murupara and Waikaremoana, Mick was surprised at the quantity of squashed wildlife. 'What sort of animals are they?'

'Possums,' I explained.

Nowadays there are as many Tasmanian brushtails impressed into New Zealand roads as there are at home. Possums were introduced in 1858 in the hope of establishing a fur trade, and in an environment that historically had no mammals whatsoever, except seals and bats, they proliferated to the great detriment of the native vegetation, especially forests. So much do they eat that some habitats and tree species are in danger of extinction. For a while the fur trade did, in fact, keep the possums in check, but the anti-fur lobby has been so successful that there is no longer a big enough market to enable shooters to keep numbers under any sort of control. These days, countless tonnes of 1080 pellets are scattered officially and indiscriminately all over New Zealand, but with limited success.

'Well, conservation issues are always more about matters of the heart—right-wingers would say dogma—than pragmatics,' Mick offered.

'The fact is, pretty much everything you'll find squashed on New

Zealand roads has been introduced, and roadkill is more celebrated that abhorred,' I noted.

Actually, that's not quite true. Nobody likes to see squashed frogs even if they are Tasmanian green bell frogs and brown tree frogs. The only other introduced animals New Zealanders seem unhappy to see dead on their roads are hedgehogs, or as Frances prefers to call them, deadgehogs. Mind you, my kids aren't always so unhappy because, if they have been squashed sufficiently flat and have had time to dry, they make rather impressive frisbees.

Suddenly, Mick slammed on the brakes. 'There's a live hedgehog now. On the road verge. Stop it before it runs off. I want to see one.'

I opened the door and got out. I was standing on something soft. Looking down I saw the slimy, rancid jelly of a long-deceased possum enveloping my jandals, oozing up between my toes. The stink was unbelievable. I went to sit back in my seat but Mick quickly drove ahead a few metres, and locked the doors. I found myself listening to him from behind a wound-up window. 'Just thought you might be feeling homesick,' he explained. 'Can't think of any smell more reminiscent of Tasmania than roadkill possum.'

'Let me in,' I pleaded.

But he wouldn't, not until I'd descended a blackberry-ridden gorge and cleaned my feet in a cold, cold creek.

Koi

A COUPLE of hours after our plane landed in Hamilton, New Zealand—on the return from a grocery-shopping expedition, while strolling across a bridge spanning the Waikato River—I found myself looking at what I took to be the biggest goldfish in the world.

'Koi carp,' offered a voice from behind. '*Ordinary* carp: the same bloody pest that you have in Australia. An ornamental form to be sure, but still bloody carp.'

I turned. Heaven forbid! It was Mouldy, the nutter I met at Lindisfarne on the River Derwent in Tasmania, the one who followed me everywhere up and down the beach wanting to talk when I wanted to fish. I read the cloth badge on his shirt: *Hamilton Bow-Fisher's Club*.

'Here John, have a shot,' he chirruped, offering me a crossbow. 'Biggest one I ever got was fifteen pounds. There's blokes in the clubrooms got em bigger than that though. You should drop by, have a drink, look at the trophies.'

I soon learned that Mouldy lived in the North Island for months at a time. He hadn't founded the bow-fishing club, but he had been associated with it more or less from its inception. His colleagues provided a steady outlet for his handcrafted crossbows and recurve bows, and they knew pig shooters who were also into bow hunting. Although making bows took up most of his time, he was now also producing and selling split-cane fly rods. He gave me his card: it had one contact address in Hamilton and another in Hobart.

The Butcher's son

IT WAS a blue-sky day at the end of summer. Mick and I called into the homestead at Papuni Station intending to ask for permission to fish the main broadwater on the Ruakituri River, but there was no-one home. Based on the tenuous premise that I'd been given permission to fish in previous years, we decided that the station owner wouldn't mind us fishing so long as we closed the gates and treated the property with the usual amount of respect.

The Papuni Road leaves the fastwater, does a U-turn, and ploughs straight back to the Ruakituri, headlong towards the broadwater. Then, near a bankside shanty, it does a hard right-hander before quietly continuing along the true left bank. We drove ahead a few hundred metres past the hut, and parked in the shade of a willow.

The water was clear enough and, fishing our way upstream, we spotted at least one good fish every fifty metres or so. The day was progressing wonderfully, when the willows became too dense for comfort. So we were forced to fish our way back downstream, all the way to the shack, which was where we met the butcher's son. He was a Maori, of the tall, tough, wiry variety, complete with muscular arms, tattered shirt and crude homemade tattoos; incomplete with teeth. In his right hand there was a three-quarters-empty can of Tui ale. It was ten in the morning. 'You've not been getting too many of my fish have you?' he said, cheerily enough.

'Well, you never get too many do you? We let 'em all go anyhow. Great spot you've got here. What's cookin'?'

'In the smoker? Eels of course. Hey, you want to have a look at my place?'

The humpy had started out—thirty-four years ago, when our raconteur was a toddler—as a small plywood caravan. In those days, his dad had been a butcher at Wairoa, the nearest town, which was small and economically depressed, and hasn't changed. He used to slaughter the Papuni herd, and the station owner let him camp on the property, first while he worked there and later, as they got to know each other better, in perpetuity. Almost immediately upon the announcement of permanent tenancy, an addition was made to the river side of the caravan: a small corrugated-iron verandah supported by thin bush poles. After a long, cold winter, this was closed in, again with second-hand roofing and minimal framing. The following winter, also bleak, necessitated the installation of a stone fireplace with crude sheet-iron chimney.

Over the next couple of decades, the building continued to sprawl—impulsively, like a small child's house-of-cards—and it now comprised several rooms, some with dirt floors, some with sections of plank flooring (no joists) and verandahs (no gutters). It was chaotically furnished with rustic furniture, much of which had been fashioned from old fence droppers, feed-pallets and the like. The final product was ramshackle, but delightfully so—clean and tidy, functional and warm.

'Don't build them like this anymore,' said Mick nostalgically, remembering a youth spent in Granville Harbour, Trial Harbour, and the Central Plateau; a youth lived before simplicity and functionality gave way to materialism and over-regulation.

'You aren't allowed to build them like this anymore,' I lamented, 'not in Tasmania, anyway.'

'You better have a beer,' said the butcher's son. He had detected the sincerity in our voices. We were friends.

The Butcher

AFTER AN hour of bullshit and tall stories, Mick and I bade the butcher's son well, and continued down the riverbank. We carefully crossed the big rapid at the tail of the pool and wandered back upstream along the far bank, stealthily polaroiding and catching more fish as we went. The broadwater, it turned out, was fully two kilometres long. It was evening when we finally reached the inflow where, to our surprise and relief, we found a suspension bridge—an unusually robust one, apparently a cattle crossing. From a high vantage midway across the river, we saw several *hinakis*, baited eel pots, lying deep down on the silty riverbed, attached by ropes to willow trunks.

We found our car and drove a couple of kilometres to the end of the Papuni Road. Fish and Game and the Department of Conservation have managed to negotiate with the owners of Papuni Station to allow a formal walking track to be maintained from this point, across several kilometres of private pasture, to the Urewera National Park. From this point, the track continues into dense native forest and terminates at Waitangi Falls on the Ruakituri River. Above the falls there are no brown trout, only rainbows. Famously, most of these fish weigh two to three kilos and some exceed five kilos.

But it was almost dark now—too late to walk to the falls—so we strolled over to a lonely old weatherboard farmhouse, presumably occupied by one of the station hands, to ask if we could set up camp beneath the willows on the pasture beside the Lockwood Creek. The house was a little unkempt but otherwise in good condition. The lights were off, the shower was running. 'Anyone about?'

'Yeah buddy. Come on in.'

I went in, turned the corner of the hall and got a full-frontal view of another wiry local, soaping his crotch. 'Ah, I was wondering if we could camp beside the Lockwood. Me and me mate were going to walk up to the falls. It's a bit late now, so we'll have to set off in the morning. Would have asked at the homestead, but there's no-one there.'

'Don't see why it'd be a problem.' He was vigorously shampooing his head now and had closed his eyes to keep out the soap.

'Thanks,' I said.

Morning arrived cool and sunny.

Originally, Mick and I had intended to camp overnight at the falls, but because the fishing in the rest of the Ruakituri had been so good, we found ourselves running out of time and decided to settle on a daytrip.

The beginning of the formal walking track looked quite intimidating. Apparently we were supposed to push our way into a blackberry thicket and ascend a cliff. A much easier option was to follow a disused but perfectly graded vehicular track which we could see gracefully ascending the distant hills all the way to the National Park boundary.

The fishing above the falls proved to be extraordinarily good. Enormous rainbows lying in heavy current were prepared to engulf our cicada imitations one after the other. We fished much longer than was exactly sensible and barely managed to get out of the forest before sunset. But from here onwards the old vehicular track wasn't hard to follow—it was perfectly illuminated by the moon, or perhaps just by our inner glow.

We were grateful that we'd left our tent pitched at the Lockwood. But before we'd managed to change into dry clothes or put a billy on to boil, we heard the mechanical drone of a quad-bike. It was difficult to figure out exactly where the noise was coming from, and we eventually concluded that the headlights were switched off. Suddenly a silhouette loomed out of the shadows. 'It's coming right for us,' said Mick with mock horror.

A dark two-dimensional figure dismounted. 'How's it goin?'

It was the butcher's son. His voice was slurred. 'You don't mind if I sit with you for a bit? I was goin to have a cone with my mate…' he pointed to the old farmhouse, '… but, well, he's not there. Probably off trappin possums.' He skolled the rest of his can, and pulled another from a carton crudely strapped to the back of his bike.

Mick, realising we were as trapped as any possum, sat down cross-legged beside the cheerless remains of last night's campfire. I was cold and wanted to get some firewood, but civility called for patience. I lay down opposite Mick and propped myself on my elbow. The butcher's son sat between us, rather shakily, on his haunches. So, there we were, a semicircle of silence in the cold and dark.

The interloper swigged his can. 'Did you find anything when you walked up to the falls?'

'Lots of big fish.'

He gave a disturbing little laugh. 'What do you do for a living?'

'Gardener,' Mick said.

'You got a bit of a green thumb then?' He turned to me. 'You?'

Journalist was not the answer called for. 'Builder,' I said, figuring that this answer wasn't entirely dishonest.

'You look like policemen.'

Mick laughed out loud, and the butcher's son seemed to think that settled the matter in our favour. 'You gunna make a fire or are we just gunna freeze our arseholes off?'

By the time I had gathered a few twigs from the willows and prepared the fire, Mick and the butcher's son had been chatting for some time. As the flames began flickering higher, I saw that our self-imposed friend had a rifle slung across his shoulder. The barrel pointing jauntily at Mick's head. It was a big calibred thing, at least a .32-30.

'I shoot pigs mainly. And red deer. Look at this...' The butcher's son was suddenly brandishing a large hunting knife. 'My old man taught me his trade. I can bone out anything, anything at all—do it so well that there's not a lick of flesh or gristle wasted.' There was pride in his voice, and intended or not, a bit of menace. He was into his fourth beer now, but apparently he needed a little something extra. He reached into his breast pocket and withdrew a small pipe. He unscrewed the cone and began packing it with pungent greenery. 'This is the best dope you'll ever see,' he bragged.

Then he looked us straight in the eye. 'You can't fool me: I know you've seen my plots up there in the hills. I've always been a druggie. Do you want some—won't charge you nothing for it.'

'Thanks,' said Mick, 'but I'm trying to give it up.'

He nodded sagely. 'Only good thing about dope is that I can scratch out a bit of a living from it. Well, I can when the bloody cops aren't giving me a hard time. Bastards. Wouldn't give me a gun licence, you know. Just because I'm a certified schizo.' He magicked a sharpening stone from a breast pocket and began honing his knife. Manically. 'I should have told you this yesterday. It's been playing on my mind all the time.' He angled the edge of his knife towards the fire to get a view of its sharpness. I saw it glint. 'No-one's allowed to fish on Papuni Station; no-one except the owners, and me and my dad. And my mate just over there.' He nodded in the direction of the farmhouse. 'In fact, he's more protective of it than anyone.'

'Sorry about that,' I said hastily. 'There was no-one at the homestead when I went to ask …'

'Wouldn't want to be in your shoes if my mate found out you'd been fishing the broadwater yesterday.' The knife glistened again. He tested the edge with his thumb, and failed to notice that he'd drawn blood.

'Well, we're sorry. We didn't kill any fish you know. And we won't fish there anymore now that we know you don't want us to.'

'I'd better be off now, leave you blokes to cook up some food. I feel better now you and I know where things stand. No hard feelings, eh?' He sounded sincere.

It was after midnight now, but the moon hadn't set. He wasn't the butcher's son anymore. He had become The Butcher. He staggered towards his quad bike, and struggled to mount it.

'Need a hand?'

'She'll be right.'

Where you goin?

'Here and there.' He was nodding toward the vehicular tack we'd walked back on. 'I often just scout about on nights like this. Looking for trespassers. People who use the road instead of the walking track, that sort of thing. Nothing else to do, eh?'

The bike revved into life, and putted out of sight. We heard it groan its way up the hills.

We cooked and ate a meal. The engine could be heard all the while, echoing faintly off the valley walls in such a way that you could never be quite sure of exactly where it was, how near or how far.

'Time to hit the sack?' said Mick.

'You see any dope plants?'

'Of course not. Did you?'

'No.'

But we both knew that, for The Butcher, the truth would be whatever sprouted in his mind.

Rental car

WE'D BEEN travelling around Hamilton on New Zealand's North Island for what seemed like ages, and still we couldn't find a sign directing us to the airport.

'You can walk at night without a compass across a forest of mountains and gorges, and know exactly where you are every step of the way. And yet you get hopelessly lost as soon as you enter the smallest of cities. I can't believe it!' We had barely an hour left to catch our plane home and Mick was getting angry. He pulled into a service station. We'd already filled the tank in preparation for returning the car, but given the amount of futile searching done since then, Mick rightly felt that it needed a top-up.

Cheap hire-cars suit me perfectly. In addition to being, well, cheap, the companies that rent them are less precious about where you drive and unlikely to fine you for silly things like minor blemishes on the duco. I use such cars exactly as I use my own vehicle at home, something I'd never get away with if I patronised one of the big-name rental-car businesses. In New Zealand, small companies like Waikato Car Rentals have wonderful staff who will happily have a car waiting for you at the airport any time of day or night, and who allow you to drop the vehicle off unattended in the carpark on your return. This way you can squeeze every drop of adventure out of your holiday without having to worry about time-consuming paperwork when you are already cutting things fine on the last day of the trip. The only problem we had this time was that the cheap car also had a cheap map, one that didn't clearly show where the airport was.

Mick was exasperated. 'You've been to Hamilton heaps of times. Can't you remember how to get to the airport?'

I didn't even know which side of town it was on. I admit it, I veg out in cities. I fob off responsibility for driving to anyone I can, and curl up foetally. I find certain places interesting, of course— museums, art galleries, coffee shops, parks, pubs—but all the stuff in between I can happily do without.

'You'll have to ask someone where the airport is.' Mick wasn't joking. Things had got that desperate.

One of the best lines in *Finding Nemo* is spoken by Dory when

Marlin opts for the headless-chook approach rather than talking to a nearby whale. 'What is it with men and asking directions?' The whole adult audience laughs, women because they understand the frustration, men because they understand the futility.

'Over there.' Mick instructed. 'They'll definitely have a give-away map showing where the airport is. Hop to it while I fill 'er up.' He was pointing to the offices of the opposition. Hertz Car Rentals.

There was no escaping my duty.

The bloke stationed at the front desk was soft and pudgy and had a ruddy complexion, even though he wasn't particularly overweight. He wore a crisp white shirt with a flamboyant necktie, and had seen fit to top himself with an immaculately manicured toupee. Actually, on closer inspection the toupee proved to be his actual hair. Still, his smile, when he saw me coming through the front door, was genuinely welcoming.

I breasted up to the counter with as much confidence as I could pretend. 'G'day mate. You don't happen to have one of those tourist maps of the town do you? So we can find our way to the airport. We're in a bit of a hurry. Plane leaves in an hour.'

'Sure. Here you go.' Recognising my accent he added jovially 'Have a nice flight back to Oz won't you. I trust you didn't take our win in the cricket too badly'.

I should have left it at that, but I felt he deserved to know how much I appreciated his helpfulness. If I'd made some self-deprecating joke about Australia's underarm problem, I'd have been on safe ground, but instead—I don't know what possessed me—I said 'You blokes are all so professional and friendly. The Hertz car we've been using for the last couple of weeks has been brilliant…'

'Oh, you've got one our cars then?' He was excited beyond anything that seemed rational. 'Thank God for that. What sort is it?'

How would I know what sort of cars were included in his upper-class fleet? Hell, I didn't even know the make and model of the car we actually had. 'I'm not sure. It's a small, white, four-door sedan.' At least I'd managed to squeeze in something truthful.

'We've got a chronic shortage of hire cars at the moment. You returning a sedan to the airport at this time is a real blessing. I'll look up the details on the computer. What's your name?'

Oh shit. 'Ah… um… I didn't actually hire the car myself. My mate did. A mate of a mate actually. Don't rightly know his real name.

Everyone just calls him, ah, Zongo.' These lies weren't very convincing, but the bloke behind the counter was too relieved to notice.

'No worries. Should be able to find it. When did you pick up the car? Three weeks ago? Okay.' He rattled through his keyboard and studied the computer screen. 'That's strange. There's no record of a white sedan being hired out around that time.'

Think. Think. 'That would be because the car was actually picked up in, ah, Wellington.'

The furrows disappeared from his brow. 'Right. I'll just call up the Wellington office's data.' He smiled at me gratefully, and once again began enthusiastically punching away at his computer.

Was there to be no end to this torture?

'Bugger,' he said suddenly. 'The computer has crashed.'

He looked so despondent that I couldn't help myself from saying 'Is there anything I can do to help?' Pathetic, wasn't I?

'You can, yes. The computer should be back up and running in few minutes. If you can get Zongo to give me a call, I just need the rego number and the details of where the car will be parked at the airport. Then I can check that the car hasn't already been allocated to someone else and get it ready for some desperate Canadians who need a vehicle by tomorrow morning.'

'Right you are,' I said. 'Think nothing of it.'

'A godsend you coming in here today,' he reiterated. 'I don't care what anyone says. Not even the underarm incident can change my opinion of you Aussies. You're a bloody decent, honest, bunch of blokes, you are.'

As I walked out via the big glass door, I realised that there was an unobstructed view from the Hertz desk all the way to our Waikato car, which was still parked beside the petrol bowser across the street. I could see Mick urging me to hurry up. I ignored his gesticulations, turned right and hurried up the street. Mick swore. Then he slammed the car door and drove off in pursuit.

Strokey

STROKEY WAS given to me by Chelsea, one of my daughter's best friends, who was upset that I was going on a two-week trip to the South Island without my family. At the time, Chelsea and Jane were both aged five.

Strokey was handmade—lovingly so—from a cheap plastic sauce bottle. He wore a coat of bright orange felt, crudely affixed with clear sticky tape, but the screw-cap was conveniently exposed so you could retrieve treasures from inside: glass gemstones, porcelain teddy bears, red dice with white spots, a Lego fairy's wand. Chelsea proudly presented him in cradled arms—no gift wrap or cellophane—and before she handed him over she tucked him under her chin, as gently as if he were a Stradivarius. 'If you miss Jane too much—and Tom and Frances—you can stroke him like this. He'll help you most of all at night times—that's when people get loneliest, you know—so don't forget to cuddle him into your sleeping bag.'

'Thanks,' I said, somewhat overwhelmed.

'Don't be sad. He's there for fun too—that's what all the jingly things in his belly are for.' She broke into a huge grin, and danced a samba around the room, shaking Strokey like a maraca. Then she passed him over and gave me a quick, coy hug.

Of course Strokey accompanied Lester and I on our trip. He explored glaciers, got up close to wildlife, played on trampolines and swings in camping grounds, sipped kiddie-chinos in coffee shops. Whenever one of us caught a trout we'd perform wild star jumps and wave him loudly in an orgasmic frenzy of pagan joy. And at night, he and I snuggled up close.

I rediscovered Strokey just prior to going on my most recent trip to New Zealand with Mick. He was on my main bookshelf, seated upon a topographical map I needed to take with me. He'd been watching over me for years from the sort of prominent position where things are too easily taken for granted, too easily forgotten. It occurred to me that Chelsea was now thirteen, a teenager. I put him under my chin, and stroked him. He seemed to lament the passing of time, the loss of youth.

***

North Island on a Shoestring—the Further Adventures of Strokey is an A5 publication bound with a cheap plastic spiral. Text and photos by Greg French. Layout and production by Jane Latham. Print run: one copy. The cover features Strokey lynched from the limb of a tree (the older Chelsea is more into gallows humour than kiddie-chinos). Inside, Strokey is to be found perilously close to boiling mud, overwhelmed by steam. There is photographic evidence of him bungy-jumping off a bridge (the shoestring again). More pictures of him canyoning, sitting atop Waitangi Falls, rolling joyously in a huge rainbow trout like a dog wallowing in roadkill, driving the car while seated on Mick's knee, getting intimate with a hedgehog, guzzling Tui ale, drunkenly vomiting treasures.

We all know that the years between five and thirteen are infinitely longer than those between thirty-eight and forty-six. Chelsea had forgotten about Strokey. When Jane and I handed over the book, she was overwhelmed with nostalgia. After a time, she danced the samba with Jane. Before we left, she gave me a quick, coy hug.

How much, I wonder, does a child change, *really* change, on the long, long road to adolescence?

Lester's rod

LESTER HAD travelled down from Deloraine to Hobart to see his neurologist. 'How's the MS going?' I asked when he rocked up at my place. It had been ten years since diagnosis.

'I haven't got MS anymore.'

I'd been witness to so many of his debilitating whammies that my optimism about his long-term prognosis had been tested almost to breaking point. Mind you, in between whammies, he'd always managed to banish the condition from his psyche. In fact, casual acquaintances often had no idea of his day-to-day tribulations. 'What disease have you got then?' I asked dubiously.

'MSNW,' he declared proudly. 'Migrant Sensory Neuritis of Wartenberg.' He went on to explain that neurologists have a whole range of new diagnostic tools, permitting MS to be divided into numerous categories. 'Basically, if you are going to be hit with an

MS-spectrum disorder, Wartenberg's is one of the better species to get.' A diagnosis out of the blue would have been devastating, but as a re-diagnosis when Lester thought he was facing something even more enduringly debilitating, it was apparently a cause for celebration. He unloaded a six pack of boutique beer.

As we sat drinking on the verandah, Lester became philosophical. 'When people say there's no reason to worry about the rich getting richer providing the poor aren't going backwards, they simply aren't being realistic. If people weren't inclined to judge their personal worth against the achievements of their peers, most of us would still be living in caves and dressed in animal skins. One of the very strange things about being human is the way we always assess our wellbeing in a relative manner. Perhaps the only reason we can face the certainty of death without an overwhelming sense of injustice is that everyone else is in exactly the same boat. All events are of variable importance depending on what else is going on in your life. Yesterday, for instance, when my daughter's cat bit the tip off my old cane fly rod, I thought it was the end of the world. Today, I'm so happy about having a less degenerative form of MS that the fate of the rod seems irrelevant. Almost irrelevant, anyway.'

'I don't understand why you're so attached to that piece of rubbish,' I said.

'Old cane rods are about as useful as a soft cock,' Lester admitted. 'But this one belonged to an old guy who used to fish the Shannon Rise alongside Dick Wigram. Could have bought it from him for all I know. Whenever I cast it, history tingles through my body. Wish I knew someone I could trust to fix it.'

***

Mouldy's Hobart workshop was, well, mouldy. And cluttered with an unbelievable amount of junk. It was also strewn with magnificent bows and, I'm afraid to admit, some exquisite cane rods.

'You're into cane then?' Mouldy inquired of Lester, with an eagerness bordering on zealotry.

'I deal in antiques,' Lester lied.

'Reckon I've got a tip-guide exactly like the one that's missing,' Mouldy declared confidently. 'Let's go into the office, shall we.'

Mouldy's 'office' was worse than the workshop. The walls were decorated with calendar girls and his desks, three of them, were covered in overflowing ashtrays.

He rummaged through one cluttered drawer and found

something unexpected. He turned it over distractedly in his hand and eventually tossed it playfully to Lester. 'Maybe you could sell these in your antique shop,' he chuckled.

'Condoms. *Use by 1979*,' Lester read out loud. 'You know what Mouldy?' he added cheerfully, forgetting that I'd never, ever called Muldoon Mouldy to his face. 'I remember being in bed with a girlfriend one dark night and reaching over into a drawer and her rolling a condom on me and us going at it hammer and tongs and then me getting up to have a piss and turning on the light and looking at my dick and seeing the condom hanging in shreds like a partially peeled banana. When we found the packet on the floor it said *Use by 1979. That* was ten years ago.'

Mouldy laughed. We all laughed. The impossible had happened: I was enjoying myself in Mouldy's company.

This happens to be Lester's gift. Wherever he goes, weirdos don't so much come out of the woodwork as come out of the closet, out of themselves. Bag ladies, paranoid schizophrenics, Liberal Party voters, conspiracy theorists, IT freaks, spin fishermen, Labor Party voters, you name it, they recognise Lester as one of their own.

In Lester's company you realise that all these people are good people, genuinely good people. My difficulty is in remembering that, when Lester isn't around to remind me.

Shacking up

LESTER DECIDED to build a shack at Wilburville, Arthurs Lake. I told him he was a fool.

When an angler goes camping and it's windy—or it rains or it snows—there's no compelling incentive to stay cooped up inside your tent, so you fish anyway, and often enough you find some surprisingly good fishing. Even if you don't, you always have memorable experiences. But what if you go to a shack, in January say, hoping for a dun day—warm, calm conditions with a bit of high-level cloud—and it snows? You know there aren't going to be any risers. The fishing will, at best, be slow and it's *so* warm in front of the heater reading your latest novel. Not only that, I told Lester, but having a shack narrows your horizons. 'Can't see you going to St

Clair with me one weekend, Lake Burbury the next, somewhere else a fortnight later, if you've got a shack at Arthurs.'

But Lester wasn't to be swayed. And really, it was no bad thing.

Shack culture is integral to the Tasmanian lifestyle I revere. When you think about it, all the great shack towns were pioneered and fostered by fishermen: Trial Harbour and Granville on the West Coast, Lauderdale and South Arm south-east of Hobart, St Helens on the East Coast and, of course, the numerous shack clusters at Great Lake, Arthurs Lake, Bradys Lake and so on all over the Central Plateau.

In New Zealand the 'shack' is called a 'batch' or 'bach', after bachelor. According to *The Macquarie Dictionary*, a batch is a 'weekend cottage' and the verb *to batch* means 'to keep house alone or with a companion when neither is accustomed to housekeeping'. But shack culture is changing.

Once, shacks were built with whatever materials you could scrounge, 'borrow' or steal, and constructed in the quickest way possible, the object being to secure shelter from the elements without having to sacrifice too much fishing time either while physically building the shack or by working flat-out in your day job to pay it off. Today, lake houses, like houses everywhere, are becoming trophy items where status and investment, or sometimes art and design, take precedence over living and affordability.

Lester didn't want Prime Real Estate, an Investor's Delight, or to Be the Envy of the Neighbourhood. He wanted a shack. He bought a block—very rocky and covered in oldgrowth scrub—right on the edge of the existing shack cluster at Wilburville.

'My place is going to have a galvo roof, and I'd like the walls clad with rough-sawn vertical board. The main living area will be a simple rectangle, eight metres by five, with a steep gable, about forty-five degrees, so there's headroom between the ceiling joists and the ridge. Out the back, along the southern side of the main room beneath a low-pitched skillion, there'll be two bedrooms, separated by a bathroom, all accessible directly from the lounge so that no space will be lost in hallways.' It was to be a very traditional floor plan.

We contacted the council, studied the Planning and Development requirements, and tried to design something that fitted the law. A few rules made sense—things like the fact that *the dwelling must not exceed 7.2 metres from the highest point of the roof to the ground directly underneath*—but most were impossible to decipher. Parameters were usually protected with foaming-mad weasel words like *substantial, reasonable, unreasonable, significant, aesthetically pleasing, sympathetic to the environment*, and we couldn't find any two planners who could agree on what any of them meant.

'Are you guys too unimaginative, or simply too lazy, to set any parameters at all?' I said in frustration.

'Discretion means flexibility,' said the bureaucrat.

'Crap,' countered Lester. 'How much flexibility can you have when you're nostril-deep in a quagmire?'

'Every requirement you have seems to be inconsistent with some other requirement,' I despaired. 'Insulation regs force you to build on the northern side of the hill, while aesthetics require that development be on the southern side so that it's not visible from the water. Bushfire guidelines force you to raze your block, while environmental regulations mean that vegetation has to be left intact. It's impossible to second-guess what you want. Just give us some firm parameters.'

'If it's too hard, get yourself an architect,' countered the bureaucrat. Inflexibly.

'Doing it yourself is part of the joy of building a shack,' Lester tried to explain. 'You know: like when you were a kid and you decided to build yourself a tree-house or fort. The last thing you would've wanted was for your dad to have supplied you with a pre-made something from a hardware store.'

It was clear that our bureaucrat had never built a fort.

'Probably never done an experiment,' said Lester as we retreated down the endless corridor.

But I set about drafting the working drawings: Location Plan, Site Plan, Floor Plan, Elevations, Plumbing Plan, Electrical Plan. Then we typed up the Specifications and filled out the innumerable forms and applications. It was all simple enough, really. Even with a pen and ruler it took less than a day.

'This satisfies all building requirements, environmental protection requirements, threatened species requirements, Aboriginal heritage requirements, bushfire requirements, and insulation requirements,' said Lester as he passed the encyclopaedic wad of documents over the counter. 'I also had it approved, and stamped, by an architect and engineer, who made no amendments to Trout's original drawings and specifications.'

'Of course there would be no amendments to my work,' I retaliated churlishly.

The bureaucrat was unimpressed. 'It'll still need approval from our planner.'

'For crying out loud,' I said in exasperation. 'What's the purpose of all this endless bureaucracy? What does it achieve?'

'We achieve Clifton Beach instead of Trial Harbour, Yangena instead of Wilburville.'

I completely lost it. 'Clifton Beach and Yangena—tar pits for pretentious yuppies and their mortgages. That's the trouble with discretion…'

'Come on Trout, let's go,' said Lester.

I ignored him. 'Anyway, you bureaucratic bastards are forever shifting the bloody goalposts. You can't have a skylight because it doesn't fit with the planning scheme. But as soon as someone important with lots of money wants to turn a well-loved park into a heap of shitty units…'

Lester grasped me by the elbow and led me away.

Eventually, though, we got the shack passed with the original proposal intact. It only cost Lester half as much money as he was planning to spend on construction.

'We'll start mid-autumn so we don't get distracted by the fishing.'

Kevie

THE STEEL rods Lester needed for the piers of his shack were twelve millimetres thick, and textured for extra grip. It wouldn't have been much trouble for Lester to have cut them himself, but he got the fellas out at the sheltered workshop to do it instead. He figured that they needed the work and encouragement more than he needed the money.

There was one bloke there, Kevie, who thought Lester was pretty cool, probably because he was the only visitor who ever paid any interest in what anyone was up to. As soon as Kevie saw Lester get out of the ute he started shouting.

'Lethta Lethta,' he spat excitedly, waving his good arm around like a windmill. 'Ya haf tah look at the new msheen we got. C'mon on c'mon.' And he led Lester down into the workshop, limping and salivating, to show him a hacksaw rigged up to a little motor. Kevie demonstrated how he could cut steel joists with his new machine. It took forever, but it was safe and the cuts were always perfectly square.

Lester was busy offering congratulations when he heard a loud insane scream echoing from the woodwork shop. Kevie noticed the double-take. He twirled his index finger airily beside his right ear, patted Lester on the shoulder and said 'Don' worry 'bout Foogle— Eee's not awl there'.

The Pook

ONE OF the many friends Lester had invited up to Arthurs Lake to help build his shack happened to be a professional builder. It turned out to be Bram, one of the blokes who helped with the restoration of the Salmon Ponds. 'You don't really expect us to be digging all these pad footings by hand?' he said, incredulous.

'There are so many floating boulders in this clay that if we use a backhoe, the holes will end up big enough to bury your car in and I'll have to spend a bloody fortune in concrete. They only have to be four-fifty deep: it won't be too hard digging by hand.'

'There are *fifty* of em,' Bram reiterated.

'It'll only take us a day,' Lester assured him. 'I'd have to supervise the machine anyway, so we'd lose a day no matter what. This way you'll keep fit.'

'I've got some jelly,' said Calvin hopefully, and Beatrice biffed him playfully.

Hayley was there too. And Budgie. And my family. And Magenta. And ten other people, including two toddlers—Theo and Lily.

'Grab one of these and hop to it or it'll be Sunday night and we'll still have nothing done.' Beatrice was pointing to a box-trailer full of crowbars, shovels and spades.

Some of the holes were four-fifty deep when we struck foundation—a crumbly gravel base—but others seemed to go on forever. A couple ended up waist high and Lester plopped Theo and

Lily into them with a few Matchbox diggers. 'Reckon you'll be able to excavate the last bit for us?' It kept them conveniently occupied for the rest of the day.

Lester's second hole was going from bad to worse. First he found several big floaters, then mush, then a spring—which explained the mush—and by mid-afternoon the hole was so big that when he knelt down he completely disappeared.

'Sure you don't want just a bit of jelly,' said Calvin.

Lester popped up like a jack-in-the-box. He had a pair of socks on his ears and an inflated washing-up glove on his head. 'Pooka Pooka,' he said. 'Pooka Pooka.'

The kids howled with laughter, so Lester disappeared down the hole, then sprung up once more. 'Pooka, Pooka. Pooka Pooka.'

More laughter, uncontrollable now.

And somehow that was how the shack came to be called *The Pook*.

Finally, just on dusk, an orgasmic cry echoed from Lester's cavern. 'Well, you can stick a fork up my arse and turn me over. I'm done.'

'Must be beer o'clock,' said Calvin, but he wasn't speaking for the majority.

'I'm going to finish this hole before I knock off,' said Beatrice, who was most of the way through her fourth. And several other people expressed similar desire, even Bram. So the holes were finished by torchlight, and by then Lester had prepared one of his famous camp meals: three meat and one veg, the veg being deep-fried potato chips.

Someone gussed up the cooking fire into a roaring campfire. There was beer and wine. And cigarettes, which Lester justified by saying 'If you're not living life on the edge, you're taking up too much space'.

'What's tomorrow's job?'

'Concrete will arrive at 8.00 am.'

'So you're not mixing it by hand then?' Bram was gloating. Boy he loved machines.

'Well it's purely practical,' Lester explained defensively. 'I'd have to get a load of aggregate, a load of cement, a concrete mixer, a generator to run the mixer, water. The freight alone would cost more than a load of readymix. I'm hoping that the chute will reach most holes, so you won't even have to use the wheelbarrow. Much. Then we just run our stringlines back across the profiles, measure the centre of each stump and insert one of Kevie's steel rods into each pad.'

Eventually we staggered off to sleep in tents and backs of utes. In the morning Lester dished up hash browns, sausages, eggs, bacon, fried onions—not too heavy, not too light—and by midday the concrete was poured and the steel in place.

Greenstone

READING THROUGH past editorials in *Fish and Game* magazine, it quickly becomes apparent that the official managers of New Zealand's trout fisheries pride themselves on their preparedness to fight for the right of anglers to have freedom of access to rivers and lakes. Indeed, the department has championed this principle at every possible juncture: whenever the concept of the Queen's Chain has been questioned; whenever farmers have tried to regulate numbers of anglers traipsing over their freehold properties; whenever there has been a potential conflict of interest with various Maori iwi. Generally I'm supportive of this stance, and because I understand that negotiating with landowners is a time-consuming and costly business, I like to contribute financially to the cause. For this reason, I always pay for a full-season angling licence, even when I can make do with a cheaper version.

Still, I do wonder about indigenous rights.

Lake Wakatipu, in Otago on the South Island, is dauntingly big and astoundingly beautiful. The area boasted a thriving tourist industry by the 1890s, even by standards set elsewhere in New Zealand today. The main town, Queenstown, now has about ten thousand residents, and services a much greater number of visitors. It glitters and bustles. Even so, development hasn't been allowed to sprawl along roadsides or up mountain slopes, and everything remains overwhelmed by natural grandeur. Adventure junkies come for a variety of compelling reasons, all of them world-class—trout fishing, skiing, white-water rafting, jet boating, river surfing, bungy-jumping, paragliding, parachuting, canyoning, mountain biking, horse riding, tramping, motorcycling, rock climbing, water skiing and wind surfing. But there are many slower-paced-attractions too:

scenic cable cars, wildlife parks, aerial sightseeing, Maori culture.

Maoris first visited the Wakatipu area in the 1300s in search of moa. The remains of a village have been found near where the Route Burn meets the Dart River, and there is a moa hunting site at Glenorchy where the Dart enters the northern end of Wakatipu. These sites, like other such moa sites, are notable for not having any fortifications or even weapons of war. But by the early 1500s, the local moa population had been hunted to extinction and the Maori returned to live on the coastlines. In *The Future Eaters*, Tim Flannery notes that the South Island was too cold to grow sweet potato, and after the moa were gone, the Maori were reduced to eating cordyline, and even bracken fern roots, a staple so poor that elsewhere in the world it is little more than famine food. Flannery believes that the constant warring between iwi only arose among the normally peaceable Polynesians following the demise of the moa, and he attributes it to the battle for food. If you didn't protect your own supplies, or steal food from other tribes, your children starved to death. And if you didn't cannibalise those who fell in battle, you didn't get enough protein to stay healthy. Who among us would behave any differently?

While the Wakatipu area was quickly exhausted of sustenance, it remained rich in pounamu, also known as jade, nephrite or greenstone. This soft lustrous stone was carved into ornaments and war clubs, many of which went on to become precious heirlooms of great mana. Collecting pounamu involved traversing treacherous transalpine trails, and expeditions took many weeks, sometimes months. One of the main routes was along the Route Burn valley. Another, hardly surprisingly, followed the Greenstone River. It is said greenstone was still being collected by Maori in the Greenstone valley as late as the 1850s, at the time Europeans began their own major explorations of the Wakatipu district.

I finally visited Wakatipu in 2005. After a few days fishing the nearby lakes and streams I walked with my family up the Greenstone. The path is used by thousands of trampers and is well formed and maintained. In places it passes over grassy river flats, but sometimes the densely forested hills close in and the track is benched into steep slopes high above the river. From these vantages we could often see good-sized fish hanging in currents at the heads and tails of pools. Often I stopped to do a few quick casts while my family walked on ahead, and then I'd scramble back up to the track and race off after them.

During one of these little asides, after hooking three good fish in the one glide, I rounded a bend in the river and noticed an angler ahead of me. I had to walk past him in order to get back onto the track, so out of courtesy I put my rod back in its carry tube and said a polite g'day as I drew alongside.

'You're not fishing are you?' he replied menacingly.

'No,' I lied.

He looked at my rod tube. 'You have to have a Backcountry Licence to fish the Greenstone nowadays, and they're all booked up.' He stopped fishing and flashed a Fish and Game ID at me. He was a bailiff, he said. Apparently I should have applied for a fishing permit way back in September when a maximum of just fifty-one permits, for trips that were to be a maximum of three or four days' duration, were made available for the two month period from mid-January to mid-March. My chances wouldn't have been good.

'I thought you guys wanted access to be guaranteed,' I said. 'Why give private land owners a hard time for limiting the number of anglers fishing their rivers, when you want to do exactly the same thing?'

'We need to preserve the backcountry experience,' he said.

But when I pressed him, he couldn't define the backcountry experience, had no idea what we backcountry anglers really value about our fishing.

I said 'I thought fishing in Australasia, as opposed to the contrived experience in the UK, was all about spontaneity. I thought we cherished the freedom to fish when the weather suits, to be able to develop a season-long intimacy with the land. Why should *any* river be made a preserve for a handful of privileged lottery winners, who are then compelled to fish from dawn to dusk in order to take full advantage of their precious time? What is so wrong with casual sport? How else do we get children or passing trampers to understand and respect our passion?' I simply could not comprehend why anyone would think that the upper twenty-five kilometres of the Greenstone was capable of supporting no more than three pairs of anglers per day. It was patently absurd, like saying that only one lane of an Olympic pool should be open at any one time, and then only for an hour a week.

'Fish can smell people,' he said, dead pan. 'If you wade across a stream, the fishing for hundreds of metres downstream is ruined for days on end.'

I wanted to tell him about the fish I'd caught a few minutes ago, the same ones he must have fished to minutes before my arrival, but I guessed that he'd only try to arrest me or something. Given the impracticalities of enforcing the law, I almost decided that it would be worth letting him try. Instead I told him about the wonderful fishing I'd enjoyed the day before on two very popular waters, the Route Burn and Diamond Creek, both smaller and much more heavily fished that this stretch of the Greenstone.

'You might think the fishing was good there, but it's completely stuffed compared to how it used to be,' he insisted.

On the Route Burn I landed six two-kilo rainbows in two hours. On Diamond Creek I caught three trophies, including a brown trout well in excess of ten pounds. 'Surely if things were any easier than that, the fishing would be worse, not better,' I suggested.

He didn't understand what I was talking about.

'Look,' I said, pointing to a spot hard against the bank, halfway up the pool. 'See that fish up there in the current. Go and walk across the rapid at the head of the pool, and let your pheromones wash all over it. Then, if I can have a lend of your rod, I'll catch it for you.'

'You can't fish, you don't have a licence.' I swear he was gloating.

'Okay, I'll go and walk across the rapid,' I said.

'No. You can't.'

But of course I could. Fish and Game has no veto over people wanting to wade across a stream, any more than it can bully swimmers, rafters or bushwalkers. And after I waded the rapid, I came back and rechallenged him to cover the trout with a fly. I think the only reason he accepted my dare was that he didn't want me to think he couldn't cast. But I'm also sure that, subconsciously at least, he didn't really want to be successful, didn't want to have his preconceptions proved wrong.

The presentation was clunky and the fly landed too heavily on the water, but the trout instantly raced through the current and snatched the cicada. The bailiff was so surprised that he struck by reflex, too quickly. He pricked the fish, but it got away.

'There you go,' I said victoriously.

'What do you mean? It just proves what I was saying. If he hadn't been aware of your pheromones, he would have taken the fly more deliberately and I would have got him.'

There was no way to win this argument. The thought struck me that if the bailiffs really were issued with legitimate backcountry licences, Fish and Game had to be stealing positions from the lottery. Either that or this bailiff was fishing without a backcountry licence—do as I say, not as I do. 'I'll be on my way,' I said. But before I left he insisted on giving me some pamphlets about the new regulations.

That night I read the propaganda, devastated to find out exactly how draconian the laws were. Even if I had won the lottery, permit holders were to be accompanied by no more than one nominated fishing partner. Fishing casually with my family—my daughter for an hour here, my son for an hour there—was now illegal.

And in an effort to airbrush away unpalatable truths about quota systems, the beneficiaries of the system were not required to cover the price of having their exclusivity assured. That cost was to be borne by mugs like me. Functional quota systems require dedicated processing, monitoring, policing, advertising and promotion. They don't come cheap, especially not when there is poor economy of scale. Perhaps you can justify such a system for trampers using the Routeburn Track where the financial burden can be diluted amongst eleven thousand participants. But you couldn't possibly get away with spreading such a huge cost over just one hundred anglers in the Greenstone valley.

Maybe there *were* more people fishing the Greenstone than most people would prefer. But as far as I could tell the 'solution' was far worse than the perceived problem. Over-regulation had instantly altered the backcountry experience dramatically, for the worse, and perhaps forever. It seemed to me that the most worrisome anti-fishing zealots now resided within the angling community itself. If that was the case, what chance did we have? I could already hear the anglers' collective voice fading beneath the cacophony of trampers and anti-trout 'environmentalists'.

The Maori were forced to fight over dwindling moa stocks. But we anglers, with the luxury of not needing to eat what we catch, have been able to embrace meaningful bag limits so trout are in no danger of disappearing through overhunting. Perhaps the Greenstone trout are better compared to pounamu, the greenstone itself—precious, but plentiful. If we unreasonably deny access to those who need its mana, how do we expect those we have cast out to respond?

The only fisherman I saw in the Greenstone valley was that single Fish and Game officer. But I did meet walkers who would have loved to have fished for an hour or so in the late afternoon if they could. And some were already talking of war. One bloke, a lure fisher, was so pissed-off with the situation that he was hankering to launch his li-lo upstream of every 'selfish bloody fly-fisher' he chanced to see. His big problem was that he couldn't find any.

Another bloke, a white-haired old timer who had fished the Greenstone since his eleventh birthday, said that if things didn't change he'd fix the bureaucrats by throwing a handful of dreaded Didymo algae into the headwaters. 'Can't wait to see how those Fish and Game bastards feel when I shut *them* out of the Greenstone.' When I asked how he could possibly bring himself to vandalise a water he claimed to love, he said 'The essential nature of the river has already been destroyed, and if delivering the coup de grâce means there's a chance that other backcountry waters will be saved the same bureaucratic fate, it might just be worth the angst'. I don't know if he made good his threat, but I do know that Didymo was discovered in the river sometime after our discussion.

The Greenstone seems to be facing yet another resource war, and I wonder if the bloodshed and angst is really going to be worth it.

Reflections

I THINK a lot about the mantras *take nothing but memories, leave nothing but footprints* and *observe, don't interact*, mainly because my imperative in the bush, trout fishing, happens to be the antithesis of these ideals. I am not alone. There are many experts in other fields who also believe that interaction is essential to the honesty and wellbeing of their relationship with nature. Of any relationship.

Karen is a close friend whom I first met more than twenty years ago when she was working as technical forester and I was a park ranger. When I walk with her, plants are everything. She'll pluck petals from flowers to show me an orchid's sex organs, grind leaves between her fingers to release their spicy aromas, dig into the ground to reveal native truffles, nibble just about any fruiting body she stumbles upon. The latter habit might be considered by some to be risky or even dangerous, but it pales against the efforts of one of my entomologist friends, Ruth, who feels obliged to deliberately experience the sting or bite of every invertebrate known (and unknown) to humanity. With her it is a case of upturning rotting logs and scuffling around in humus. Looking, poking, prodding. Mind you, if she finds some impossibly luminous nematode or planarian which can't be needled into attack, then Ruth, too, is likely to consider her discoveries ripe for tasting.

I find myself privileged to have such passionate people sharing their love of nature with me, showing me things I never thought existed, making my world ever more complex.

Sometimes I am surprised in other ways. I've long suspected that many bushwalkers actually find gadgets—digital watches, GPSs, EPIRBs—more interesting, more real, more important, than the bush itself. Photographers, for example, always seem to have an unhealthy preoccupation with technology and artificial points of view. But then along comes Brad, who shows me how the viewfinder forces him to appreciate light, and detail, and the perspectives of animals bigger and smaller than humans. After a week in the bush with him, I found myself noticing things—natural things, important things—I never knew existed.

Stewart is a respected musician who owns and operates the locally famous Red Planet recording studio in Hobart. We got to know each other simply because his children, Chelsea and Jake, happen to number amongst my kids' best friends. Anyway, this story really starts when he and I were walking along the Rodway Range in Mount Field National Park, on our way to Lake Hayes. I was going there in the hope of catching some wild rainbow trout. The fish in this lake are often large and always spectacularly coloured—striped bright red on the sides and peppered with numerous black spots on the underbelly and chin. Stewart, however, was thinking and talking of other things, largely in response to an idle comment I made about Budgie's worsening deafness.

'Babies hear frequencies ranging from about thirty hertz to twenty thousand hertz. By the time you are a teenager, the upper limit has already been reduced to eighteen or nineteen thousand. At our age, you and I probably struggle with anything above fourteen thousand. The whole of the audible range comprises just nine or ten octaves.'

The last point seemed ridiculous.

'An octave is the distance between a soundwave of one length and one of exactly double that length. It's an exponential thing, a bit like that theoretical primary-school maths problem where you have to figure out how many times you'd have to fold a newspaper before you'd end up with a tower as high as the moon. Kids are always amazed to find that it only takes something like forty folds.'

'I still find that amazing,' I admitted.

'And here's another thing, the octave is actually divided into twelve equal parts, but in Western music we traditionally only used seven of them, you know: do re mi fa so la ti.'

'Why?' It seemed like the obvious thing to say.

'Because combinations of notes only sound good if they are mathematically compatible. You can divide a twelve-part scale into quarters and thirds, but not into fifths, so the fifth note is discordant and we don't normally bother with it. Same sort of thing with the other missing notes. But you could theoretically divide an 'octave' into as many or as few parts as you wanted, and if you combined those tones into clever mathematical packages they would still be pleasing to the ear.'

We had descended into a native herb field, a flat lawn completely surrounded by boulder scree. 'Stop,' Stewart said quietly. I stopped. He made a short, sharp clap with his hands. The sound was strangely comforting. Then he used his voice to reproduce bird calls, drum beats, jungle rhythms, heartbeats. The sounds had extraordinary warmth. Even when Stewart stopped making noises, when everything became quiet, the atmosphere accorded a sense of mystical wellbeing.

'I don't normally like quiet,' I admitted.

'I know. I remember how on-edge you were during that thick snow fall at February Plains. Do you know why you felt that way?'

I supposed that it was because I couldn't see.

'You didn't feel nervous the night before when we walked in pitch-black darkness from Wurragarra Creek to Lake How, did you? It wasn't that you couldn't see in the snow—you were scared because you couldn't hear.'

I didn't think I had let my discomfort show on that trip. Stewart had exposed a private embarrassment.

• *Artificial* •

'You know how horses go a bit crazy on windy days, running circles in their paddocks—it's because in their heart of hearts they are still plains animals, still at risk of attack from wolves and lions. They can't hear predators when the grass rustles noisily all around them, so they experience a kind of sonic twilight filled with creepy shadows and echoes of dread. We haven't had the wild animal totally domesticated out of our souls yet either. We don't like the fact that we can't hear potential predators. Nor do we like being unable to communicate. It's not just you Trout—the silence of falling snow makes everyone feel a bit creepy.'

'Hearing's not that important to me,' I said sceptically.

But Stewart insisted that people use a primitive sort of echo location, me more than most because I was so attuned to sound when I was fishing.

'On February Plains, I wasn't scared in that little rainforest where the trapper's hut is,' I countered. 'And it was perfectly quiet in there.'

But apparently it wasn't as quiet as I thought. 'In there, the soft mosses and leaves offered quite a lot of absorption—airwaves would vibrate the delicate vegetation and much of the sound would dissipate as heat. But even mosses are not as effective as thickly falling fluffy snow…'

I'd never thought about the entropy of sound before, but it made sense. The low end of the spectrum is something you feel rather than hear. The boom of a base drum, the rumble of heavy machinery. I remembered an earthquake in the Cox River in the Blue Mountains which produced a silent sound that physically took my breath away.

'Anyway,' Stewart continued, 'tree trunks and limbs always reflect some sound, so the forest still gave us some feedback.'

It occurred to me that if we like to hear reflected sound, why did so many artificial environments give me the heebies. 'That restaurant we took our families to last week—why did I find the noises so annoying? You know: cutlery on china, glass bottles on polished tables.'

'Those noises are in the harsh part of the audible range, about two to five thousand hertz. Sure, this is also the intelligible part of the spectrum where we can best identify pitch—which is why we use it when we speak—but it can be quite grating. In the restaurant the sound was reflected off the ceramic floor-tiles, the mirrored walls, the metallic fittings, the glass windows. Not only that, but the space was so small that high-energy sounds didn't have time to dissipate. They bounced off the flat surfaces and reinforced each other, creating standing waves of the sort which, to our souls, are as terrible as those in stormy oceans.'

I remembered taking a dinghy through the mouth of the Gordon River, where wind-driven waves and the incoming tide confronted the outflowing river, creating a life-threatening maelstrom. I shuddered. But considering the water analogy further, I asked why sound travels so well across lakes at night.

'Well, if conditions are calm enough, sound rolls unimpeded across the surface tension enabling us to talk to each other across kilometres of water, and that seems pretty wonderful. But usually it travels too far before reflecting, and because we have to wait so long for feedback, it can also make us anxious. What we really like is sound that's reflected off lots of multifaceted surfaces so that the noise that comes back to our ears is mildly chaotic, but still decipherable, subconsciously at least. It's called pink sound—white sound with all the harsh static rounded off, soft as a newborn baby. It helps if the reflecting surfaces are further away than in the restaurant because then the sound's energy is reduced. It also helps if there are air cavities between the surfaces in which some of the sound can be absorbed.'

Like the boulder field we were resting in, I realised.

'This would make the perfect recording studio,' Stewart concluded. 'We spend millions of dollars creating concert halls, incorporating all the theory about absorption, diffusion, reflection and audible ranges, and never come close to what we have right here. I guess we like the way we hear sound in the bush because this is where we really belong.'

I asked Stewart if he liked recording music as much as he liked being 'in the wild'.

'Yes I do. Except when people want me to build up their songs from two-bar sound grabs. Mind you, I understand what your Irish mate, Matt, meant when he said that music should be something you do, not something you play on your stereo. Playing music, dancing to it, is what makes it real.'

Which, of course, is why I prefer fishing to looking passively at nature from the sidelines of a boardwalk. My involvement with the wild has to be physical as well as cerebral. It has to be a celebration of my bestiality, not a denial of it.

When we finally got to Lake Hayes, the fish were gorging themselves on gum beetles, slurping them noisily one after the other. Whenever I was casting to one, I remained perfectly aware of others to my left and right. I always knew exactly where I should put my next cast—which direction, how far away—even though I couldn't see the quarry.

'You're as blind as a bat,' said Stewart.

It was a heartfelt compliment.

Wall frame

ONE WEEKDAY in May, Lester and I went up to The Pook to lay the blocks and fill them with concrete, and the following weekend he rallied a bunch of mates to help with the frame.

'Where did you get the timber from?' asked Budgie.

'There was one big stringybark in the middle of the living room, so Trout and I hired a portable mill and chopped up the whole thing into four-be-twos.'

Magenta was astounded. 'I sort of know that wood comes from trees, but timber is something I get from a hardware store.'

Bram was critical, of course. He hated the way green timber bled wherever it was nailed, found it unpleasantly wet and sticky.

'Would you prefer that green timber was an unyielding material like steel, or artificial like plastic?' Budgie barked. 'Would you prefer to work with *immaterials*? Soulless things? Dead ones?'

'Don't be effin daft. But I hate the way it shrinks, the way the movement makes doors stick and the joints on your architraves come apart.'

'I'll tell you what I hate,' said Budgie, and no-one doubted him. 'I hate the modern preoccupation with perfection. I hate the way kiln-dried timbers have had all the life baked out of them. I hate the fact that it comes perfectly straight and square, with smooth-planed surfaces that never exceed catalogued dimensions by more than a fraction of a millimetre.'

'I once heard Peter Timms talk on gardening,' I added quickly, hoping to defuse the situation. 'He reckoned that the joy of gardening was bound up in the fact that it is essentially futile. You weed and prune knowing full well that next week you'll have to do it all over again. It's the process of weeding that is important, he stressed. The closeness to the earth, the dirt and manure, the smell and toil. He lamented the *Backyard Blitz* mentality. What was the point of static perfection, he wondered.'

'Just like building a cubby,' agreed Lester.

'It's also one of the reasons we fish,' said Budgie. 'You know, the fact that it's essentially futile.'

'Well it's futile when *you* fish anyway,' said Lester.

The bearers were five-by-threes, laid in rows five feet apart. The floor joists were four-by-twos, spaced at eighteen inches centre-to-centre. 'It a funny thing,' noted Frances, 'builders and trout fishermen must be the only people in Australia who still talk imperial.'

'Christ alive!' shouted Lester.

'Did I say something wrong?'

'A bloody ant—an effin jack-jumper—just stung me.'

'Don't sting, they bite,' insisted Bram.

'Don't tell me what I do and don't know about insects. I'm a fly fisher, remember.' And with that Lester pulled a carpenter's rule from his back pocket and began prodding the offending beast.

'What did I tell you?' gloated Bram as the jack-jumper grabbed at the plastic with its pincers.

'Keep watching. See—he's arching his arse around. There—he's trying to sting the ruler.'

'Be buggered.'

'What are they doing?' asked Magenta who'd just returned from the long-drop.

'Converting inchmen to metric,' said Budgie.

'Didn't know you had a sense of humour,' said Bram, humourlessly.

'I don't,' Budgie retaliated, biffing him round the head so hard that his ear shone red.

There was more disagreement when it came to putting down the tongue-and-groove floorboards.

'That looks more like what I'd buy from the hardware store,' said Magenta.

Bram was aghast. 'You can't put them down first, not before you have the place fully framed and weatherproof. First decent rain, they'll swell up, make the joists bow upwards and wrench the frame to fuckin bits.'

'Look Bram, we'll just broom some sealer over them,' said Lester patiently.

'But they'll stain and crack and look old.'

'A sight better than having a high-gloss artificial look,' said Budgie.

'And I like to have a platform to work on,' Lester added.

'Suppose you're goin to tell me you don't have a nail gun?'

'Yep,' said Lester proudly, picking up a stack of four or five boards and laying them end for end along one edge of the floor frame.

Almost straight away, much to Bram's delight, Lester found nailing dry hardwood more troublesome than he expected. There was a twang as a two-inch nail speared past Frances' ear, followed immediately by the dull splod of steel on flesh. 'Kevie see blood,' screeched Lester melodramatically, jamming his thumb and index finger into his mouth.

'I see that being a caring health professional doesn't mean you can't take the piss on blokes in the sheltered workshop,' said Magenta.

'Look,' said Budgie. 'I'll show you a few tricks for nailing. Bloody nail guns have turned you all into a bunch of pussies. Throw us a hammer.'

Lester threw it, hard.

And Budgie caught it, nonchalantly. Then, after quickly satisfying himself that the boards were properly cramped, he weighed Lester's hammer approvingly in his right hand, and collected a fistful of nails with his left. He knelt on one knee. Without looking, he used the thumb, index finger and middle finger of his left hand to select one nail from the bunch.

He had started the nail off with a solid hit, not a tap, which sank the nail a full quarter-inch into the timber. The next blows were harder still—two, three, FOUR. And before the final hit, his left hand had already selected the next nail, and turned it around. He sped along, musically, effortlessly. Soon he had finished the first row and, without looking for a reaction from his audience, was immediately onto the next.

Before long, everyone was getting into the swing of things. 'It feels good,' Lester agreed. 'Like sending out a double haul. The timing and rhythm are sort of sensual.'

'Pah. If you don't have a gun you are not in the game.'

'What is *the game*, Bram?' Budgie exploded.

Stunned silence.

'Look,' apologised Budgie. 'I understand why people invent tools to do meaningless tasks, like washing nappies. But why for beautiful tasks like nailing? Next thing you know they'll invent a machine to have sex for you.'

'They already have,' said Magenta.

'Tell me more, Magenta,' said Lester suggestively.

'Well, I do have a rather good story on hand,' said Magenta. 'The other day I was visiting my mum, helping her clean out the old shed at the back of the house. There was this Bakelite thing, with a couple of metres of electric cord and a 240-volt plug at the end. It was about the size of a large cucumber and covered with perished black rubber, which was sort of hanging in shreds, like tentacles. I had to look at it for a minute or two before I realised what it was.'

'And what was it?' said Bram innocently.

That night there was another roaring fire, beer and talk. The conversation revisited nailing, fly casting and genital vibrators and settled into deep study of the nature of rhythm.

'One of the lads at the sheltered workshop is such a munt that all he can do is sand table tops, and he can only do that in time to music. When there's not much work on they play blues for him, and when there's too much they play old LPs at seventy-eight revs per minute.'

'Talking of music, what's say you blokes sing us a song?'

'Why not,' said Bram, who along with Lester and Calvin was a member of the Meander Men's Choir.

'What sort of music do you blokes do?' asked Magenta.

Actually, they specialise in working songs, primarily ribald sea shanties. They linked arms and began swaying in time like a ship in a steady swell, like seamen hauling lines.

Nellie's in the kitchen bakin' duff
With the cheeks of 'er arse goin' chuff chuff chuff

Next day, after another cooked breakfast that was, according to our chef, 'just right', we began preparing the wall frames. Lester and I paired four-by-one-and-a-halves for the top and bottom plates, cut them to length and laid them out like a map on the floor. Frances and Magenta marked the positions of the studs; the others cut the studs to length and sorted out the lintels and wall battens. Then we all got to work nailing the studs to the plates with four-inch bullet-heads. 'One thing about green timber,' Bram conceded, 'it's as easy as hammering matchsticks into play-dough.'

'Speak for yourself,' said Magenta angrily as she struggled to straighten yet another bent nail.

'These walls weigh a bloody ton. There's no way we're going to lift them without a fuckin crane,' Bram complained when the first wall had been finished.

'There's no occupational health and safety inspections on this site, Bram,' Lester scoffed.

'Some health professional you are.' But Bram helped, along with everyone else, and after lots of grunting and swearing the walls were stood up, gang-nailed together, plumbed and straightened.

That night around the campfire little Lily approached Lester with her left hand forming a crude cylinder and her right hand cupped on top. 'Open the lid,' she giggled.

Lester opened the lid.

'Put your finger in. Stir it around.'

Compliance.

'Take it out… close the lid.'

A strategic pause.

'THANKS FOR CLEANING THE TOILET!'

Laughter from all the kids. And the adults too, who of course had done the same thing when they were kids. Even Beatrice was smiling—perhaps it was the gin and tonic.

'I was thinking,' said Budgie out of the blue. 'We'd be a lot better off if we all had prehensile tails. It'd make working on the roof a sight easier.'

'Interesting,' agreed Bram. 'If our ancestors had tails, why did we lose them? Maybe Darwin was mistaken, maybe the theory of evolution is plain wrong.'

'*Evil-ution*,' said Beatrice, only half in jest.

'Lizards lose their tails all the time,' said Calvin.

We were completely drunk.

Silkscreen sign

BUDGIE, CALVIN and I arrived at the carpark at the end of the Mersey Forest Road in Calvin's old Torana, still going weakly fifteen years after I first rode in it. It was 8.00 pm, which in October is just on dark. A kilometre or so into the forest, at the place where the Jacksons Creek Track forks away from the Chapter Lake Track, there was a rather imposing registration booth. Budgie cursed.

'What's wrong now?' said Calvin impatiently.

'Bureaucrats gathering stats.'

'So?'

'They're trying to stop us going into the bush. They can't sell this idea to anyone without some kind of science, or pseudo-science, to back up their case. They need statistics.'

'What if the stats don't support their case?'

'All statistics will support their case. A small number of walkers using the track: a good reason for keeping numbers at current levels or lower. A large number using the track: ditto. And since they'll use anything against us, the only thing is not to give the bastards any data at all.' He doused the logbook with meths and set fire to it.

An hour later, on the edge of the Plateau, on the boundary of the National Park, kilometres from any road, our torches illuminated a highly reflective silkscreen sign: 'Fuel Stove Only Area!'

This set Budgie off on another tirade. 'How can anybody think that this fuckin metal sign is more natural or less confronting than a campfire? It defies sanity!'

'Maybe they are worried about escaped fires?' Calvin offered.

Budgie looked around at the cold sodden ground and rolled his eyes melodramatically. 'I used to burn these signs. Poetic justice. But the bastards must've cottoned-on. Look at this!' The post was made of steel, and set in concrete. 'Bastards. Bastards, bastards, BASTARDS!!'

'Nothin like a challenge,' said Calvin.

I set off ahead of them and gained a couple of hundred metres before the inevitable 'BOOM!'

It was about midnight when we arrived at the tier overlooking Lake Meston. The fragrance of pencil pine smoke forewarned us that the hut was already occupied.

'Well, at least they've saved us the trouble of unblocking the fireplace.'

This was yet another thing that pissed Budgie off. Parks and Wildlife bureaucrats had arbitrarily decided to seal the fireplaces in the Meston and Junction huts so now they were cold and cheerless, damp and musty, barely functional. It was something that stuck in my craw more than Budgie's.

Caretaker

THE COMMUNITY Huts Partnership Program came about through intense lobbying by the Mountain Huts Preservation Society Inc., an affiliation of people who were appalled by the Parks and Wildlife Service's cavalier attitude to European historical heritage in remote areas. Most offensive were the various internal departmental reports which advocated dismantling huts, sealing them off, not undertaking maintenance in the hope that they would simply rot into the ground and, for structures that had suffered fire damage or vandalism, a refusal to allow reconstruction or repair.

Things are a bit different now, but only because community groups, having given up on so-called consultative processes, have taken to political lobbying. Whereas arrogant bureaucrats can't be voted out of office, arrogant politicians can—and they know it.

Although I've never been involved with the Mountain Huts Preservation Society, the Parks and Wildlife Service approached me out of the blue and asked if I wanted to be the official, albeit unpaid, caretaker of the Meston and Junction huts. I didn't really know why they picked me, but I agreed to do the job anyway, and the district ranger for Mole Creek arranged to meet me at the Junction Lake hut so that we could carry out a joint assessment of what work should be done.

The walk to Junction Lake takes five to seven hours, some of which is fairly steep. I chose to use the Jacksons Creek Track, which was reasonably well defined. The only dodgy bit was just a kilometre from the start, at the Jacksons Creek crossing. The 'bridge' was nothing more than a fallen tree—very old, rotten and slippery with only a single strand of loose fencing wire for a handrail. I chickened out and waded through the ice-cold current. The rest of the trip was uneventful, but when I got to Junction Lake I was perfectly alone. I waited for two nights, and still no-one turned up. Oh well, the fishing was good.

It turned out that the ranger had lost his game of Russian roulette with the bridge. It crumbled beneath him, and plummeted several metres onto the boulder-strewn stream bed. Thankfully there was someone with him at the time, and he was hauled out of the shallow water. By the time I walked out of the bush, he was safely in hospital having his face reconstructed.

A few months later, after he had returned to work, I contacted the ranger and we organised another meeting, at Lake Meston this time. The weather was wet and cold, and when I arrived at the hut there was no-one to meet me. Déjà vu. Perhaps he'd had another accident.

The Meston Hut is nestled on a high bank a few hundred metres back from the water's edge. Even in the early 1980s, when I first visited the area, the stunted eucalypt forest had a dense tea-tree understorey, but you could see parts of the lake quite well. Now the vegetation was so thick and high that you could scarcely see any water at all. I was thankful that the hut was in a glade, that marsupials kept the immediate surrounds as open as a golfing green and held the dark, dank understorey at bay. I set up a small pyre in the fireplace, put a billy on to boil and prepared a curry. Then I had a snort of port. Late in the evening, figuring that the ranger wasn't going to turn up at all, I wandered down to the lakeshore to have a fish. After dark, a luminous fly cast over the lip and retrieved slowly along the bottom usually gets results.

The instant the track left the glade, it became so overgrown that tea-tree scraped heavily at my raincoat, showering water over my face and hands. Boy, it was cold. The lake, it turned out, was unusually high, flooding the silty beaches, backing up into the trees and scrub. And there, in front of a small forlorn tent on an islet of boggy ground, rugged-up like Mawson, was a man. He was huddled over a small cooking stove, but it had gone out. He wasn't moving. Perhaps he was so insulated from the outside world that he couldn't sense my presence. Perhaps he was dead.

'Hello,' I said cautiously, as if addressing a ghost.

He startled. 'Hi there. Greg is it?' It was the ranger.

'You're not staying in the hut?' I asked.

'Horrible chilly damp things. Prefer to be out here.'

Each to his own.

We talked for bit, but it was raining now and a chill wind was whipping in off the lake. 'Come on up to hut,' I suggested. There's a fire going and all.'

'No thanks. I'll catch up with you tomorrow.'

The ranger knocked at the door early in the morning. The first thing he said was 'Well, we'll have to do something about that fireplace, won't we'.

No doubt about that. Originally the fireplace and chimney had been framed with saplings, and clad with flat sheet-iron. This design was quite popular with trappers in the post-war period, and providing you kept the fires to a sensible size, they seem to have been unaccountably safe. However, these days a lot of bushwalkers aren't used to lighting fires, much less using rustic fireplaces with internal timber frames. In the few months since my last visit someone had built a gusser that had burnt the framing right away. Not that this fact was immediately obvious—the flat iron remained exactly as it had always been, held together at the seams by the very nails that had affixed it to the framing.

'We'll have to seal the fireplace off,' he said, trying overly hard to secure my agreement.

'It's pretty safe at the moment,' I suggested. 'I mean, there's no framing left to catch fire.'

'If we don't seal it off, someone will eventually burn the whole hut down, and we will lose this glorious heritage.'

His false sincerity grated terribly—only last night he had been telling me how much he hated huts. I guessed that his real problem was with people collecting firewood from the bush. It was a case of ideology taking precedence over pragmatism. The reality is that in eucalypt forests there is always enough limb-fall to supply firewood without damaging the environment.

As I saw it, there were a few problems with sealing the fireplace. Without fires, huts are colder than tents and unattractive to camp in. They soon become clammy and musty. And anyway, I don't think the backcountry huts should be kept as mere museums. Surely their true value lies in their ongoing functionality. 'We could install a wood heater inside the current fireplace,' I suggested.

'Too expensive, too much work.'

'I think you'll find that it would be pretty easy to raise the funds privately.'

'There would be environmental problems associated with fuel collection.'

'Perhaps one of the local angling clubs, bushwalking clubs or hut preservation societies would be prepared to fund fuel drops?' I proposed.

'The Department would never agree to it, and I have to say I don't blame them.'

There was no point arguing the toss. 'The real point,' I said, 'is that I'm in no position to endorse your proposal. I'm just one person, and the Department invited me to do this job, so I don't represent the community at all. What say I help you work up all the options, then we present them to all the local interest groups and get them to decide what they want, and what they can afford?'

The ranger didn't seem very keen to talk about hut maintenance after that. But he promised to contact me again as soon as his busy schedule allowed.

I visited the hut a few months later. To my complete surprise, the fireplace had already been sealed-up. An entry in the hut log revealed that the Department had wasted no time in implanting a more compliant caretaker. Nobody had bothered to tell me.

In the same vein

BUDGIE AND I were fishing Tasmania's Macquarie River when two different mayflies landed on the back of my hand, a black spinner and a red one. 'Hey Budgie, look at this.'

He rubbed his eyes, but they seemed more watery than before.

'You alright?'

'Yeah… Sometimes I get sparks in my eyes.'

'Perhaps you should have yourself checked out for retinal detachment?'

'It's not that. But my eyes are always playing up on me…'

I looked more closely at the spinners. 'I just love Lai's mayfly painting,' I offered. 'You know, the one of the wing where…'

'Lai was intrigued with the way I always talked about the beauty of mayfly wings. The delicate veins used to remind me of bridal lace, of rivers viewed from mountain tops, of paths untravelled on a map. I was optimistic then, romantic. Life was good.'

'You're not optimistic now?' It was rather a silly question.

'At night when I close my eyes I see the veins on my retina. I'm sure it's not normal—scares the living bejesus out of me. You know, Trout, when Lai was alive my ill health would have reminded me of a red spinner's wing. Now the wing reminds me of my ill health. It's an ugly turnaround.'

His words chilled me. One of the conclusions Lester had reached after years of working in geriatrics and palliative care was that happy people died graciously, while unhappy people clung-on to life desperately, even as terminal illness caused their misery and hopelessness to spiral out of control.

'As for the black spinner's wing, these days it reminds me of crazed pottery, perished rubber…' Budgie lamented.

'When I was a kid,' I interrupted, 'whenever I heard about someone perishing—usually they were lost at sea or in the highlands—it scared me witless. *Perish* was such a horrible word. I imagined my skin splitting, contracting, going flaky. Couldn't imagine a worse way to die.'

'When I was a kid,' Budgie reminisced. 'I read a story about identical twins, one of whom was fascinated by the prospect of death. He imagined that the gentlest way to go would be to swim offshore, in a straight line, way out to sea; to keep swimming and swimming, rhythmically and steadily, until sleepy exhaustion dragged you back to your watery beginning. Dying at sea is a common fascination isn't it. You know, captains going down with their ship and whatnot. Did you ever see *Whale Rider*?'

'Drowning? Is that how you'd like to go?' I asked sceptically.

'No! Couldn't think of much worse than being out in the icy-cold briny, tumbling in the waves, struggling, choking. If you changed your mind ten miles from shore, there'd be no way out. Your last minutes would be filled with unbearable panic… When the time comes, I think I'll just walk off into the Western Lakes, in bad weather. Walk and walk until cold and gentle exhaustion take me over. I'd feel safe in the knowledge that I could always save myself if I wanted. When the point of no return came, my body would be comfortably numb and my mind psychedelically misty... It's more than a fantasy, you know. I've come close to dying in the high country, in Canada and Mongolia. I know what it would be like.'

'I wouldn't let you do that to yourself,' I said lamely.

'What you really mean is that you wouldn't want to let me do it to you,' Budgie suggested.

'Are you really as selfish as you pretend you are?'

'I'm captain of my own ship,' he said.

'Yeah?' I was angry with him now. 'What sort of Captain insists on taking the passengers down with him?'

He didn't respond.

I tried to change the subject. 'What about Lai, Budgie? What was she thinking when she painted that picture?'

'I've told you before. She was in awe of the fact that mayflies found immortality by sacrificing themselves for the next generation.'

'There you go then—she was into life, wasn't she? She wouldn't like you getting all maudlin...'

'She couldn't have kids, Trout.' The pain in his voice was almost unbearable. 'There was no next generation for her... If she could have passed on her passions to anyone—if she could have kept guiding— she'd have been happy enough. But... fuckin bureaucrats...'

His eyes were more watery than ever now, and our conversation leaked dry.

Larson's fish

BUDGIE WAS at the wheel and I was his passenger. We were driving along Tasmania's north-west coastline on our way to do some sea-trout fishing. Budgie seemed to be playing a game of Space Invaders, using the release-button on the tip of the hand brake as a makeshift gun. When I asked, he explained that he was lining up a spot on the windscreen, a dried droplet of splattered insect or something, with the first letter of the numberplate on the desperately slow car in front of us. If the alignment remained true while he pressed the trigger, the car was vaporised. Otherwise, the shot was deemed to have missed. I tried it myself. Getting a direct hit was harder than it sounded, so the car didn't vaporise and Budgie was forced to overtake. As we rounded a corner and crossed back onto our proper side of the road, late-afternoon sun suddenly hit me square in the eyes. I pulled down the visor. There was a Larson cartoon pinned to it, a picture of a fish taking a dubious step out of the primordial ocean. The caption read 'One small step for fish, one great leap for…'

'I once entered a short story in a national competition, and won,' Budgie offered without context. 'It was about a Kokoda soldier who smuggled a fly rod in his pack and managed to preserve his own sanity by sneaking off to fish for rainbow trout in places like Eora Creek. It was a true story too, even if the bloke involved reckoned I went in so heavy on the irony and metaphor that he could barely recognise himself. The cash prize wasn't huge, but I got praise and the story was published in an anthology along with the eleven runners-up. I was so excited. I rang my adoptive mum. She said she was really happy for me. She reckoned she knew how good it was to win because she had once won third division in the lottery. I'd never felt more alone—drifted off into depression even before the phone call finished. And it ended up being a bloody short conversation, I can tell you.'

'At least *you* know it was good,' I reasoned.

'Perhaps not as good as I thought. Later on, I discovered that trout weren't introduced to New Guinea until after the war. I still wonder if the old digger was lying to me, or if there had been earlier, undocumented liberations.'

'Ever write anything else?' I asked.

'I had this idea for a novel. Submitted a few chapters and an outline to a publisher, and they liked it enough to give me a contract and an advance.'

When I asked him to outline the thrust of his story, he exhaled deeply, blowing smoke all over the windscreen. He was in the mood for storytelling. 'It's always struck me,' he began importantly, 'that as prophetic as the golden era sci-fi writers proved to be, there were some things they consistently got wrong. Like the idea of the super computer that goes mad and takes over the world.'

'Well that was really just them ripping-off Mary Shelly's story…'

'No, no. I think the authors genuinely found the concept spookily fascinating. You know, the idea of a monster being set amongst us by a psychopath—a mad scientist, a fascist government, whatever. But for me the scary thing is that the monster is not imposed on us by anyone. We set it upon ourselves. No-one's really got the hang of that.'

I was about to urge him on, but he didn't need any encouragement.

'People love technology, love being monitored and controlled. We have random breath testing and speed guns and unfettered video surveillance not because Big Brother wants it, but because we want it.' A sign—*Penguin Rookery Under 24-Hour Video Surveillance*—flashed by the driver-side window.

'My story,' Budgie continued, 'involved the idea of an all-powerful computer which wasn't foisted upon us, but into which we were happy to meld.'

It's almost come to pass, I realised. The Internet is the sum of millions of willing contributors, and contains a store of detailed knowledge beyond human comprehension. We all feed it and are nurtured by it. We're not in the least bit scared of it, not even as we become more dependent upon it.

'My story was written long before the Internet existed,' Budgie stressed. 'I essentially predicted things as they are today, but I went one step further. I thought, what if we didn't have to tap into the computer manually? What if our brains were seamlessly linked to it? What if we could think up a connection, and scan the Net with our minds? I'm more certain than ever this will eventually happen, and probably in the not too distant future.'

'We wouldn't stand for it,' I said hopefully.

'You're wrong, Trout, and you know it. We'd accept it as readily as twitchers accept video surveillance of penguin rookeries. It'd probably start relatively low-key: the ability to download basic principles of grammar and arithmetic. Why should anyone be condemned to spend decades of their life learning things manually if the whole lot could be downloaded in an instant? If you are slow at basic maths, why shouldn't you download the capacity to be as good as the class dux?'

'Surely people accept that it is the manual process of learning that is important and fun and exciting—the very thing that makes us human.' My argument sounded lame, even to my own ears.

'You'd be laughed out of town,' Budgie retaliated. 'It'd be like trying to argue against stem-cell research.'

'I certainly wouldn't argue against that,' I admitted. 'I'd pretty much do whatever it took to halt Lester's MS, or MSNW as the case may be.'

'Of course you would. So would I. That's my point. We won't stop it because we don't want to. What I hate, though, is how all this technology makes us all more alike, less defined by our so-called deficiencies, less different. To what end, I ask. What are we aiming for? What is the ultimate goal?'

I asked Budgie how deeply he was beholden to technology. When he finally decided to answer, his voice was leaden with regret. 'I got pretty heavily involved with the test-tube baby thing.' Each word became more introspective. 'I couldn't put up a convincing argument—not even to myself, let alone Lai—that anyone should be denied the right to be a parent. Even knowing that the success rate was mind-bogglingly low, that the number of people who were damaged exceeded the number of people who were successful, I still agreed to Lai's plea. If the technology hadn't been there, I think Lai and I could have accepted the inevitable. But the mere fact that there was a chance, no matter how improbable, meant that there was no closure—no normal grieving process, no learning to get on with our life. What the hormone treatment did was devastating. It's a long, long descent, Trout, for those of us forced to watch loved ones spiralling into depression…' Budgie seemed on the verge of tears. I probably should have asked more about Lai. Instead I asked him about the title of his unpublished book.

'The working title was *Artificial Intelligence*. Nowadays that would imply more efficient or superior intelligence. But I wanted my title to imply fake or misleading intelligence. If I had to name the book now, I'd drop the reference to intelligence altogether and just call it *Artificial*.'

'Did you ever finish the novel?'

'Oh yes. A hundred times.'

I laughed.

'The problem was that, any way I looked at it, the ending was hopeless. I simply couldn't dig up any romantic stuff à la *Star Trek*. Not for me the idea that individuals find eternal salvation from an expanding sun by journeying into space. In the future that I created, the individual became meaningless, as insignificant as a cell of our own body. As for ongoing space exploration and trade, why? Eventually we'll master nuclear fusion or some other limitless source of clean energy, and then we'll be able to manufacture any element, any compound, any*thing* we want. Why bother looking for rare minerals on other planets when you can build everything you want from hydrogen molecules? As for curiosity or academic pursuit, eventually we won't have to travel to find it. The Hubble telescope has already looked so far back into the past that we are on the cusp of observing the big bang. With refinement, there's no reason why we won't be able to see events that happened on the surface of distant planets. As for the feeling of exhilaration that comes from actual travel, we know enough about the biochemical nature of our brains to be able to manufacture that as well.'

'Budgie, you're way too bleak.'

'That's what I mean—that's why I couldn't give the publishers a manuscript. There was no message of hope. For Christ's sake, I was bleaker than Orwell. I simply couldn't conclude that the stars offered salvation to humanity. Space travel may offer opportunities for some sort of human-induced life, but it will be something unrecognisable, something decidedly *in*human.'

'You're out there.'

'Well it was a sci-fi novel, it had to be *out there*. Anyway, I felt an overwhelming sense of loss while I was writing it. I realised that no-one is listening. Orwell presented Big Brother as powerfully as it is possible for anyone to write, and even though the book is widely read, well respected and well understood, we ignore the message completely. The only ones who seem capable of acting on the content are bad guys. Look at the Iraq war. Freedom Fries for Victory Coffee. The neutering of language—terms like *collateral damage* and *illegal combatants*. The torture. The essential lie that precipitated the whole thing in the first place. David Hicks being imprisoned for merely thinking about doing something that wasn't even a crime at the time.'

Budgie was getting me depressed now. 'Do you think every generation loses part of its soul to progress? To environmental degradation and the over-regulation that comes with overpopulation?'

'I suppose that the young, who have no memory of the things lost, find it exciting. I watch on in despair. I think I know how tribal elders felt watching the bison vanish from the plains, and rainforests disappear from the Amazon. Sometimes I feel I am witnessing the death of fly fishing. At least the part of it that sustains me—communing with wild fish in wild environments in my own good time. Bureaucrats seem hell-bent on turning it into some sort of contrived circus event.'

'Hey Budgie, you just told me that the ether of the universe preserves everything. That's got to be a comfort, the idea that nothing is lost forever.'

He grinned.

'What did you do with the manuscript?'

'Wouldn't have a clue. It's laying around in my house somewhere, I suppose.' He noticed my scepticism. 'The fact that it wasn't published doesn't bother me in the least. I'm not one of these blokes who takes his writing so seriously that he commits suicide in the hope his work will be discovered in a supernova of posthumous glory. For me the joy is in the doing. Once it's finished I've no more need for people to read it than I need them to read the cryptic crosswords I've solved. The idea that you can gain some sort of immortality through your work is a myth. Take Shakespeare—no-one really knows who he is, do they?'

I supposed that he could be Christopher Marlowe.

'No, no: I'm not talking about that. Who is either of them? They're just names, just symbols. Nobody knows them, not in any meaningful way, not like I know you or you know me.' He paused for a bit, then pulled down his own visor and said 'Here's a bookend to that cartoon above your head'. I found myself looking at another Larson artwork. It depicted the course of evolution, beginning with a fish emerging from the primordial ocean, following its progress through various amphibious and simian stages, and finally arriving at the epitome, Man. Represented as an angler proudly displaying a dead fish.

Roof frame

THE NEXT working bee wasn't until August. Lester was standing on the ceiling joists when we arrived, hoisting up the ridge boards, wearing naught but adult incontinence pants. 'Kevie scared, Kevie poo himself,' he explained, much to Tom and Jane's delight.

'Are you going to take those nappies off?' asked Frances.

'How much more of me do you want to see? Actually I've got a dose of psoriasis.' The blotches on his skin were quite prominent. 'Vitamin D's what I need: sunlight. And sun at this time of the year is precious. I intend to soak up all I can while I can.'

Frances rolled her eyes at Beatrice. 'We can start running the electricity cables.'

'You know how to do that?'

'Been with Trout a long time now.'

The rafters were large—six-by-twos—so we didn't need intermediate supports. 'The roof space needs to be as uncluttered as possible,' explained Lester. We had only just finished cutting them when Budgie arrived.

'Hey Budgie, I'll put a cuppie on; you help Trout,' said Lester magnanimously.

Budgie and I started sliding the rafters up onto the ceiling frame. 'Time for the ridge,' I said.

'How do you put that up?' asked Beatrice

'It's much easier than it looks,' said Budgie. 'Mind you, it'd be bloody handy if we had a third arm.'

The roof was pitched by lunch time. Lester was ascending a ladder, when he hit his head on a rafter. 'Shit!'

'What you need is an eye on top of your head, like those tuatara lizards in New Zealand, only more developed,' Budgie suggested.

Lester wasn't in so much pain that he couldn't voice his frustration. 'Budgie, have you got any idea what we'd actually look like if you were in control of human anatomy? Go and get the drill and screw the battens down for us will you?'

'Screw them down? What's wrong with nails? Trouble with building inspectors these days is that they've never built houses. Book learning is all they have. They have no feel for timber, no confidence to use discretion.'

'Well, they would be held responsible if the roof did come off,' said Frances, exasperated.

'Litigation again. My point is that the roof *wouldn't* come off, so there would be no litigation.'

The atmosphere around the campfire that night was more relaxed. Lester has false top teeth—from an unfortunate encounter with an irate miner at the Tullah pub—and by pushing them forward with his tongue he performed a hilarious impersonation of his mother-in-law. Then, taking them completely out, he imitated the old hermit who lived down the road. Beatrice was laughing along with the rest of us. 'I used to think you were being cruel,' she admitted coyly. I saw Calvin secretly squeeze her hand.

Lester quickly changed the subject. 'Frame inspection tomorrow.'

Budgie was ready for a rant. 'People don't just tolerate Big Brother, they encourage it, love it.'

'Don't tell me you're against building inspections too?' said Calvin.

'Should be optional. If formal inspections are valued by the community, a Certificate of Inspection would be valuable at the point of resale. If you didn't have a certificate to show that the house had been inspected, a potential buyer could make up his mind whether or not to buy the property.'

'Hidden defects could be dangerous.'

'I'll bet none of the early shacks around here were ever inspected, and as far as I can see everyone lives in them safely enough.'

'Security is a myth. Life's either a daring adventure or nothing,' said Lester.

'Who's quote is that?'

'Beats me.'

The building inspector arrived late in the afternoon, in a giant 4WD. Lester approached, introduced himself, and shook hands as if everything was perfectly normal. He was completely naked, except for his nail pouch.

'Nice nail pouch,' said the inspector.

He was one of the better bureaucrats—knew his stuff, was friendly and helpful. When he left, Lester announced that the frame had 'passed the test' and was ready for the insulation wrap.

'Bloody insulation requirements,' spat Budgie.

'For God's sake; what's wrong with insulation?'

'I like my house to cool off at night, especially the bedrooms. I like the act of getting up in the morning and lighting the fire, the feel of radiant heat evaporating the chill. I like, always, to be aware of the weather and world outside.'

'I like to keep the outside *outside*,' said Beatrice defiantly.

'What right has a building inspector got to tell me to be energy conscious when he drives around all over the place in a bloody great petrol-guzzling truck of a car...'

'Hey, it's starting to snow,' Frances announced.

'Well, Budgie,' I said, 'get busy wrapping. Lester, Frances and I will screw down the roofing iron. With a bit of luck we can have the place weather proofed by tomorrow night. Unless you'd like the snow and wind inside the house as well as the cold.'

By dusk the snow was beginning to settle, and the wind, coming in squalls, made sitting around the campfire a bleak affair. 'Bloody weather,' said Lester. 'I was hoping we'd get to do some wet-fly fishing; it is the opening weekend of the trout season after all.'

'Don't be silly,' Frances countered. 'You're so obsessed with the shack now, nothing will distract you until it's finished.'

'Hey, we could play fiery footy instead,' suggested Calvin. 'With all this snow there'll be no chance of starting a bushfire.'

'Cool!' said Tom and Jane.

So straight after tea—more meat—Lester took a toilet roll, saturated it with meths, and set it alight. He kicked it along the driveway towards Tom. It whooshed through the air. Tom kicked it to me; I caught it in my hands and passed it on in an instant before it had a chance to burn my skin.

'You are the most irresponsible lot of people I've ever met,' Beatrice lamented.

'You've got to admit, surely, that it's spectacular,' said Calvin. 'And everyone's having fun except you.'

'It's no example to set for Hayley.'

'She's a smart kid. Don't you trust her?'

Beatrice went back to the fire.

By the end of the next day the house had been wrapped and roofed, exactly as I had predicted.

'Trout declared guilty of completing something within his estimated time,' said Calvin amid applause from everyone else.

'There's a first time for everything,' said Lester philosophically.

'Including the fact that we're in danger of running out of beer.' So several of us went to the pub at Great Lake.

'How you goin with the shack Lester? Living in it yet?' asked the barman.

'Will be tonight, not that the Council knows anything about that.' The whole room tittered.

Later, in the car on the way back to Arthurs Lake, Budgie opined 'Funny, isn't it, how you can talk about disregard for Council regs in public without fear of reprisal. It proves my point about the bureaucracy being completely out of step with community expectations'.

Lester ripped into the cardboard wrapping surrounding a slab of cans. 'For God's sake Budgie, have a beer and learn to relax.'

Qualicum

WE WERE vaguely aware of the old couple as soon as we got out of the car at the small camping ground, but we were immediately distracted by a scattergun of potent sounds: spray, the rapid disturbance of wet shingle. A few metres behind our allocated campsite was a small levee. Looking over the embankment, we were surprised to see dozens of giant salmon sprinting through an ankle-deep rapid. It was a moment so powerful that a whole bunch of horrible clichés actually occurred: time stood still, our breath was taken away, our hearts beat audibly.

We had arrived in Vancouver city the day before, after flying from Hobart half a planet away. This morning had also been consumed by travel: through ugly city traffic to the ferry terminal, over the Strait of Georgia to Nanaimo, and then to the Little Qualicum River. Here, a friend had assured me, I'd be able to catch a quick swag of small coastal cutthroats, thereby sating my immediate need to catch some wild Canadian trout, and freeing up my soul so that I could enjoy the next few days doing things that my wife, daughter and son needed to do: sea kayaking, bear watching, halibut fishing.

I didn't expect this—not mid-afternoon on our second day in Canada, at the first water we came across. The creek was tiny, no more than a modest fly-cast wide, and the water was improbably low and clear. Weren't salmon supposed to run after a spate? My first impulse was to stare. My second impulse—fifteen minutes later when the flurry had ended—was an intense (if unaccountably belated) desire to catch one of these leviathans. On a fly.

It was going to be a difficult task with a six-weight trout rod. Most of the animals we were looking at were fifteen to twenty-five pounds, plenty were about forty, and some must have been fifty to sixty. There was no doubt in my mind that they were spring salmon, the doyen of Pacific salmon species, the most majestic and most revered. The ones we call chinooks in Australia and quinnats in New Zealand. The ones Canadians refused to call king salmon because 'only the bloody Americans would feel the need to be so arrogant', and 'only *they* would disdain charm, embrace the mundane'.

By the time Tom and I had fixed up our fly rods with indicators and heavily weighted Glo-bugs—the sort of rigs we use for pre-spawned rainbows in New Zealand's Tongariro River—another group of salmon was running the rapid. The holding pool from which they emanated was scoured into our side of the river. However, this bank was cliff-like and overgrown with scrub. 'You'll have to wade across the rapids and walk down to the long shingly beach on the far side,' said a gravelly voice close beside us.

It was the male half of the couple we'd noticed when we first arrived. My word he was old. I glanced around for his wife. Their campervan was parked within metres of our tent-site. She was hobbling shakily, on a walking frame, struggling to cover the few steps from the car door to the picnic table. I could scarcely believe that she'd been allowed out of the nursing home.

Also, I was too revved up to be interested in civility. 'Thanks,' I muttered and headed off.

Halfway across the creek, a third group of salmon made a dash for it. They shot out of the narrow current at the head of the pool like a single torpedo, but fractured across the rapid so that by the time they reached us, individual fish were metres apart. I kept thinking: force equals mass (very big) times acceleration (very fast). If one of these things hit our shins, there was every chance that bones would be broken—ours, not theirs.

'Imagine that old crone wading across here,' said Tom, and we laughed.

The place to cast a fly was in the head of the pool where the fish were resting up. Tom immediately caught a small cutthroat and gloated melodramatically about being first to catch a Canadian trout. I cuffed him playfully. Soon, though, we were hooking the intended quarry. With a lot of side strain we could shepherd them into the calm water on the edge of the main current, and sometimes they would come enticingly close to the bank, but invariably they would sidle back into deeper water. Slowly, though, over the course of ten minutes or half an hour, we would begin to entertain thoughts of victory. Then a group of fish at the head of the pool would erupt into the rapid, and almost instantly the fish being played would hear the call. Totally oblivious to the fact that it was still hooked, it would burst into life and race off after its brethren. A six-weight rod proved to be an insignificant restraint. All the flyline would peel from the reel, then all the backing, and finally the ten-pound tippet would ping like cotton.

The momentum of the running salmon was phenomenal. Over the course of the afternoon, several fish (not ones we hooked) mistimed bends in the river and ended up floundering around on beds of dry shingle, metres from the water's edge. Some of these we were able to rescue, and it was a humbling experience, like assisting beached dolphins and whales.

One group shot round a bend out of sight and minutes later came hurtling straight back down stream, current-assisted. One individual zoomed smack-bang into the middle of an emergent boulder and promptly expired.

'Do you think they were panicked by a bear or something?' I asked Tom.

'I didn't think there were supposed to be any bears in this area?' he replied hopefully.

We kept helping as many salmon as we could, yet we kept fishing for them too. By nightfall we'd taken several more cutthroats, but only one spring salmon. It was as good a fish as could possibly be hoped for when using trout gear: a chrome specimen of about ten pounds. Yet it was a strangely unfulfilling experience. Perhaps a bigger one would give us a better buzz?

After tea, after everyone else had gone to bed, I wandered back upstream, fishing with a luminous Glo-squid fly. Moonlight enchanted the banks, and a sort of eerie silence began to overwhelm everything but the rush of salmon. Raccoons, weasels and minks could be seen, scampering over smooth shingle seeking out fresh fish carcasses, which despite our earlier efforts at salmon rescue, were by now dotted all over the place. I became intensely aware of my aloneness, of my vulnerability. Could it really have been a bear that scared those salmon earlier in the day? Would I round a corner and confront an angry grizzly? Would I flee into the forest, run headfirst into a tree, and promptly expire? Or simply be ripped to shreds? I realised that I honestly didn't care. I wound in my flyline and kept walking. I was intensely aware that I was alive; that I was living, *really* living.

***

The old man accosted me shortly after sun-up while I was boiling a billy. He was awake because his wife needed tending. She was awake because she was in pain. I was awake because I'd never gone to bed.

'You've tired of it then.'

It was a statement, not a question, but I answered anyway. 'Sort of got the feeling that now they're back in the river they've made it—they've earned the right not to be fished.'

'Everybody gets to that point sooner or later. That's why you've had the fishing to yourself.'

It was clear that the salmon were sacred to him. 'You don't sound too upset that I've been ransacking your temple?'

'I've been where you were. You can't impose an endpoint on anyone. Everyone needs to take the journey for themselves. It's the journey that's important.'

I felt that he'd let me into his church under false pretences. 'I'd still happily catch the salmon if they were offshore,' I cautioned.

'Me too.'

I asked him where he was from.

'I'm living in Victoria these days,' he said, referring, I eventually realised, not to the Australian state but to the capital of BC. 'But I was born here at Qualicum Beach. Phoebe too. We came to this site on our honeymoon, sixty-eight years ago. The salmon were running to spawn, just like now. Our first child was born exactly nine months later. I was an engineer and we've lived abroad most of the time since then; Minsk and Rio, and lately Tokyo where both our son and daughter have put down roots. Never used to think too much about home. Then, when Phoebe's Parkinson's got bad, homesickness hit big time. Our children—they're always your children even when they're approaching three-score and ten—begged us not to go. Mum was too frail, they said. The journey was bound to kill her.

'Ryan! You talkin about me?'

The old man looked over at his wife, lying on a banana lounge, and chastised her lovingly. 'You're supposed to be resting.'

'How can I be at rest. Absurd. Specially when I'm shaking like an electric sex-toy.' She laughed out loud at her own joke, and we laughed with her, and then we realised she'd become completely silent. The old man walked to her urgently, then came back. 'Asleep,' he said.

I looked at his Phoebe, weary and battle scarred, swaddled in white blankets as if cocooned in the sort of fungus that commonly engulfs dying salmon.

The sound of yet another rush of fish came from the river.

Ryan said 'If I were a romantic I'd tell you that Phoebe won't die here, that nothing ever does, that everything that comes here is reborn. The truth is, we came back because we were compelled to. I don't know why'.

'You're happy though?'

He tested some words out loud: *invigorated, content, glad.* 'Relieved,' he finally decided.

He seemed relieved just to have acknowledged it.

Bear aware

IN BRITISH Columbia you are more likely to be abducted by aliens than attacked by a bear. I'm serious. Each year hundreds of people report being forced onto interstellar craft, always ones that look like saucers or cigars, in order to have their bodies and minds examined by bug-eyed anthropods. Most years, no British Columbians report being menaced by bears.

Strangely enough, considering the aforementioned statistics, Canadian governments haven't funded so much as a single fridge magnet suggesting that people be alert, not alarmed, about the prospect of unsolicited anal probes. But they have spent countless millions of dollars on Bear Aware programs.

The publicity about bears has had a remarkable effect on people's perception of risk. I was surprised, then bemused, and finally saddened, to see people walking in remote areas carrying what looked to be military grenades strapped to their belts, conveniently close at hand, inconveniently close to their genitals. They turned out to be super-sized canisters of capsicum spray. Their owners walked briskly with military menace, blowing metal whistles like drill-sergeants, shouting abrupt warnings to imagined enemies. 'Yo Bear! ... Yo Bear! ...YO Bear! ... Yo BEAR.'

Even in suburbia, Whistler for instance, people out for a stroll looked remarkably like extras on the set of a Rambo movie, ready to defend British Columbia from bears *wherever they may be*.

Despite mass-media coverage, and the mass hysteria which accompanies such coverage, the curious fact is that confrontations with bears happen so rarely that even people who have no qualms telling you about their ordeals in outer space baulk at the prospect of feigning a bear attack. They are worried that you might take them for being nutters.

I have to admit that I'm not immune to irrational fear. I was scared during the whole of the plane flight from Hobart to Vancouver. Not because of possible terrorist attacks. Simply because, to paraphrase Douglas Adams, jumbos seem to me to stay in the air in exactly the same way that bricks don't.

I was scared, too, when I saw the size of our hire-car. The only vehicle big enough to carry five passengers with hiking gear was an SUV that was also big enough to carry a platoon of marines. Apparently no-one in Canada had heard of a station wagon.

The most scary thing of all was the prospect of driving a military assault vehicle across a big strange city at night on the wrong side of the road after thirty-six hours of uninterrupted awakedness. I delegated responsibility to Frances.

I have to say, though, that my fear of cars, while admittedly wimpish, is certainly not irrational. Each year almost a thousand British Columbians die in cars on their way to rivers, mountains and towns, and many more than that get maimed trying. No-one seems to give much of a damn. There are bears to worry about.

The bush is my natural home, a place where I am never scared. Not in Tassie, not in New Zealand, not in the Americas. Is that because I am ineffably naïve? Karen, my botanist friend, who had come to BC with me, Frances and our kids, suggested, sarcastically I think, that it is because of my long-held boast that I'm not afraid of death.

Well, being unafraid of death doesn't mean I'm not scared of dying. As I've just admitted, I'm appalled at the prospect of being incinerated in a plane as it plummets out of the sky, terrified at the likelihood of being pulped and sliced by metal and glass on a noisy highway, and devastated by the very concept of being connected to a life-support system in the sterile confines of a hospital.

But some prospects of death do not worry me at all, and most of these would occur in the bush. Don't think that I don't know what I'm talking about. I've almost died while rafting Tasmania's wild rivers, while wading across flooded streams in New Zealand, while traversing alpine moors in severe blizzards. And even on the occasions that I have really believed death to be imminent— especially on those occasions—I've experienced an ethereal peace. Death by bears? A bit violent for my liking, but hey, worse things happen.

When hiking in British Columbia's backcountry, Frances, Karen and I made a point of selecting relatively unpopular trails where we, and the local wildlife, were unlikely to be bothered by shrill-voiced people armed with capsicum spray. And we'd walk as quietly and smoothly as possible. In this way, as we ascended forests of Engelmann spruce, we'd mingle with small herds of mule deer. On the tree-line, we'd round boulders and come face to face with Rocky Mountain goats. Then, while sitting perfectly still on patches of rock scree, we'd find ourselves surrounded by busy pikas and inquisitive marmots.

Along river banks and lakeshores, we'd often sneak around a corner and find a steaming bear-pat made by an animal that we'd surprised, evidently terribly so, seconds before our arrival. Sometimes the bear prints would be so fresh that they were still filling up with ground water. But, despite our best attempts, we never actually saw bears unless we went looking for them in well known feeding stations— below a waterfall, say, on a major salmon river.

Nonetheless, because we were always very quiet, because we remained acutely aware of everything around us, we did get to see more than our fair share of moose, most of which were wading in marshes and grazing on aquatic succulents.

Moose attacks happen to be much, much more common than bear attacks. Admittedly they are still less likely to be reported than instances of alien abduction, but at least the reports that do come to hand are verifiable. Usually there are reliable witnesses, intriguingly grotesque injuries, or actual bodies. Yet the authorities only tell you to beware of moose in a very generalist sort of way, and even then it's usually an afterthought, perhaps at the end of a Bear Aware pamphlet. 'Oh and remember that all big game is potentially dangerous, so it pays not to get too close to, er, elk and other, er, things.'

Although we saw moose in marshes and sloughs, they prefer to eat saplings and young branches. In fact the word *moose* is an Anglicisation of *moz* which is Algonquin (local Indian) for 'twig eater'. It stands to reason that moose have to eat twigs during ice-over, but even in summer woody materials—principally shoots, buds and bark from deciduous trees like willows, poplars and aspens—comprise more than half of everything they consume.

British Columbia's forestry practices are a global disgrace—massive clear-felling operations on a scale usually witnessed only in third-world economies that have been brutalised by corrupt and amoral governments. Strangely enough though, the moose, perhaps uniquely amongst Canada's big mammals, has benefited from this mismanagement. As degraded as the forests may be, the sheer scale of the regrowth has resulted in a bonanza of moose food. Unfortunately, as areas of clear-fell regenerate and mature, moose are forced to retreat back into remnant stands of old-growth, and numbers are now so abnormally high that the new arrivals cause major environmental damage. Most environmentalists, even the fundamentalists (not to be confused with animal-rights activists), accept that culls are necessary. So the provincial government issues permits to recreational hunters, enabling them to bag one moose each per year. More people want to kill moose than there are available permits, so a lottery system has been implemented. Most hunters are successful two years out of three.

What subset of people do you think are most likely to be attacked by moose? Preoccupied anglers? Novice campers? Arrogant hikers? Enthusiastic photographers? Curious canoeists? Brash foresters? Optically challenged hunters? Your guess is as good as mine. Unlike information on bears, no analysis of moose attacks is readily on hand for public consumption.

In Revelstoke we met up with Anna, a friend of a friend who was doing research on caribou—the critically endangered woodland variety, as opposed to the more robust tundra strain. Unlike moose, woodland caribou have been devastated by forestry operations. The herds on Mount Revelstoke and in the Glacier National Park, as well as those on other mountains, have been reduced to just several hundred individuals apiece, and they are now geographically and genetically isolated from one another. Anna managed to get radio collars on about fifty animals and tracked their movements for a year. Almost half didn't make it through the winter. Guess what killed them? Avalanches.

'Not what you expected then?' I said.

'It would have been convenient if the caribou had died in clear-fell areas whilst trying to migrate from one mountain to another,' Anna replied. 'But one thing I've learned as an ecologist: if your research delivers the results you expect, you've most likely overlooked something. If it delivers the results you want, you've rigged things.' She looked so sad. 'At that rate of death, the herds will be extinct in just a few years. Why should they be so susceptible to avalanches? It doesn't seem to make sense. It could be that the caribou are forced up to the snowline because there is no food left lower down. It could be that global warming has made the snow less stable or less predictable. I just don't know.'

She did know an awful lot, nonetheless, including the rationale behind the Bear Aware programs.

'Bears love the sorts of food that people like so they are attracted to campsites, and once they learn the connection between people and tasty food they simply won't go away. These bears start to harass people for treats. Soon they are ripping into tents, smashing car windows. Everyone complains, and some people actually do get mauled. In the past, park managers tried relocating problem animals, but bears are so territorial that most refugees ended up dying. In the not-so-distant past, so many bears were translocated that some local populations actually became extinct. Basically, an aware bear—that is, one aware of human behaviour—is a dead bear. So I guess you could say the Bear Aware program its more about protecting bears from people.'

'And moose?'

'They prefer twigs to picnic hampers, and they're shy, not

inquisitive. They tend to avoid campsites and never become a problem.'

'Why are so many people killed by moose then?'

'Well they are quite happy to defend themselves if they feel threatened. And each year at least ten thousand hunting permits are issued, so I suppose they have every right to feel threatened.'

Sturgeon

IT WAS inevitable, I guess, that my son Tom would rebel against me. Don't get me wrong. At fifteen, he still loves fishing. It's just that he'd prefer to target things other than trout, things exotic and mysterious, things his dad knows nothing about. So when we decided to go to Canada, I knew he'd be on the lookout for some very un-Australian angling opportunities.

'How do giant spring salmon sound?' I suggested enthusiastically.

'Okay, I suppose. But come on Dad, admit it, they're really just another sort of trout.'

Then a friend of ours, Danny Rimmer, who lives in Tasmania but was raised in British Columbia, presented me with a bundle of BC fishing magazines, and it was here that Tom discovered the existence of the white sturgeon, the largest freshwater fish in North America.

Tom researched frantically, and then presented me with the case for hiring a fishing guide:

'You really need to fish from a seaworthy boat to have any real chance of success. The best stretch of river is huge and treacherous—the water eddies and wells, boils and rolls, sucks and churns. Marc Laynes of Cascade Fishing Adventures is one of the founding sturgeon guides. Not only that, he operates out of Chilliwack, which is little more than an hour's drive east of Vancouver via Highway 1, bang smack in the middle of the prime stretch of sturgeon water. He and his wife have their own modern accommodation on site: Chilliwack Mountain Bed and Breakfast. Can we do it? Please?' Then, in desperation 'They also specialise in salmon. After I've caught a sturgeon, we could spend the rest of the day fly fishing up a tributary like the Vedder'.

As chance would have it, Danny and his eight-year-old daughter Katie were in BC the same time as us, so we invited them along. We arrived at the B & B the evening before the big day, and within minutes of meeting Marc and his wife, Maggie, they felt like old friends.

Finally, after a restless night dreaming about what was to come, it was morning. By 9.00 am we were on the Fraser, and Marc was using a landing net to scoop a rancid salmon carcass from the water surface. 'Bait,' he explained. He handled it with rubber garden gloves, pliers and scissors while we huddled in the bow holding our noses, trying not to retch, begging him to hurry up.

Five species of salmon utilise the Fraser, seven if you include rainbow trout and cutthroats. Some literature I've read suggests that sturgeon prefer to eat lampreys, but clearly they attain their massive bulk by taking advantage of the same resource that sustains everything else in these parts.

Live salmon were constantly jumping clear of the water. We were watching one skip skip skip across the water surface when, in a jolt of panic, it rocketed skywards—two metres into the air. We realised suddenly, but not as suddenly as the fish itself, that it had landed on top of a hungry harbour seal.

Dead salmon drifted down currents and washed up on riverbanks where they were scavenged by bald eagles and bears. Others settled on the riverbed where, we were informed, they were hoovered up by sturgeon.

Marc anchored in an appropriate current, dropped three lines overboard, and straight away the rods began to dibble dibble dibble. 'Nothing to get excited about yet—they're just small pike minnows.' Then, after an anxious forty minutes, there was a long slow bend in one of the rods and Tom set the hook.

The fish did nothing for a few seconds—it was just a dead weight that might easily have been taken for a snag—and then it raced away, screaming off line. Five minutes later the sturgeon rose vertically from the water. Up up up it came until it was a metre clear of the surface. Then it fell sideways, made a short run and leapt again. Finally it dove deep and we didn't see it again for five minutes until it was right alongside the boat. Here, it seemed to go from full strength to exhaustion in an instant.

'A small one,' said Marc, wondering if we would be disappointed.

As if! It was an impressive four feet long. But more than that, it was wonderfully prehistoric. 'It's like someone's given me the chance to hug a stegosaurus,' said Tom, unable to hide his delight.

We studied the primitive fish for a full minute: the four barbels, the bony scutes along the spine and lateral line, the strange sharklike skin, the feel of its cartilaginous body. It was very much the equal of being up close to a wild moose or bear. We were still staring in awe as Marc and Tom gently set it free.

After this first fish, it seemed to me that there was no downtime at all between strikes, but perhaps that was just because there was such an air of expectation. Anyway, we were always being entertained by salmon and seals. Not only that, but every now and then a sturgeon would rise spectacularly of its own accord. How could we possibly have gotten bored?

When Danny finally brought a specimen of two-hundred pounds alongside the boat, Marc asked us if we'd like him to manoeuvre the boat into shallow water so we could hop in and get a classic photo of the sort commonly seen in local fishing magazines—standing in a row, waist deep, struggling to support the fish's bulk. But everyone wanted to release the sturgeon as soon as possible, mainly so that we could keep on angling.

Marc then asked if we would like to spend the rest of the day fly fishing for salmon in the Vedder River. Tom and Katie looked at me venomously, before yelling in unison 'More sturgeon!'

Then, pandemonium!

Tom was solidly hooked into a monster. How big? 'Not quite as big as yours, Danny, but *big!*' Tom grunted. 'Strap the bucket around my waist. Quick!'

After ten minutes the fish leapt out of the water. It was huge! A harbour seal, as impressed as we were, moved in beside us, and stayed there. The fish took a back-breaking forty-five minutes to bring alongside the boat. But even when it was brought to within a metre of the murky surface, it remained invisible. 'I just want to see it,' Tom exclaimed. Much later, the fish played itself out; and Tom—shaking, exhilarated, almost as exhausted as the fish—was able to examine his prize: a genuine trophy.

Marc got me to hold the dumb end of a tape measure on the fork of the sturgeon's tail while he traced the rest of the tape along the lateral line to the tip of the nose. 'Ninety-three inches!' he lamented.

'Just three inches short of joining the eight-foot club.'

But such trivial statistics mattered not one jot.

'If you were still allowed to kill these primitive monsters, would you keep the odd one for flesh or caviar?' Tom asked Marc as they released the catch.

'What do you think?' Marc replied.

Doukhobor

THE ROCKIES lie more than a thousand narrow, convoluted kilometres from Chilliwack, so there was no chance of driving the whole way in a single day. When Frances and Karen recommended that I decide how to break up the trip, I suggested camping a couple of nights in Cathedral Provincial Park, an alpine wilderness. Here we would find iconic American fly fishing, plenty of scope for day-walks, botanic variety and lots of wild animals. Because Jane hates walking up steep mountains, and this would have been a doozey, I even went so far as to arrange for a vehicular ascent into the heart of the park, an option made possible by virtue of the fact that there is a rugged access track to a small private in-holding on the shores of Quiniscoe Lake. This had to be organised a couple of days in advance, something I'm always loath to do because timetables are such an impediment to spontaneity, but I figured that it was a small price to pay.

At Hope, we turned off Highway 1 onto Highway 3 and found ourselves surrounded by country so arid that it felt like desert. We were passing through one stark rocky gorge when Tom thought he saw a mountain goat. We got out of the car and, looking high, scanning the cliff-face, we eventually located a whole family of them. But apart from that joyous incident, I was happy when we crossed the Similkameen River and reacquainted ourselves with forests. The aspens flanking the Ashnola River were bursting with autumn brilliance, and beyond them, extending up the hillsides were ever-thickening stands of Douglas fir and cottonwood.

We arrived at the carpark at the foot of the Cathedral mountains right on time to be picked up. Amid twenty or so parked cars we spotted our transport—a Mercedes Benz Unimog truck, a troop carrier so battered that it may well have seen active service in the South African army. The only sign of life was a chipmunk sitting on the driver seat. Perhaps he was our chauffeur.

While we unloaded our backpacks, a car pulled up on our right-hand side. Two men got out and introduced themselves. Don was a journalist with the *Daily Courier*. His mate, Jim, was quieter and didn't tell us much about himself at all. Then another car parked on our left side and two more men joined our group. Len, stocky and thickset, was in his late sixties. He was extremely excited about the prospect of hiking around the lakes, because he hadn't been up in the high country for almost three months. His son, Eugene, a gentle soul, seemed more blasé about the prospect of hiking. We got the idea that he was only there to look after Dad.

We trooped our belongings over to the Unimog. On closer inspection, the old vehicle looked like it hadn't moved in weeks. Even the chipmunk had given up on it and was now hopefully inspecting our communal pile of gear—nine full backpacks, half a dozen daypacks, several shopping bags full of food and alcohol.

Just when we were wondering if we were going to be picked up at all, an old work-horse of a Land Cruiser came bumbling down the mountain. It had just five seats: two in the front, three in the back. The driver wound down his window. 'Name's Norm,' he said enthusiastically. Noting that our gear had been piled up beside the Unimog, he added 'We won't be using that bloody heap of crap. You'll have a more comfortable ride in this'. Then he twigged to how many we were, and conceded jovially that on second thoughts it might not be such a comfortable ride after all. He hopped out of the four-wheel-drive, quickly shook our hands, and had a closer look at all our gear. His demeanour seemed to suggest that there were more passengers than he expected, but apparently there was no question of leaving anyone behind.

He undid the back door of the Land Cruiser, then reached into the back and lifted up part of the floor, creating one more row of seats. There were eight berths now, but not much boot-space. 'We'll just have to strap stuff on the roof,' he said brightly. No-one dared point out the glaring absence of a roof rack. We just watched as he reached under the driver's seat and extracted a bunch of old ropes; all knotted, too short and too frayed.

'I'll have better tie-downs than that,' offered Len, who quickly proceeded to produce a stunning array of brightly coloured nylon cords from his ancient rucksack. Norm and Len, bonded by their love of old ropes, began stacking our packs onto the roof, crisscrossing their rigging this way and that, moving so fast that you could scarcely believe there were just two of them. They fairly swarmed over the car, like ants on roadkill. All the time, Norm busied himself by shouting instructions to Len, and Len busied himself by ignoring him and talking to us. 'I left home for a rest and look at me, working like a maniac. You know why I had to get away? Because everyone kept asking after my wife. She left me last week. I didn't see it coming. Honestly. Have no idea why she would want to leave a lovable old man like me. Ah well, her loss.'

Eugene tilted his head in our direction, even managed to fit in a sigh of resignation, but his father wasn't about to relinquish command over our attention. 'Just before she left me, my wife was harping on about how I never helped with the shopping. Well I've been doing it myself for the last week, and I have to say I don't know what she was complaining about. It hardly takes any time at all. Mind you, I suppose that could have something to do with the fact that I only buy bread, milk and whiskey…'

Suddenly we were all being ushered into the Land Cruiser. Norm took the driver's position, of course, and Len the front passenger seat, of course. Don was sandwiched between them, on the centre console facing the back. In the next row were Jim, Karen, Jane and two rucksacks. I was in the row behind that, with Tom, Frances and Eugene, all of us nursing day packs. The boot was jammed so full that we soon found ourselves fending off cascades of fruit and cutlery.

The track was steep and rugged. Norm warned us that it climbed fifteen hundred metres over fifteen kilometres and would take about an hour. 'But the place where we stop, the lodge, is just five-minute's walk from the Quiniscoe Lake campsites.'

Don asked Len about his accent. 'East European?'

'Russian,' he conceded. 'My forebears were Doukhobors.'

We soon learned, whether we wanted to or not, that the Doukhobors, or spirit dwellers, were Christian pacifists who traditionally lived in small communes. In the mid-1700s they began questioning the dictatorial nature of the Russian Orthodox Church.

Surely, they reasoned, God resides in everyone and it is up to the individual to work out how to live harmoniously with his fellow man. Who needed churches or, for that matter, governments? For this heresy the Doukhobors were banished to Russia's cold wastelands, but they continued to thrive. In 1898 and 1899 more than seven thousand of them emigrated to Saskatchewan. Then between 1908 and 1913 their leader, Peter Verigin, led them westward to British Columbia where they founded the outpost of Castlegar.

If Len was any example, and I had no doubt that he was, the Doukhobors remained a friendly but fiercely independent people. All of us in the far back seat were too busy enjoying his narration to ask questions, but Karen somehow managed to catch his attention. 'Where's Castlegar? What's it like?'

'You'll pass through it on your way east. It's a sprawling town of some seven thousand people not far north of the Washington border, about halfway between here and the Rockies, on the junction of the Kootenay and Columbia rivers.'

All the time that Len had been telling us about the Doukhobors our driver, Norm, had been talking over the top of him, giving a running commentary about the landscape and wildlife. From time to time I even paid cursory attention to what he was saying. Like when he noted the clinal transition from Douglas fir to lodgepole pine and Engelmann spruce. From here on there was little understorey and Norm told Jane that she should keep an eye out for a cougar. Instead, she spotted the first patch of snow.

Don, the journalist, took this lull in Len's monologue to ask us about bushfires in Australia. He was surprised that we were advised to stay home and help save our properties, not to evacuate. 'Australia is full of bushfire-prone environments,' I pointed out. 'So we have experience on our side. We've actually found that most people die in their vehicles while trying to out-run a fire front. I reckon managers in British Columbia are overly cautious simply because they are unfamiliar with the situation, the same way New Zealanders are overly scared of snakes.'

'I reckon we'll have to learn to live with fires soon enough,' Don responded, before going on to tell us about an article he was working on regarding the sorry plight of the forests.

The massive dieback of British Columbia's lodgepole pines was first noticed in 1993, and now gigantic swathes of forest, cumulatively covering an area one-and-a-half times as big as Tasmania, are dead. The damage is caused by mountain pine beetles which, although native, have reached plague proportions. We had already seen the destruction from the air, and found the scale and enormity of the problem to be quite soul destroying. Historically, winter temperatures used to fall below minus thirty-five degrees Celsius for weeks on end, and the majority of the beetles would die off. Now the winters are warmer and most beetles survive. The livelihoods of some twenty-five thousand families are directly affected, and many rural communities are facing extinction. There aren't many climate-change sceptics left in British Columbia, that's for sure.

'Dead forests are prone to wildfire,' Don said. 'I'm researching the effect that fire will have on human health and safety. I'm beginning to wonder if the immediate loss of jobs in the timber and tourism industries will end up being the least of our worries.'

'It's a bit hard to believe in global warming just now,' Jane joked. We had just been hit by a veritable blizzard.

Quiniscoe

BY THE time we got to the Quiniscoe lodge, the snow was twenty centimetres deep, but the latest flurry was drawing to a close. Despite the cramped conditions, our cosy carload had become one big happy family, and I daresay we would have continued to sit and talk except that the view outside demanded immediate attention.

Quiniscoe Lake was exquisite in white, the towering granite peaks providing a grand backdrop, the small forests of Engelmann spruce, sub-alpine fir and balsam fir along the water's edge holding the promise of delightful shelter. But Jane found the ground itself to be even more riveting—the fresh snow was already laced with little footprints. She and Tom quickly set about using an animal-tracks guidebook to identify squirrels, chipmunks, porcupines and mule deer.

We all walked to the little registration hut, and asked the ranger to allocate some tent-sites. 'Just wander around and use whatever ones you want,' she said cheerily. 'We have to allocate sites in summer when hundreds of people visit every week, but in autumn, especially this late, you'll virtually have the place to yourself. In fact, I'm locking-down for the winter at the moment. Next week there won't be any official presence up here. The first of the permanent snow will settle soon after that, then the place will be abandoned by almost everyone for nigh on seven months.'

We were allowed campfires, she said, but because trees were so scarce, we had to buy our firewood. She had a big store of it for sale in the lean-to shed attached to her office.

There were thirty or so tent-sites in the forest flanking the shore of Quiniscoe Lake, but they were clustered together in groups of three or four so that small groups could share a picnic table and a fire-ring. Somewhat reluctantly, our three parties split up and dissipated into the forest.

Frances, Karen, Tom, Jane and I managed to find a secluded cluster of three tent-pads. Nearby was a battery of wire-mesh lockers that resembled fish-safes on stilts. These caches proved to be essential for protecting food from animals. Although there weren't any bears up here, there were dozens of mischievous squirrels and chipmunks. And whiskey jacks—birds so accustomed to campers that they would happily sit on the palm of your outstretched hand.

Frances, scraping snow off our tent site, called out excitedly 'Trout, we're not the only ones calling this place home'. I looked over in time to see a chipmunk poking its head up from a hole that it had burrowed underneath the timber border of our earthen tent pad.

While Karen and the kids set up their own tents, and I made a fire, we were serenaded by the took took took of woodpeckers, their heads hammering faster than tuning forks. The Canadian backcountry was even better than I had imagined—more spectacular, more exhilarating.

Not everyone was as excited about the environment as we were, however. Nearby there was an unoccupied tent, looking forlorn under the weight of fresh snow. Apparently the owners had surrendered themselves to the creature comforts of the lodge.

It was dark by the time we had set up camp, but after tea we took a torch and looked in the outflow creek. It was full of fingerling-sized trout. I picked some up in my hand. At last I had encountered the fabled westslope cutthroat, the fish that featured in so much of my favourite American fly fishing literature. Trout were not native to these lakes—Norm told us that they had been introduced in the 1930s—but they were now maintained entirely by natural recruitment.

The next day we walked for half an hour to Lake of the Woods, which is surrounded by dense stands of small fir trees. Despite the snow, rising cutthroats scoffed our Carrot flies in spectacular fashion. Tom and I caught twenty or so from fifteen to twenty-two centimetres long. They were all old fish with big heads, but exquisitely coloured. Then we moved on to Pyramid Lake where the Lyall's larch, a deciduous pine, had recently turned yellow. The fishing here was the fastest I've ever witnessed—a fly cast anywhere on the water surface was often taken immediately and hardly ever lasted more than a minute. The fish, all cutthroats, were just as small as those in Lake of the Woods, but what fun!

On the third day, we walked to Ladyslipper Lake. Here, the scenery was dominated by stark granite outcrops and glacial till. But the glaciers themselves had retreated back beyond the ridgeline and, despite the snow, you could sense that things were much warmer than they should be. The lake itself was deeper than the others. Despite the absence of silt and weedbeds, it produced 'trophy' rainbows up to about a kilo, but I found myself more interested in the wildlife, especially the pikas and marmots.

I would have loved to have walked onward to the remote Haystack Lakes where, Len had suggested, there was a largely forgotten population of tiny golden trout. But time was running out, so we decided to return to camp. By the time we had descended back down to Quiniscoe, the snow had largely melted and the rodents were out in full force, scouting for food. We watched closely as a chipmunk picked up a soft fluffy Engelmann spruce cone in its forepaws, and started plucking away at the cone-scales to get at the seeds, leaving the debris piled up in a neat little pyramid. Jane was gushing that it was 'sooo cute' when suddenly we heard Len and Eugene. They were beckoning us over to their old and dodgy tent. I noticed that they had rigged up an extra fly, a blue plastic tarp that sailed above their camp like a giant Steller's jay. It was suspended miraculously by means of myriad ropes tied to myriad branches.

'Eugene decided I needed more sustenance than milk and bread,' said Len, offering us some borscht and meat-filled cabbage rolls.

'I notice he hasn't weaned you off the whiskey,' said Karen.

'It's only for medicinal purposes,' Len insisted.

'How do you explain all these bottles,' I laughed, looking at the pile of empties stacked neatly beside the fire ring.

'I'm a sick man,' he explained jovially.

Dolly Varden

AFTER CATHEDRAL, we needed another break. I would have loved to explore the St Mary's Alpine Provincial Park or the Kokanee Glacier Provincial Park, but the walking would have been a bit tough for the kids. The Top of the World Provincial Park seemed a better bet—there was a gentle trail, just seven kilometres long, leading through a tall conifer forest to a public cabin beside a lake filled with wild cutthroats and bull trout.

I caught my first bull trout at Fish Lake. It was pathetically small, less than a pound, but after catching dozens of cutthroats it came as a welcome surprise. Two Americans witnessed the capture and came over to admire the little fish, the lithe body and lemon spots. The older bloke introduced himself as Chuck and his younger companion as Jefferson. 'His Ma and Pa named him after our third president, the great and noble Thomas Jefferson; wanted him to turn out statesman-like. He's shattered their dreams, he has.'

Jefferson laughed.

We talked for a bit and I followed them back to their camping area, an official if largely empty one, a hundred metres or so south of the public cabin in which I was camped with my family. Their tent was one of only three, though there was room for at least fifteen. Their rucksacks had been hoisted high up a bear pole, a large permanent contraption that looked like a metal maypole. I mused that the process of retrieving lunch was rather reminiscent of the lowering of a flag. Chuck invited me to share a pot of coffee and said contemptuously 'They can call bull trout what they want, they'll always be Dolly Varden trout to me'.

Jefferson disagreed. 'I like the fact that they have been reclassified. It means there's one more trout species I can claim to have caught.'

'It's only an academic difference,' Chuck insisted. 'Nobody can tell the difference between one and the other. And I like the name Dolly Varden, not just because it's the one I grew up with but because it's more romantic.'

No doubt about that. Dolly Varden, a character in Charles Dickens' *Barnaby Rudge*, was a name applied to a type of calico cloth widely used in British Columbia in the late 1800s. Because the colour and patterning of the fish were deemed to be reminiscent of the fabric, it ended up with the same moniker.

'The name *bull trout*,' Chuck scoffed, 'just refers to the fact that they are inclined to have large heads in proportion to their bodies. Pretty unflattering, isn't it, considering what a fantastic sport fish they are? So why change at all, I say?'

According to Jefferson, the fact that the fish formerly known as the Dolly Varden comprises two distinct species was discovered accidentally when some researchers were looking for a DNA signature they could use to differentiate Dolly Varden trout from Arctic char. They ended up identifying not two, but three, distinct lineages. 'It seemed to the researchers that, rather like Atlantic salmon (*Salmo salar*) and brown trout (*Salmo trutta*) in the British Isles, these fish did not interbreed successfully, even when they shared the same spawning beds. Their assumptions were tested in hatcheries and found to be more correct than they had supposed.

'Usually trout species from the same genus, such as brown trout and Atlantic salmon can be made to produce a high percentage of viable offspring, even if such progeny turn out to be mostly sterile. The two varieties of Dolly Varden, while indistinguishable to humans, proved to be as incompatible as brown trout and brook trout (*Salmo trutta* and *Salvelinus fontinalis*), which belong to different genera. Yes, you can produce hybrids simply by squirting milt from the male of one species over the eggs of the other, but the fertility rate is low, there is a high degree of mutation, and those that survive are sterile. No-one could have guessed it. No-one did.'

So, in the aftermath of this research, the name Dolly Varden was retained for the variety that was predominantly coastal (*Salvelinus malma*), while the inland type (*Salvelinus confluentus*) got stuck with a nickname that had long been used by some locals but not much loved by anyone else.

Morphology, the physical appearance of trout, turns out to be a frustratingly poor way of identifying one species from another. Most trout-fishing fanatics would be aware of the marble trout (formerly *Salmo marmoratus*) which is native to the rivers that flow into the Adriatic Sea between Italy and the Balkans. It is a unique animal, rather like a brown trout in overall shape and proportion, but smothered in lemon spots and squiggles, like char. It is much rarer than it once was, its last stronghold being the wild rivers of the Slovenian wilderness, notably those in the Soča watershed. The thing that brought it to the brink of extinction was the introduction of brown trout. It wasn't so much a matter of competition, as rampant inbreeding—the hybrids have proven to be fully fertile. Given that brown trout do not occur naturally in Adriatic watersheds, should the two species be reclassified as one? Well, they have been—DNA mapping suggests that for all intents and purposes the two fish are genetically identical.

Jefferson didn't like what I told him about marble trout. He lamented that many of the American trouts were also being lumped together. He told me that the golden trout, the exquisitely beautiful *Oncorhynchus aguabonita*, the state emblem of California, is now considered to be nothing more than a sub-species of rainbow trout. 'I don't know why I ever bothered hiking out to such remote places in search of the goddam thing. Certainly wouldn't have done if I knew I was just chasing common old rainbow trout.'

It turned out that Jefferson's quest for golden trout had taken him into the furthest reaches of some of the most spectacular wilderness areas in America—the Haystack Lakes in the Cathedral Mountain Provincial Park, Michele Lake on the fringes of the Banff National Park in Alberta, the alpine fringes of the Waterton Lakes National Park, the headwaters of the Kern River in California's Sierra Nevada wilderness. How could he possibly regret having done all that? 'Surely,' I protested, 'whatever classification the golden trout ends up with it remains as different from a rainbow as a marble trout is from a brown?'

Chuck agreed. 'Taxonomy is such an artificial exercise, it means nothing in the end. They clump things together this year, split em apart the next, arguing the toss with each other the whole while. Been doing it for centuries, will still be doing it for centuries to come.'

'But it's not arbitrary, not at a species level,' Jefferson pointed out. 'If fish that look different from one another can interbreed successfully over multiple generations in the wild they are, by definition, exactly the same species and there's naught you can say that will change that simple fact. And the thing about DNA mapping is that we can predict which fish can and can't interbreed without actually having to make them do jiggy jiggy.'

He was right. In fact, DNA mapping has become so refined that we can now trace genetic lineages with absolute certainty.

'Did you know,' Jefferson added by way of example, 'that we've proved without doubt that President Thomas Jefferson had sex with one of his slaves?'

'You're pulling my leg,' Chuck protested.

'No. He must have believed that no-one could ever know what he had done. He certainly fooled my parents. But more than two centuries later, we found his genetic imprint in his slave's great, great grandchildren.'

'And these days,' I saw fit to point out, 'we can use DNA mapping to see what creatures were mating with what other creatures not just centuries ago but millions of years ago.'

'So you see Chuck, there is no ambiguity any more,' Jefferson insisted.

But actually he might be wrong on that point. The Kerguélen Islands are a French outpost, near Australia's Heard Island, in the Southern Ocean halfway between Australia and Africa. Whereas Heard is sub-Antarctic, the Kerguélen group is just far enough north to be temperate, and it provides ideal habitat for introduced salmonids. Both brown trout and Atlantic salmon thrive in the local streams, and it has been discovered that they readily interbreed. They don't seem to do this anywhere else in the world, so can they be considered to be the one species? I'm pretty certain that all the hybrids will prove to be sterile, but what if I'm wrong? If taxonomists did end up grouping them together would it matter? The next time I caught a tiny half-pound brown trout from a Tasmanian rivulet, would I feel like I'd landed a hundred-pound sea-run Atlantic salmon from the fjords of Norway?

As an angler I have a deep desire to explore the unknown, to broaden my skills. Tracking down different species is certainly an attractive novelty, but I am well aware that trout behaviour is influenced much more by environmental factors than quirks of ancestry. Consider the different experiences offered by brown trout hammering whitebait in estuaries, brown trout midging in windlanes on a highland lake, and brown trout tailing on the flooded verges of a lowland meadow.

Landscapes have shaped people as well as trout, and we too have become noticeably different from one another, both in looks and culture. The fact that we remain the one species means that there is a bigger bond between us than might otherwise be the case, but surely it is our dissimilarity that remains truly valuable? After all, our differences, more than our commonality, lie at the heart of why we are inspired to travel and interact with the rest of the world. Perhaps we should learn to appreciate them much more than we do.

Northern nights

DESPITE ALL the travel I've done over the years, my trip to British Columbia was my first to the Northern Hemisphere. I was surprised at how quickly I adjusted to little differences like driving on the wrong side of the road, and even more surprised at how I struggled with the big differences, the cosmic ones.

At home I never wear a watch, never need to. I'm always subconsciously aware of the position of the sun in the sky, even if conditions are cloudy. Nor do I often need to use a compass, not unless the sky is obscured by a forest canopy. Until I encountered the northern sun, I never realised how innate this sense of time and direction had become, how lost and vulnerable it was possible to feel when your intuition abandons you. And, boy, did mine abandon me. The fact that the sun followed a southern path across the sky was totally bewildering, leaving me with a feeling that east was west, and north was south.

By the second or third week, I could calculate time and direction by looking closely at the sky, but I never got to the stage where I could *sense* the where and when of things. I was very much a stranger in a strange land, and I felt it.

The night sky was even worse. At home I often walk cross-country at night, and even though I only have a schoolboy's vocabulary of the major features—Southern Cross, Pleiades, Orion, Scorpio,

Magellanic Clouds, Mercury, Venus, Mars, Jupiter—through a process of subconscious osmosis, every speck has become desperately familiar. I found the northern sky completely incomprehensible. I was unable to divine the time of night, time of year; unable to get my bearings.

One evening at Fish Lake in the Top of the World Provincial Park, after everyone else had gone to bed, the thick clouds that had blanketed us all day inexplicably parted like curtains in a theatre, revealing the entirety of the heavens. There were fewer stars than I was used to at home, but in the rarefied mountain air they were crisp and close. I lay on my back across the little jetty in front of the cabin, and found myself trying to make some sort of deep peace with the universe. I hadn't done this for a long time, not since I was a teenager.

Even though the stars were as clear as I've ever seen them, they still twinkled, and although I know this is an optical illusion, it felt as if I was watching them struggle against their own gravity. Which is something they actually do. The energy they use to maintain this fight is released by way of fusion, the melding of simple elements into bigger ones. The endpoint is iron; to build atoms bigger than this you need to add energy to them. When the energy in a massive star is almost consumed, and gravity can no longer be held at bay, there is a sudden contraction followed by a cataclysmic explosion. Clouds of dust are hurled into space, full of more complex elements than existed in the original stars that formed just after the big bang. They eventually coalesce and form second-generation stars such as the Sun, planets such as the Earth, animals such as caddis-flies, trout and humans.

I scanned the horizon for Mars, the red planet, the one that is quite literally rusting away. I couldn't locate it, but while I was looking I did see several falling stars which, of course, are not stars at all, just space debris, hurtling red-hot through the atmosphere. When I was eight or nine I found a fragment of a meteorite that I had seen explode in a paddock the night before. Museum staff told me it was composed of iron, and that prehistoric people struck flint against meteorite fragments to produce the first manmade fires. At Fish Lake it suddenly seemed delightfully poetic that fire was gifted to humans from the stars, that early people used starlight for cooking, warmth, safety and comfort. I marvelled that the stars are so important and yet so unreachable, so uncontrollable. No wonder they lie at the hub of so many religious beliefs. What exactly, I wondered, did the Druids make of the night sky? The ancient Chinese astronomers? Copernicus, Galileo and Kepler? Buddhist monks? The Pope? Indigenous Americans?

I usually pretend to my more learned friends that the main reason I do not dismiss outright any of the world's gods is that I simply cannot think of a decisive experiment that might support any argument for or against them. But, at the Top of the World, I realised that the truth is more pagan and illogical than that. Looking at the heavens the way I was, I could feel the presence of my history, my ancestors, my creators. Perhaps it was because I knew I was looking into the distant past—the light from most of the stars above me was hundreds or thousands of years old.

With radio astronomy, it is possible to see much further back in time. Astronomers have actually witnessed the cusp of the big bang, the beginning of time some 13.7 billion years ago. I couldn't help but wonder how the ancients knew that the universe records everything that ever happens, that all events are retrievable if you learn how to read the stars. How did they know about the big bang, that in the beginning there was light?

I thought about the other ways we have of looking into the past, relived my conversation with Chuck and Jefferson about genetic imprints. My thoughts turned to the concept of judgement day. Despite the enormity of the universe above me, I still couldn't see any reason to believe that my morality would be best judged by anyone other than myself, but I did find it disconcerting to know that the cosmos was busy recording every single thing I did, and that someday humanity, or its usurper, might be able to retrieve and examine my every deed. Why not? After all, we are constantly being reborn as higher, more complex beings.

Now that I thought of it, the parallels between evolution and reincarnation were also quite stunning. What other concepts did ancients understand, if only obliquely? How about the idea of the soul, the belief that there is a separate entity secreted deep within our very being. Could they possibly have been aware that the mitochondria in our cells were originally free-living organisms that ventured inside larger single-celled organisms? That they became trapped there, and replicated alongside their hosts, even as the single-celled organisms evolved into multi-cellular ones?

Of course, I was being whimsical. But I also know that many things will never be understood by humans, just as some things will remain beyond the comprehension of Fish Lake's cutthroat trout and caddis-flies. As we delve deeper into the nucleus of the atom— beyond nucleons, beyond quarks, beyond string theory—we uncover layer upon layer of exponential complexity. I think all physicists end up battling a sense of futility, a realisation that in the end the universe is, after all, utterly incomprehensible.

Then again, as the American astronomer Carl Sagan is famous for saying, we are quite literally 'star stuff'. Maybe embedded in each of us are layer upon layer of universal truths. Maybe we should place more trust in intuition. After all, I rationalised, that's how I tell time and direction in the southern hemisphere. By and large, it's how I fish.

Afterglow

THE TOP of the World exceeded our hopes. On our days there, we played so hard that everyone slept in until mid-morning. Everyone except me. I was always up at daybreak. I'd fish myself into a state of nirvana, and still get back to the cabin in time to cook everyone breakfast. After that, I was happy to climb mountains, look for marmots and pikas, stalk moose. In the evenings I'd coach the kids onto fish of their own. And after dark, after everyone had gone to bed, I'd stay up late and often just sit on the lakeshore, looking at the silhouettes of the mountains and listening to the sounds of the forest.

In the Tasmanian wilderness I would have scraped the remains of our curry into the bushes, where it would have been quickly devoured by birds and ants. But in British Columbia, it was important not to leave food scraps or even unclean cutlery anywhere near our camp lest they attract bears, so I did the washing-up in the lake off the end of the jetty, same as everyone else. The thought struck me that, although Fish Lake was a reasonably popular hiking destination, the silty lake bed around the jetty had been perfectly clean when we arrived. What happened to everyone's food scraps? Were there eels in the lake? I stood up. There was sufficient night-glow to see where I was walking, even to make-out my fly rod leaning against the north wall of the log cabin, but not enough to see into the water. I turned on my torch and aimed it over the end of the pier where we had washed our dinner plates. A dozen or more cutthroats were scavenging about, and there was hardly anything left, not even rice. The trout must do quite well on this diet because the fish I was looking at were easily the biggest I'd seen. Whereas most of the ones we'd polaroided in the daytime had been half-pounders, many of those swimming below were well over one pound. One old fellow with an outsized head was double that size.

I switched off the torch and walked over to get my fly rod. The small dry fly I'd been using to catch risers at dusk wasn't going to be any use. I needed something that would sink two metres. A weighted nymph, perhaps.

I opened my wet-fly box and saw a galaxy of dull lights, a regiment of Glo-flies. It seemed prophetic somehow, given my recent musings about the night sky, so even though none was as heavy as I would have preferred, I tied one on and charged it up with my torch until it was as bright as a supernova.

There was no need to cast the fly. I just made sure that the leader was pulled past the end of the tip-guide and lowered the fly into the water, much as I would have done if I was a child bait fishing for native tiddlies with a bush pole. The fly fluttered slowly to the bottom, a single point of brightness in the black water, twinkling like a falling star. Suddenly the little light lurched sideways, then up towards the surface, then sideways again. I gave the line a tug, and a cutthroat fingerling flew up out of the water and landed on the deck at my feet. Giggling to myself as I let it go, I dared shine the torch back on the hotspot, and was relieved to see that the big fish were still there.

So I recharged the fly and had another go. Down, down it fluttered. Then all of a sudden it went out, instantly like a shooting star. I lifted the rod tip, and this time set the hook into something decent. I kept fishing in the same manner for an hour or more, watching the fly sink, striking the instant it winked out, and caught a fish on every single attempt, until finally I landed the big fellow and was happy to call it quits.

Strange, I thought, that the cutthroats were so eager to take something that resembled nothing in nature. No foodstuff, anyway.

Could they have taken it for a star? Was it possible that fish might be as curious about the night sky as humans are? Did they, like us, harbour a primordial desire to embrace the place from whence they came?

Cutthroat management

MY INTEREST in writing was inspired by the debt of gratitude I felt to the authors who had fostered and sustained my own awareness of fly fishing. In the 1970s, when I was in my teens, there weren't many good, modern, local authors. Once I'd read David Scholes and John Sautelle, I was forced to explore works written overseas. Contemporary English stuff felt very contrived and twee, but I found natural sympathy with many American authors, including Joe Brooks. His *Trout Fishing* (1972) introduced me to wild cutthroat trout, huge bull trout and the overpoweringly exotic Rocky Mountains, images which have captivated my imagination for decades. So my trip to the Elk River in the East Kootenay region of British Columbia was not so much a holiday as a pilgrimage.

In New Zealand, the Elk would be described as a medium-sized river. It lies upstream of a dam which has withheld the advance of exotic species like rainbow trout, and is renowned for its 'pure' and wild population of westslope cutthroat trout (*Oncorhynchus clarki lewisi*).

The Elk is one of several East Kootenay rivers noted for its drift-boat opportunities, and in order to get access to a boat it was necessary to use a guide. By chance, the guide we picked, Russ Trand, turned out to be a friend of a friend. (The world is truly a small place.)

In 2006, for the first time ever, some inland waters in BC, including those in the East Kootenays, became subject to Classified Water regulations. If you are a BC resident, this is almost irrelevant—you simply buy an annual Classified Waters Licence and fish where and when you like. Visitors, including Canadians who live a few kilometres away in Alberta and rightfully consider the East Kootenays to be their own backyard, are now forced to pay a hefty tax which is levied per person, per day, per river. Personally I found the law to be a major inconvenience, mainly because I hardly ever know where I might want to stop when travelling from one destination to another. Curiously enough, some people have suggested that the new regulations have resulted in *increased* angling pressure because people who used to be happy with a spot of casual fishing while the family ate lunch now feel compelled to get their money's worth. They now set aside special days and fish manically for hours on end. As I was about to do.

Since rising fish are the name of game, and the insects don't begin hatching until the sun hits the water, Russ suggested a late start. Accordingly it was almost 10 am when we set adrift near Hosmer, some fifteen kilometres above Fernie.

Russ uses a McKenzie-style drift boat. These narrow-beamed fibreglass dories have several advantages over the rafts commonly used in Australia and New Zealand. They provide a more stable platform from which to fish, are drier underfoot and have better storage room (which means less stuff on the floor for your flyline to get tangled in). Additionally, the ingenious leg-bracing system, which enables standing anglers to carry on casting even while shooting rapids, is much more secure than anything I've seen on rafts. Dories are faster across current, and easier to manoeuvre when ferry-gliding; and while not quite as durable as high-quality inflatables, they are virtually impossible to puncture. If all that isn't enough, they also feature an anchor at the stern which is conveniently operated by the guide from the rowing position at the centre of the boat.

Although the fish were yet to be seen on the surface, Russ insisted that Frances and I begin prospecting with a tiny dry. 'Why not a nymph?' I asked.

'Dries are fun—clients get to see the take.'

Russ made sure that we concentrated on shallow water near the edges of the main currents, not in fast water at the heads of pools. 'Cutthroats behave exactly like browns, not at all like rainbows.' And within minutes, joy of joys, we'd boated a couple of magnificent three-pounders. Can you imagine the exhilaration?

This early success should not have surprised me as much as it did. A short way downstream we got out of the boat to spot from a high bank, and I counted forty-five big trout along eighty metres of bank.

How many more were hiding offshore on the mottled bottom under cover of swirling currents? Well, the population has been reckoned at three thousand catchables per kilometre.

We were soon catching fish hand over fist, ranging from one to four pounds, all chunky animals with broad shoulders.

Russ had many fallback options to compensate for poor casting and mending. Chief amongst these was quickly dropping anchor. Don't worry about that missed chance—cast again. And again and again if necessary. And eventually the fish you put down would rise to the fly. I'll admit that for a couple of 'hard' trout, I resorted to nymphing, often with immediate success. Russ voiced mild disapproval at this, and at first I was puzzled. Why was the match-the-hatch ethos so strong, not to mention refined, on a water where it was unnecessary?

Yet I soon found myself adopting Russ's methods. You see, with such easy fishing you soon start looking for challenges. It's one thing to use an indicator nymph to dredge up an unseen cutthroat, or even get one to rush from the depths to attack an improbably large Chernobyl Ant. But it's quite another to tempt a seen fish to the surface with a tiny midge pattern: the slow rise through intense current, the contemplative sip, the victory! And when the fish are engulfing giant orange October caddis, you just *want* to use an imitation. By mid-afternoon I was totally won over by the local methods. And by the scenery—the autumn hues of the aspens, elk on the riverbank, beavers scuttling along the riverbed, fresh bear prints in the silt.

By the end of the day we had covered ten kilometres of water. And during the whole drift, I saw just one other angler, a bloke on crutches who was committed to fishing the headwater of a single pool. Too much angling pressure? You've got be joking.

'What are you doing tomorrow?' Russ asked.

'Want to guide me again?' I teased. He knew I couldn't afford it. I'd paid so much in angling fees and licences to city-based bureaucrats that there was simply no money left to spend in the local community.

Anyway, Russ wasn't allowed to guide any more this season. He'd just used up his quota of days, which had been arbitrarily set at ninety percent of what he had achieved in 2005. And here's the rub: effectively there is no limit on the total number of people allowed to fish on the Elk. The quotas which have been set for BC residents greatly exceed historical or likely use, and in any case residents are not required to submit any record of where or when they fish. The law is a reaction against the very notion of guiding. It is even more stupid when you consider that only twenty per cent of all use is guided anyway, and that fishing pressure across the board is increasing incrementally rather than exponentially.

'I'm desperate to try a walk-and-wade fishery,' I answered. 'What do you think of the St Mary River, Michel Creek, the Bull River, the White River?'

'They're all superb. But, tell you what, I'm going to fish the lower Wigwam tomorrow. Why don't you come along? The bureaucrats can't stop us fishing together as mates, and I'm sure you'll return the favour when I visit Tasmania. Since we're not using the boat there'll be room for your son, Tom, too.'

Getting to the Wigwam was going to involve an hour-long walk, and when we arrived at the trailhead early on a Thursday morning I was surprised to find several vehicles already in the carpark. 'This is the result of the recent almost-total ban on guided fishing on the Wigwam,' Russ explained. 'My quota here has been reduced to a ridiculous three rod-days per year, effectively just one or two days of guiding on fifty to seventy kilometres of water. Unguided anglers now assume they can avoid the "crowds" by coming here. The Elk itself, being a bigger river, is the one you'd have least qualms about popularising. Yet the regs have encouraged people away from the Elk onto smaller rivers. It won't matter, though. There's plenty of room for everyone.'

The instant we arrived at the river we spotted a couple of dozen bull trout stationed deep down in heavy current. Despite their size—typically five to ten pounds in the Wigwam, up to twenty-five pounds elsewhere—'bullies' were once considered trash fish. Perhaps this was because of their piscivorous habits. Not only were they reluctant to rise to the dry fly, they ate fish that did. Nowadays, thankfully, fly fishers' tastes are more eclectic. 'Will an indicator nymph rig work?' I asked Russ hopefully.

'Well you can use a nymph, but you're not allowed to use an indicator. Or to use jig heads, or to use putty weights.'

Say what?

'Here, have one of these.' He handed me a ridiculously large streamer, legally weighted with lead. 'Fish it down and across.'

My very first cast was eagerly accepted by an eight- or ten-pound bully. After a long fight, I proceeded to quickly hook another three fish. I cannot convey the excitement. Thirty years after reading Joe Brooks, here I was replicating some of the most thrilling stuff he'd written about.

I felt I could have caught a tonnage of char, but Tom had found us a distraction. Shimmering brilliant red in the tail of the pool were hundreds of spawning kokanee, a small landlocked form of sockeye salmon (*Oncorhynchus nerka*). Large cutthroats and immature bull trout were amongst them, feeding on eggs. These trout would readily accept a dry fly, but only if a kokanee didn't eat it first. Just why the salmon, many already spent and fast approaching death, were so eager to feed is anyone's guess.

We fished on. In deep water and shallow water, fast and still. All day we fished. We caught mainly cutthroats, but also whitefish and rainbows. Even a cuttbow, a naturally occurring hybrid which displayed the cutthroat's head and tail as well as the classic pink stripes of the rainbow. I think such fish are infertile. In any case, their sheer strength puts any pure cutthroat to shame.

By nightfall the four of us had fished precisely four pools, about four hundred metres of river. We never did see the anglers who must surely have fished the same stretch immediately before our arrival, and at no stage did I feel that fishing could have been better had the water been rested for a day or two. In fact, after working our way to the head of a pool we frequently found ourselves going straight back to the tail, either to get another crack at a fish we'd put down, or simply to try a different fly or target a different species.

The whole regulation thing intrigued me, particularly in light of the almost institutionalised distrust of fishing guides in New Zealand. Here are some facts:

Up until the late 1980s, catch-and-kill was the usual ethos amongst Elk River anglers. Since cutthroats are so easy to fool, most of the bigger fish were being quickly cropped off. Relatively few fish survived long enough to reach twelve inches long, while ten inches was average.

With the advent of guided fishing in the 1990s, the profile of the Elk was raised considerably. It was the guides themselves who pushed for catch-and-release fishing, and this proposal was finally accepted by locals following a devastating flood in 1995. Each year thereafter, the total number of fish increased; so too did the average size. And, believe it or not, this remarkable improvement in fishing occurred in tandem with increased pressure from both guided and unguided anglers.

The response to this recovery was curious. Rather than get excited, some locals began to worry that the Elk would become too attractive to outsiders.

But who is an outsider? Well, according to at least one vocal member of the Rod and Gun Club (a local lobby group), an outsider is anyone not born in Fernie. Russ, understandably, was unimpressed. 'I was born in England, my daughter was born in Fernie. You're saying we shouldn't fish together? Is it reasonable that we should all be restricted to fishing waters within a few kilometres of our birthplace? Is parochial selfishness a fair basis on which to formulate fishing regulations?'

As for another claim—that guides are commercialising the recreational fishery—compelling analogies can be drawn between guides, tackle-store proprietors and the manufacturers of flylines. 'Anyway, I don't guide primarily for money. I do it because I enjoy passing on my passion to others: to my family, my friends *and* complete strangers.'

What about authors? When one disgruntled local discovered that Joe Brooks had inspired me to fish the Canadian Rockies, he declared that all fishing texts should be burned. Had he ever read *1984* or *Fahrenheit 451*? Given his attitude to books, I decided probably not.

It may be counterintuitive, but increased fishing pressure on the Elk has resulted in much-improved fishing conditions. The real threats are environmental (the Elk valley is rich in coal and lumber) and political (in 2000 the US Fish and Wildlife Service petitioned to include the westslope cutthroat under the protection of the *Endangered Species Act*).

There is a fundamental lesson here for Australians and New Zealanders. The only way we can counter the actual threats to fly fishing is by recruiting more fishing fanatics, not by marginalising them. Not only is coaching and guiding a great joy, it is a form of enlightened self-preservation. This, then, is my plea: if you can't, or won't, teach other people to love fly fishing, then for heaven's sake let writers like the late Joe Brooks and world-class guides like Russ Trand continue the crusade on your behalf.

Driving me mad

WHEN WE travel to cities as a family, I'm the most obliging person you'll find. Honestly. I'll pretty much go anywhere anyone suggests—and have a bloody good time while I'm about it.

But when I plan to go bush, particularly overseas, it's *my* desires that are at the forefront of my mind. I'm aware that this selfishness can be a problem, so I try my best to pick destinations where there's something for everyone. I thought I had got the balance pretty right at Vancouver Island, the Fraser River, Cathedral, the Top of the World and Fernie. Now, it was up to the others to choose how we would spend the last half of the trip. My only request was that we didn't spend too long in the car or get bogged down in towns. Jane wanted to see bighorn sheep in the Banff or Jasper national parks. And elk, and moose, and Rocky Mountain goats. Frances wanted to canoe on pristine alpine lakes. Karen was interested in alpine herb fields and climbing glaciers. It all sounded good. Except for the road distances. But then, I supposed, we should find some nice camping along the way.

I left Fernie in good spirits, and offered to sit in the universally despised middle-back seat, where the towering scenery was hidden from view and passengers swayed as if they were strapped to the mizzen of a square-rigger in a storm. I hate being in cars anytime, so this was no real impost, but I guess I still hoped I would get brownie points for being magnanimous.

We drove. And drove. Past famous fly waters like the Oldan River, beside glorious streams that had no reputation whatsoever but were bound to hold secret fishing delights. Even when we called in at idyllic picnic spots, there was barely time to eat lunch before we had to be back in the car for more and more driving. Although I couldn't see much from where I was, I pined for the streams I couldn't fish, for the mountains I couldn't climb, the forests I couldn't smell, the rock-glaciers I couldn't explore. I felt like a tourist, felt that everything was passing me by, felt myself getting depressed.

It was dusk by the time we got to Banff, and with nowhere secluded on offer, Karen and Frances eventually settled upon one of the park's big camping grounds. I should have been more appreciative of the superb management strategies, like the fact that the rec-vehicles and Winnebagos were kept to separate areas out of sight or sound of people who preferred to pitch a tent. And the fact that the forest was filled to brimming with wildlife. Instead I lamented the design of the tent-sites, which were made of rock-hard clay and slightly domed. No doubt they were good at shedding water, but they were terrible for sleeping posture.

As usual, I got up before everyone else, at first light. The camping area, though full of hundreds of campers, was unbelievably quiet and clean. The toilet blocks and picnic tables were tidy and not even too garish. The shelter of the forest radiated serenity, and the people upheld the peace. The only sound was the scurry of squirrels, chipmunks, whiskey-jacks, blue jays and woodpeckers, all of which were happy to walk up to you to be petted. I should have been relaxed and happy. But I regretted the fact that there were no walks nearby. No mountain climbs. Certainly no streams or lakes. I sat waiting for the others to wake. I waited and waited. Frustration morphed into sullenness.

As my friends have grown older, they have become more tolerant. For me, the reverse is true. On his deathbed my father said that he would like to think that he would never judge his children, but if he did, he thought he would be more inclined to judge us on the things we didn't do than the things we did do. 'Whatever you do, make sure you don't have any regrets when you lay yourself down to die. Don't make the mistake of thinking you've been allotted three-score and ten. You can die just as easily in your twenties, thirties, forties.' He was fifty-six at the time.

I think my outlook on life would have been the same, even if he hadn't said what he did, but in any case I've lived my whole life on the presumption that I will be dead in one month's time.

As I sat, bored and frustrated, in the Banff camping ground, it occurred to me that perhaps we should not be encouraged to measure our relative ages in years or months. Time travels at different speeds at different times. Remember the length of the days leading up to your pre-school birthdays? On the basis of perceived time, the only measure that really matters, we are probably halfway through our allotted spans by the time we reach puberty. Three quarters by adolescence. Nearly at the end by thirty or forty.

I continued to sit, more bored and more frustrated. More convinced than ever that there was no time to waste, more passionate than ever before about optimising what remains of my life. And less able to do anything about it. One way to stretch your perception of time, I suppose.

We eventually drove off about mid-afternoon. With no set destination, or objective, our time got frittered away. Not all of the chaos was anyone's fault. We decided to walk up a remote glacier, only to get caught up in the first cold-snap of the season, the one that heralds winter ice-over and necessitates road closures that will last months at a time. Forced to move on, and then move on again, we inevitably arrived late in small towns where the local grocery stores, blitzed by other refugee hikers, offered little in the way of variety, and any remaining accommodation was usually depressingly tatty.

When we finally got somewhere where there was still a chance to walk or raft or climb, someone would come down with a fever. So we'd drive on to yet another contrived campsite or isolated room. I had become very sullen indeed. I didn't have any desire to make everyone else feel miserable, but nor could I bring myself to say cheery things—it would have been as hard as telling someone you love them when you really just needed to break it off. So I said nothing which, of course, was worse. It was a downward spiral.

The worst of it was driving on past such glorious places. Yoho. Glacier. Revelstoke. I remembered times when I was so hard-up for money that I couldn't feed myself properly, when walking through the exquisite aromas outside restaurants was about the purest form of agony I had experienced.

We stopped at Kicking Horse Pass, where the Canadian Pacific Railway completes two huge spirals through steep mountains of solid granite. The fact that they were built by hand with migrant labour in the late 1800s was one of the most humbling revelations in my life. Even Karen was finding the car trip to be a bit painful and she commented that she would prefer to be on the train. 'At least we could relax, drink good wine and enjoy the scenery.' But for me, being trapped on the train would be like being sentenced to a purpose-built purgatory, the views of paradise specially designed to heighten my desperation. At least with the car we could stop when we wanted to. It wasn't much of a consolation though. I wanted to go home.

Animal farm

JANE'S PASSION for wild animals is as crucial as my passion for wild waters. Before leaving Tasmania she had made a checklist of all the wildlife she hoped to see in the Canadian bush, and she collected more ticks than her dog Halla does when running in the bush in early summer. The only iconic animal we hadn't seen by the time we left the Rockies was a raccoon. Bearing in mind that they pretty much only live in the south-western corner of British Columbia, and we were compelled to spend the last day or two of our holiday driving about the Interior, this was beginning to become a problem.

Just before Kamloops, we found ourselves approaching a small wildlife park that purported to display 'all the animals native to British Columbia'. 'We should be able to see a raccoon in there,' Karen said optimistically to Jane, who was in danger of becoming as sullen as me. She received a grunt by way of reply.

'I know its not *in the wild*, but it might have to do,' cajoled Frances.

'Better than nothing, I s'pose' Jane conceded ungraciously.

It proved to be one of those rather depressing roadside reserves where the enclosures are small and the settings unstimulating. The animals looked happy enough though. Perhaps it was just that I felt so dour that they seemed happy by comparison.

Thankfully there was a raccoon exhibit. Jane ran on ahead, and I set off after her, even before Frances had finished paying for the tickets. The first raccoon we saw was a metre long and must have weighed at least fifteen kilos. I had no idea they grew to such size. A big brushtail possum, the size I expected raccoons to be, is never more than half a metre and four kilos.

Jane was beaming, ecstatic. I smiled, despite myself. In fact I almost felt bad about feeling better. I remembered being a kid wallowing in my own grumpiness, being really pissed-off when someone tried to make me laugh, especially if they almost succeeded. Could I really claim to have matured much during the last forty years?

Between Jane and the raccoons' cyclone-mesh enclosure was a waist-high barrier designed to deter people from getting too close. It was nothing more than a hitching rail really. 'Dad, do you think the operators would mind if I hopped over so I could push the lens through the mesh to get a good photo?'

'I'm sure they'd mind,' I said. 'But I can't see any staff around, and I won't stop you.'

Rather nervously, Jane hopped the fence and took a few quick shots. They weren't as good as she wanted, so she waited, hoping for the raccoons to reposition themselves, glancing about nervously all the while lest she be spotted by a worker. Suddenly Mr Fat barked and stampeded. Jane, momentarily overwhelmed by fear, turned clumsily and fell over her own legs.

Laugh! I nearly ruined our bonding session.

My daughter scowled at me venomously, but she remembered that there was a mesh barrier that prevented the raccoon from reaching her. Then she saw the funny side of things, and suddenly we were laughing together.

Not far from the raccoons was a grizzly bear. It, too, was imprisoned behind mesh, two layers this time. 'You won't be able to get a close-up unobscured by wire this time,' I warned.

'Unless I do what that bloke is doing,' Jane replied, pointing to a young man hiding in a bush. He had his compact digital camera sticky-taped to a long stick that he'd scrounged from under a nearby tree. It had already been pushed through the first screen and was now being manoeuvred through the second. The photographer realised he'd been spotted and smiled at Jane. She smiled back. A secret bond between wildlife paparazzi.

Eventually the camera made its way to within a metre or so of the sleepy bear's nose. 'Awesome,' Jane whispered. The man tipped his hat indulgently. The bear lunged.

The photographer startled, his arm flailed. He very nearly lost his camera. Jane and I roared laughing, but unlike Jane, the stranger didn't regain composure. He flashed us a look of sheer fury. The bond between him and my daughter was broken. 'Didn't really like him anyway,' she said as we walked away, and I cuffed her playfully on the shoulder.

The bison, mountain goats and moose were not so grumpy as the raccoons and bears and didn't need to be imprisoned behind mesh. Furthermore, they seemed to know exactly how to pose for tourists. Jane spent long minutes composing each of her photos, and took some clever close-ups of nostrils, ears and eyes.

Then we moved on to find wolves, cougars, lynx, coyotes, badgers, porcupines, and bighorn sheep.

And then we went round the whole lot again.

We eventually caught up with the rest of the family at the tearoom near the entrance gate just before closing time. 'You look happier,' Karen said to me, amazed and relieved. 'I thought you hated this sort of thing?'

Jane and I looked at each other knowingly. You can't possibly stay grumpy when you're sharing time with passionate people who are enthusiastically doing the things they love best.

Nerka

SOCKEYE SALMON are the most colourful of salmonids, at least when they have advanced well up the rivers and are long rid of their oceanic silvers and greys; heads pea-green, bodies brilliant red.

Budgie had told me that they pack themselves so tightly into the rivers, braids and tributaries that from the air the waterways look like veins on the wing of a red spinner mayfly. He said that there was a likelihood of our trip coinciding with a famous run on the Horsefly River, and encouraged me to go there. When the decision had been made to travel north through the Rockies and back through the Interior Plateau, I fancied that we might do just that. Now that I was in Kamloops, the idea seemed less attractive. We would have to detour hundreds of kilometres north, and I was sick to death of driving. I didn't even mention the idea to the others in case they decided it was a good one.

Coincidence is a funny thing. While in the wildlife park, Karen had got talking to the tea lady and learned of a salmon run nearby in the Adams River. 'What do you think, Trout?' she said enthusiastically as we walked back to the car.

I was less than thrilled. Perhaps, despite my good time with Jane, I wasn't quite rid of my deep-blue funk. 'Another tourist trap, I suppose,' I said churlishly.

'Apparently not. The lady in the shop said there were no facilities, no gift shops, no fees.'

'But the spawning only lasts a couple of weeks and big runs don't happen every year, so the chances of it being worthwhile probably aren't that good.'

'Stop being such a negative pain in the arse.' Karen was smiling. She could sense the optimism flickering deep within my core.

When we arrived at the Adams River parking area next morning, it was like turning up at a poorly maintained country sports oval where everyone was getting ready for a small agricultural show. The cars, mostly utilities and pick-ups, were splattered with hay and horse shit. Interspersed amongst them were several yellow school buses, all stereotypically Canadian, with long noses and rounded windows, a design essentially unchanged since the 1950s. Some looked like they had been built in the fifties. The only thing that distinguished one bus from the next was its length, a physical feature that enabled you to determine with uncanny accuracy the size of the school from which it originated. The kids themselves were chatting excitedly, trickling out of the buses like molasses. Instead of prissy uniforms, they wore workaday clothes, like everyone else. The younger ones squabbled and laughed, the older ones flirted. Although we hadn't quite stopped driving, a friendly carnival atmosphere was already permeating our car.

I noted with a sigh of relief that there were no permanent buildings, only a row of dirty white canvas marquees, all square, with a single pole propping up the centre of the roof.

A cheery man, rotund and jovial, in a woollen lumberjacket and clay-coated gumboots, beckoned Frances to wind down her window. He introduced himself as Bryce, and advised us where to park so we wouldn't find ourselves hemmed in later on. 'Don't like to tell people what to do, but it's the peak of the run in the dominant year. Hundreds of cars will arrive shortly, and there'll be chaos if we don't organise things a bit.' His voice was soft and strangely heartening.

'How much to get in?' Frances asked.

'We don't like to ask for payment, but during the peak of the run we do have to employ people for the carpark and hire port-a-loos and stuff. So it is nice if you can donate a dollar or two. Mind you if you were really hard-pressed, we'd let you in anyway.'

We paid gladly.

On the short walk across the clearing I thought about how unusual it was to see strangers saying cheery hellos to one another.

As soon as we reached the bushland at the end of the carpark, we could see the river, thirty metres and more wide, shallow enough that you could wade across the rapids. It was perfectly red with salmon, a life blood that didn't so much flow as ripple, heave and splutter.

Some visitors seemed transfixed. Others moved upstream alongside the fish. Some even donned wetsuits and drifted silently amongst them. There was a good deal of talking and pointing, even squeals of delight, but everyone seemed to behave in a way that enhanced the spiritual atmosphere.

Our route to the riverbank led us to a deep pool, scoured into the bend of the river, where thousands of fish were resting up, bottlenecked. We stayed there mesmerised for almost an hour before we forced ourselves to move down to the tail of the pool to watch new arrivals spraying up the shallow rapids, hundreds at a time, their humped backs blistering out of the water, redder than sunburn. Then we followed a well-worn path upstream to the best spawning shingle where fish were paired up, shivering against each other, side by side, spawning. Here the substrate was so fine and flat that the brisk current failed to riffle the surface. A millpond view. The salmon were so brilliantly red that even a colour-blind person like myself could sense their luminescence.

The attendant we met earlier moved in beside us. He could tell that we were enthralled, and said softly 'The Roderick Haig-Brown Provincial Park was gazetted in 1977, specifically to protect the spawning beds, and encompasses just over a thousand hectares on both sides of the stream between Adams Lake and Shuswap Lake. The salmon hatch here, migrate to Shuswap Lake, live there for a few months, and in spring they go all the way downstream to the ocean where they wander for three years before returning'.

'How long does it take them to swim back upstream from the mouth of the Fraser?' Tom asked.

'They travel the whole four hundred and eighty-five kilometres in just seventeen days.'

I did some quick mental arithmetic. These fish were passing through Chilliwack on exactly the same day we were fishing there. We were reacquainting ourselves with the very same salmon we saw escaping the gauntlet of harbour seals, sturgeon and anglers. Only now could I begin to comprehend why the sturgeon were able to attain such gargantuan size.

'Sockeye come every October,' Bryce continued. 'All the way from the ocean up the Fraser, then up the Thompson, before passing across a bit of Shuswap Lake and into the Adams. There is a sub-dominant year, when the run hits about three hundred thousand fish, then there are two dud years. But every fourth year we get just over two million spawners. You're lucky. This year has seen the best dominant run in living memory. My guess is that two million have swum-up already and that a million more will arrive over the next week.'

'I'd better get my rod out of the car,' said Tom.

Bryce appreciated the joke. 'You could get a rod if you wanted,' he said seriously. 'No-one would stop you from fishing for rainbows, or whitefish, or Dolly Vardens.'

We looked hard. There were some rainbows. And spring salmon. Perhaps pink salmon and chums too, though it was hard to tell if they weren't just small springs. 'Why isn't anyone fishing?' Tom asked, incredulous.

The attendant smiled, an encouragement for Tom to follow his gaze around all the people, across all the fish. And suddenly Tom understood.

Although it was the first week of the run, dead fish already littered the banks. Many had been mutilated by scavengers, but none were putrefying. That would happen soon enough. You can read all you want about how important salmon are to the ecology of the Interior Plateau, but I doubt anyone can fully comprehend the scale of things until they witness it for themselves. Millions of tonnes of nutrients retrieved from the ocean, delivered hundreds of kilometres inland. Eaten by black bears and bald eagles, otters and mink, and defecated into the surrounding bushland. Without the salmon there would be total ecological collapse. Social and economic collapse too. No wonder the sockeye are so revered and celebrated.

It was hours before we went back to the carpark and marquees. I looked in some of the interpretation tents. The exhibits were a bit crude, rather like the ones at Liawenee in Tasmania, but bigger, more pagan.

Displayed in one tent was a large aerial photo of the salmon, taken earlier this very day. The river, its braids and tributaries, looked like veins on the wing of a red spinner.

Mature salmon and mature mayflies, I realised, are equally desperate to squeeze every last drop of life from their bodies, the enthusiasm of their last hours being essential not just for themselves but for the wellbeing of their kind.

Dan buildin'

LARGELY BECAUSE of the time we had spent in Canada, it was mid-October before we could organise a weekend to clad The Pook. The Tasmanian highlands were a sight warmer than they had been in August. Unusually warm, in fact.

Lester was at Wilburville when I arrived, installing the wood heater. So was Calvin, without Beatrice, which shouldn't have been noteworthy—after all, I was there without my family. But it bothered me anyway.

When Budgie arrived, Calvin and I got him to help Lester install the heater while we began nailing up vertical boards. The work was a good distraction. But, as we toiled away, it became apparent that Calvin was bothered by something more immediate than domestic disharmony. 'Jock itch?'

'Nah. Look at this.' Calvin undid the front of his jeans and, beneath his big hairy scrotum, sewn into his underpants, was a cluster of buttons. 'Beatrice's handiwork, I reckon,' he said despondently.

'Why don't you snip the bloody things off, or if that's too much trouble, just throw your undies away?' I asked.

'Well, you know, she's gone to so much trouble, seems a shame to waste all that effort.'

'Never picked you to be the sort who was into self-flagellation,' I said.

'I think I *must* be into self-flagellation. Beatrice and I have bought a new house and I've spent every night after work moving furniture. And now I'm up here at Arthurs. With you bastards.'

'They say moving house makes you a prime target for divorce,' came Lester's jovial, if somewhat muted, voice from inside the living room.

'Divorce? That'd be the easy option. At least I'd only have to move half the bloody furniture. Any bastard that reckons futons are good for your back has obviously never tried to load one onto a ute.'

'Isn't there a rock group called Self-Flagellation… no, wait a minute, Machinegun Flagellation?' said Budgie, who had just walked out of the living room onto the verandah.

'Fellatio: Machine Gun *Fellatio*,' Calvin corrected with a giggle.

'Did you know,' I offered, 'that when Machine Gun Fellatio played at one of the unis in Melbourne, they were forced to bill themselves as Machine Gun?'

'Funny, isn't it,' agreed Budgie. 'Machineguns, are acceptable, fellatio isn't. Killing: good. Pleasure: bad.'

'I heard a story that Christa Hughes, their lead singer, did a send-up of *Puppetry of the Penis* at the Melbourne Comedy Festival. Apparently she called it *Muppetry of the Muff*. That didn't go down too well at the uni either,' Calvin ventured.

'Makes you wonder what happened to raging against the machine, doesn't it?' Budgie despaired.

'Talking about muff,' said Lester, who was now somewhere inside the roof cutting a hole in the iron for the flue, 'Magenta was amazed to learn that blokes can tell when women are ovulating. Started getting all self-conscious, wondering whether or not we could all smell her. Then she had this idea that if pheromones are such an attractant you should tie flies out of pubes.'

'Already been done,' I said, looking at Budgie. 'But tell me, do *you* think smell is important to trout?'

'Intuition tells me so.' He was sounding even more muted than when he was in the lounge.

'What is intuitive isn't always correct,' expounded Budgie. 'Think about Euclid.'

'What about bloody Euclid?'

'Well, you know Euclidean geometry?' Budgie said.

'Yeah, yeah,' Lester replied impatiently. And then, feeling the need to prove himself, 'He wrote his manifesto about 300 BC or something and apparently it's still the basis of modern mathematics'.

Budgie pounced. 'Ah, but it's not. You see, it's all built around the idea that mathematical proofs can be reduced to fifteen or seventeen "self-evident" truths, axioms and postulates, things like: *the shortest distance between two points is a straight line*. There is no proof for an axiom or postulate—you have to take it on faith. Well, one day a couple of mathematicians, just for a lark, wondered what would happen if you didn't take it on faith. They had a lot of fun buggering around with maths pretending that Euclid was wrong. Non-Euclidean maths it's called now.'

'I'm sure that did the world a lot of good,' said Calvin.

'Well, Einstein actually used this new maths to account for a whole host of anomalies that were seen both amongst the heavenly bodies and inside the atom. And what he came up with was relativity. It turns out that the shortest distance between two lines *isn't* a straight line.'

'I think about heavenly bodies all the time,' admitted Calvin.

Lester poked his head up through the roof, through the hole he'd just finished cutting for the flue. 'Hey,' he said impatiently, 'do you think you can work out the shortest distance to the beer fridge?'

Then he slipped, disappeared and re-emerged, eyes on stalks.

'You look like a bloody meerkat.'

'Looks like someone's installing a suppository.'

'Doctor told *me* to take suppositories once,' offered Budgie. 'Haemorrhoids, you know. For all the good they did me, I could have stuck em up my arse.'

'Knew a guy at Strahan once who had arse-grapes in big purple bunches. Someone told him to dry them out with meths…'

'Hey, there's a *dun* up here on the ridge cap.'

A dun! The mayfly hatches were clearly going to be early this year. Suddenly the pressure was on to finish building The Pook as soon as possible.

Funny bone

NOTHING SHOCKS me anymore. Least of all the fact that Lester wanted this ugly old kitchen bench—nowhere near square, plywood all blistered, whiffing of mould—to be fitted into his brand-new shack. I started barking instructions. 'Lester, after I've slithered on my back along the middle shelf into the back end, you and Budgie and Frances will have to push the cupboard so that the bench-top presses hard into the corner. Then I'll do my best to get a screw into a stud somewhere. Where did you get this heap of bloody junk from anyway?'

'The local tip.'

'The *tip!*'

'You sound shocked,' said Lester gleefully.

'He sounds more pissed-off than shocked,' said Budgie, just as gleefully.

In my effort to squeeze through the small corner-cupboard door, I found myself attempting a sort of limbo manoeuvre. 'I'm bending over backwards for you Lester. Don't give me a hard time.'

Everyone giggled. Then Budgie started reading out world events from the newspaper which just happened to be lying on the bench-top in front of him. Murders, tortures, deforestation, bombings, you name it. He was trying to get me to concede that I could be shocked after all.

'Magenta convinced me long ago that there is nothing so terrible that humanity hasn't done it, often on an unimaginably large scale,' I replied. I had contorted myself right into the back of the cupboard by now; no mean feat with a torch in one hand and a large electric drill in the other. The shelves had been painted numerous times over the years, I observed, but not the undersides. Déjà vu.

When I was a small child, and my mum and various family members were painting our kitchen, I pointed out that they had overlooked the underneath of the bottom shelf.

'Doesn't need to be done,' said an uncle curtly. 'Get out of my way will you.'

I had no intention of moving until someone told me why it didn't need to be done.

'Because it can't be seen,' my uncle said.

'But I can see it.'

And everyone laughed. Except me. I was hurt, and promised myself I would never forget what it was like to be three; promised so hard that I can still remember the incident as if it were yesterday. And now here I was, amazed to be looking at Lester's cupboard from the inside, from my long-forgotten child's perspective.

Suddenly I was aware of someone undoing the fly of my trousers. I was out of the cupboard in an instant.

'Can't be shocked?' said Lester victoriously.

Apparently he was being hilariously funny. I wouldn't know. I was on the floor, flat on my back, not laughing, wiping away the blood that was dripping down my forehead. I found myself taking my mind off the pain in my funny bone—I'd banged that too—by looking at the floor and the ceiling and the mat and the skirting and the cornices in a way I hadn't done for decades. The view I had of the world made me feel like a fish in a bowl. Waves of pain radiated through my elbow. I began to go limp and watery like an actual fish. Is it possible for a human to know what a fish sees and feels? I mean, if I couldn't properly recall the way I had viewed things at various stages in my own life, what chance does anyone have of comprehending the way other animals, or even other people, perceive anything at all?

The next day Lester and I went out to the Nineteen Lagoons. My elbow still hurt, so much that I even tried casting left-handed. Boy, did that feel gangly. Was this what it felt like when I was first learning to cast? I had forgotten so many things.

I went back to casting right-handed, but my performance was impeded by pain. I didn't miss the fish by much, just enough to spook them. In the Western Lakes, the difference between a very good day and an atrocious one can be a fine line indeed. I had forgotten that too.

'If my arm doesn't get better soon, I'll go to the doctor. Do you reckon she could help, give me a cortisone injection or something?'

'Steroids?' said Lester. 'Greg French, the drugs cheat?'

Dumb comment, I thought. But it did make me wonder what I'd do if fly fishing were subject to Olympic regulations. If having a secret cortisone injection meant the difference between being able to do what I love—or at least being able to do it at the level of proficiency I have come to savour—or having to do what I hate, living a life of dull drudgery in an office in a city somewhere, would I cheat? 'Look,' I protested, 'the whole drugs-in-sport thing is not as black-and-white as it seems. Why is having an anti-inflammatory unacceptable, but having an elbow reconstruction perfectly alright? I mean you can't tell me that reconstructive surgery isn't performance enhancing. Anyway, there's a strong argument that everything you ingest enhances your performance. Try going without food for a few days and see how well you do. And why should diabetics be able to take insulin if people like me can't use cortisone?'

'Insulin just brings diabetics back to normal. It doesn't enhance their performance so much as level the playing field.'

'Cortisone would just bring me back to normal,' I insisted.

'Anyway, you miss the point. All elite athletes are abnormal. They all have physiological anomalies that enable them to outperform everyone else. There is no such thing as a level playing field.'

Lester gave me a troubled look and said 'You would cheat, wouldn't you? If that's what it took?'

He wanted me to say no. But I couldn't.

Optimism

MY ELBOW played up for longer than I thought normal, and I wondered if the slow recovery time was just an unavoidable aspect of growing older. Anyway, it prompted me to go and have a check-up—the old forty-thousand-kilometre service, as Lester called it, even though I was a couple of years over the forty mark.

All right then, five years over.

I got a fine bill of health from the GP. And the dentist. And then I went to my optometrist, Andrew. The gadgets they use these days! Things that puff air at your pupils, things that take instant digital photographs of the blood vessels in your retina, things that flash pinpoints of light in your peripheral vision. I needed to talk in order to take my mind off it all. 'I was laying down on my back amongst the poa tussocks in the Western Lakes yesterday, looking up at the sky.'

'Playing ink-blots with the clouds, were you?'

'No—well yeah, that too—but mainly I was just taking the time to look at things the way I did when I was a kid. I wondered things when I was little that I haven't wondered in a long, long time. Tell me, why is the sky blue?'

'For the same reason that sunsets are orange—because we live in a rainbow.' Did I tell you that Andrew is a dyed-in-the-wool romantic? 'The atmosphere is a prism. When the sun is overhead, the light passes through a relatively thin layer of air and we are bathed in the blue part of the spectrum. In the morning and evening, when the sun is low on the horizon, light passes side-on through the atmosphere, through many more kilometres of air, and we shift towards the red end of the spectrum.' Even though he is a romantic, he can justify his view of the world so well that you can't help but end up being as optimistic as he is. 'Your eyes are fine for now but you'll probably need bifocals in a year or so.'

That sounded like I was getting really old.

'No, it's just what happens to short-sighted humans. The rest of us hit forty and need reading glasses. People like you get a few extra years grace, but then you need bifocals.' He went on to explain how the lens of the eye hardens as we age and our muscles simply can't squeeze it into focus anymore.

'But I can still spot trout better than any of the young guns,' I protested.

'You have several advantages. First, being colour-blind you're used to distinguishing one object from another by differences in shading. No doubt you are better able to notice subtle movement during low light, when the rest of us start to lose colour vision, simply because you've never been able to rely on colour anyway. Not only that, but movement is something best picked up in our peripheral vision, and yours is extraordinary. That's probably because of your pupils—they are the biggest I've ever seen.'

'So what you are saying is that I fish well because I'm some sort of freak, not because I'm good at what I do?'

He was amused. 'I didn't say you weren't good at what you do.'

'What I mean is…' I couldn't really figure out what I meant.

Book of Pook

THE FINAL inspection at The Pook was undertaken by a different bureaucrat, a complete bastard.

'The splashboard behind the sink isn't wide enough.'

'The splashboard is painted timber. The walls are painted timber. How can it possibly make the slightest difference whether or not there's any splashboard at all?'

'If it's not sealed properly, it'll get damp and breed germs.'

'Germs? You've watched too many Domestos ads.'

'People don't realise how dangerous germs can be.' The bureaucrat was poker-faced as he said this.

'Enlighten me.'

'Take cats, for instance. Shouldn't be allowed as pets. Their stools can cause toxoplasmosis in pregnant women. Very dangerous.'

Lester had had enough. 'Have you ever gone down on your wife?'

The inspector was stunned into silence.

'Try it, try living life on the edge.'

As the inspector was getting into his car, Lester looked at me and declared him to be an oxygen thief. I had no argument there. 'But on to more important things,' he declared. 'I've made a visitors' book: *The Book of Pook*.'

There was an introduction on the inside front cover assuring readers that 'No vegetables were killed during the production of this shack'.

Inspector's gift

LESTER AND I were at The Pook cleaning out his dinghy when we discovered a long-forgotten fish carcass under the false floor. Hell, it stunk.

'Reminds me of bear turds,' I said. Then I went on to explain what happens in British Columbia in the fall. 'The bears that frequent the streams along the Westslope of the Canadian Rockies mainly eat berries and their poo smells quite pleasant, like fermenting wine. Closer to the coast the staple is salmon, and the turds are simply rank. Things are at their very worst towards the end of the salmon run, when the bears are scavenging rotten carcasses from the riverbanks.'

Lester prodded the trout. When alive it had barely been of legal size, and now it was little more than a limp sack of mush. 'I fantasised about sending that bloody building inspector a turd in the mail,' Lester confessed. 'I thought it might be traceable, though. Figured they might have special forensics methods. Like matching up the rifling on your stool with the haemorrhoids in your bum.'

I laughed.

'But now you mention it,' Lester continued, 'this fish would be as good as a turd.'

So we got to work and carefully shovelled the putrid thing into a zip-lock bag. Then we put the package into a padded post pack. 'I should squeeze in some Super Glue before I seal the thing up,' Lester surmised. 'That way, when he undoes the package the plastic will be sure to tear open, and hopefully the fish will slosh out all over his desk …'

'… and then leak down onto his lap,' I elaborated. Woo hoo!

That was when Frances and Lester's wife Astrid turned up. 'You are not really going to do something that puerile and childish and illegal are you?' It was more of a command than a question.

'Of course not,' I stammered.

'Working up the idea is as cathartic as the real thing,' Lester explained. Lamely.

The girls ended up building a huge pyre from framing off-cuts, and on top they placed a funeral platform made from a short length of highly flammable vertical board.

That night, the inspector's gift was ceremoniously borne to the platform, and after Lester had uttered some well-crafted words recalling the bureaucrat's achievements, a eulogy which brought everyone to tears—of laughter—the pyre was solemnly lit.

There's a lot to be said for cleansing rituals.

1979 revisited

LESTER'S SHACK was finished, and Calvin and Beatrice were there alone. It was summer and Calvin was expecting a dun hatch, but it snowed, so they stayed inside reading novels beside the wood heater. As darkness approached, Beatrice lit some candles. Calvin found himself studying the shimmering light reflecting from her soft cheeks.

'You're beautiful,' he admitted after a time. He meant it too.

She blushed. 'Don't make me uncomfortable.'

'We used to have something good though, didn't we. What happened?'

She exhaled, and he put his hand on her thigh, reassuringly. 'It was good, that thing we used to have,' she admitted.

He kissed her.

'Lester's bound to have some condoms around here,' she said weakly.

Calvin went into the bedrooms, looked in the bedside tables, came back out to the kitchen, scratched around in the drawers, then noticed a little cupboard near the heater. 'This feels hopeful,' he said holding a small packet up to the weak flickering of firelight.

'Come here,' said Beatrice.

Recycled

NO-ONE WILL ever open a coffee shop or sell 'pancakes by the ponds' at the Inland Fisheries Service's new fish hatchery and rearing unit in New Norfolk.

This was my first thought when I delivered my son, Tom, for work experience, something which had been easy to organise given my previous history as a hatchery officer at the historic Salmon Ponds.

I couldn't help but notice that there were no lawns, much less any established trees; only a large area out the back suffocated with concrete and bitumen. Nor was there a quaint weatherboard hatchery with eight-pane timber window frames overlooking earthen ponds and tranquil grounds. Rather, there was a large metal shed reminiscent of an aircraft hanger, without any windows at all. The light inside was artificial. 'It's better than natural light,' explained one of the hatchery officers, a friend of mine. For the staff or fish, I wondered.

Inside, the tops of the holding tanks were so far above the bare concrete floors that you needed a ladder to reach them. Tom and I climbed up and looked inside. The fibreglass ponds were smooth and shiny, without the slightest hint of algae, let alone weed or silt. Clinically sterile.

'Must be a bit awkward to feed the fish?' I said conversationally after climbing down. But it turned out that the feeding was now done by computer-operated machines that delivered optimum doses of nutrients at specially calculated intervals throughout the day. What a pity, I thought. In my time, handfeeding the fish had been one of the small joys of the day.

I soon learned that in our brave new world the new breed of fish managers don't really manage fish at all. They manage machines and gadgets. Manage to completely divorce themselves from the essence of the natural world.

The water itself is recycled, which sounds environmentally friendly but isn't. At the Salmon Pond the water was gravity-fed though the hatchery from the Plenty River, and returned back to the river. The cost, economically and environmentally, was close to zero. I guess that there must have been some sort of increase in the nutrient load of the Plenty downstream of the hatchery, but there were no algal blooms or other observable environmental problems.

In the new hatchery, the water was being constantly pumped and filtered. A mechanical power failure would have been disastrous, so a backup power plant had been built. As for aeration, this was done by another plant, which extracted oxygen from the air. Furthermore, since metal sheds are hot, there was a cooling plant as well—a giant fridge, no less.

I protested to my friend that the whole operation seemed unnecessarily complicated, especially since it is widely acknowledged that the stocking of Tasmania's wild fisheries is of dubious benefit anyway. I was assured that it was a state-of-the-art facility, and in order to convince me of how wonderfully advanced it was, I was shown the dials and screens that constantly monitor ammonia levels, nitrate, oxygen, temperature, water flow and other variables too numerous to list. This is what now occupied the devotions of fish managers—nothing so mundane as the fish themselves.

'The necessity of twenty-four hour surveillance is an advance on the old way of doing things?' I asked rhetorically. 'Everything is so mechanical,' I lamented.

'No it's not,' my friend objected. 'The water quality is largely maintained by a biological filtration system. The filter maintains its own population of specialist bacteria. Some eat ammonia, others eat various nutrients. If we keep conditions just right, the bugs breed up in tandem with increasing waste levels and die off as soon as their work is done, maintaining a perfectly balanced chemical environment.'

If only it was so simple. Bacteria populations are prone to go berserk at the least provocation. 'No doubt you have to monitor the bacteria as well as everything else,' I said sceptically. 'And how about wild bacteria? I've read that they can be as destructive as wild yeast in your home brew.'

'We have to sterilise any eggs that have been collected from wild fish,' my friend conceded, and by the tone of his voice I guessed they had already encountered problems. It turned out that fish eggs collected from wild spawners at Great Lake had been soaked with an 'acceptable' dose of disinfectant, formaldehyde, and all had died. It was a bit of a problem, to be sure, but it most certainly wasn't the fault of the new hatchery, our guide insisted. Perhaps the water in Great Lake was so warm over summer that the eggs, which at that time of year are at a critical stage of development inside the females' bodies, were unable to acquire sufficiently thick shells.

I doubted it. The water in Great Lake may have been slightly warmer than normal last summer, but it was still much, much colder than that in many other sustainable trout fisheries.

In truth, most of the current crop of managers probably prefer to farm and release large quantities of domestic trout—they are easier to rear than wild fish. But while the certainty of a put-and-take fishery filled with tame trout that will eat pellet-flies year-round can be as titillating as a one-night stand, it can never amount to anything more. Real fly fishing—for wild fish in wild environments—is something else altogether. Aficionados come to understand that the goals we work hardest to achieve end up being the ones we value above all others. For most of us, fishing for wild fish in wild environments leads to the most sustained and rewarding of marriages. This is why wild-trout fisheries, such as those in Tasmania, deserve reverence.

I was more than underwhelmed by the new hatchery; I was heartbroken. 'It has come to this then,' I lamented to my friend. 'The victory of artificial things over natural ones.' He didn't know that I was in the thick of writing the final chapters of this book.

But actually, in this case, the artificial hasn't a chance of winning. We don't need the fish; it is a political gesture, not a practical one. If you think I'm wrong, consider the fact that no-one travels halfway around the world especially to catch someone else's domestic rainbows. But a great many people travel such distances in order to do things like fishing for dun feeders at Arthurs Lake, or to walk into the Western Lakes wilderness.

For those who make the counter-argument that stocking programs are not for visitors but for locals, are they suggesting locals deserve a mediocre experience? In any case, the new hatchery is too labour intensive, too complex, too expensive, too limited in its capability to be of much long-term use. 'How did someone ever convince Treasury to part with the money for a white elephant like this?' I said.

'Easily my friend,' my friend insisted. 'The artificial hatchery is *better* than the Salmon Ponds.'

'In your dreams,' I replied.

And in my nightmares.

Seventeen

FRANCES AND I met at a rather debauched party at Strahan on 17 June 1989. Exactly one month later we tentatively celebrated our strengthening friendship by walking alone to Lake Ina, in Tasmania's Western Lakes wilderness. Every month since then we have taken time to stop whatever we're doing to acknowledge the seventeenth, sometimes by bushwalking, sometimes by going to a romantic B & B, sometimes by simply having a wine at home. Twelve little anniversaries each year. Soppy?

Anniversaries, and I'm not talking about ones once acknowledged out of a sense of duty or obligation or inevitability—heaven knows there too many of those—are times of reflection as well as celebration. Are we happy with where we are? Have things changed for the better or worse? Where to from here? Traditionally, I suppose, the first two big anniversaries are the ten-year and twenty-five-year celebrations. For Frances and me, the biggie was always going to be the seventeenth. We were drawn like salmon back to where it all started, back to Lake Ina, even though we now prefer other lagoons and tarns in the same general area where there is no prospect of mechanical intrusion.

On 17 June 2006, we drove almost two hundred kilometres along the Lyell Highway, all the way from our home near Hobart to the beginning of the Clarence Lagoon track, despite the fact that the weather was worsening the whole time. By the time we stopped the car, the snow was inches thick on the ground. We ended up driving back the way we came and having a more sedate but no less romantic weekend at home.

We had another attempt a few weeks later, and once again we were foiled by the weather, torrential rain this time.

When we finally did get a free weekend with passable weather, we were well into the trout season. Things were still very wet, but at least the wind wasn't too bad.

The first four kilometres of the walk is via the vehicular track to Clarence Lagoon. We used to be able to get the family sedan across the small creek at the start of the track, but over the years it has become a sort of semi-permanent tarn, which is a bit of a pity because the next two kilometres are negotiable by conventional car, and I don't especially enjoy walking on roads. Mind you, the route obviously gets much less use than it once did. In fact it was quite overgrown with moss and tiny eucalypt seedlings.

Until a few years ago, Clarence was one of only a few fisheries in Tasmania, all remote, where you could find brook trout. The novelty was a big attraction. More recently, the Inland Fisheries Service has been stocking domestic brookies into waters all over the place, and for most people Clarence no longer seems so unusual that it warrants the special effort needed to get there.

A crude, loose-rock dam, constructed by anglers across the outflow in the mid-1980s causes floodwaters to break the lake's banks, and it was sad to see that the few grassy campsites at the south-eastern corner had eroded back to bare clay. On the other hand, environmental conditions along the rest of the southern shoreline had actually improved over time.

The lake wasn't breaking its banks today, but the outflow stream was very high nonetheless, and barely fordable. Luckily, we found a length of rope amongst some abandoned tarps, and by tying one end to a tree, we were able to use the other to steady ourselves. What a relief not to have to abandon our trip yet again.

In the late 1980s, off-road vehicles were sometimes driven illegally over the buttongrass flats flanking the eastern shore, but no-one had done this for years and the ugly black bogs had all but completely rehabilitated. Lovely.

From the northern end of Clarence Lagoon we compassed our way towards Kenneth Lagoon. Halfway there, as soon as we had crossed the arbitrary line that separates the high-conservation-value World Heritage Area from the no-conservation-allowed State Forest, we entered a scrappy patch of cabbage gums, and were devastated to find that the understorey had been completely trashed. A few trees had been sawn down too, though none in this copse would have had any value as timber. They certainly couldn't justify the money spent constructing the huge ugly road we eventually encountered. This, I realised was the infamous Lake Ina coup. It is pronounced ee.nah by Forestry Tasmania, which is technically correct, but totally contemptuous of Tasmanian idiom. The locals have called it eye.nah for decades.

The logging on the outskirts of Lake Ina, while small in scale, was remarked upon by many in the popular press as clear evidence of a deliberate ploy by Forestry Tasmania, a government-owned and operated corporation, to take roads to the very remotest extremities of our State Forests so as to undermine their wilderness value and any future claims for inclusion in reserves. It is all so narrow-minded, so short-sighted. So utterly soul destroying.

At least it hadn't been clear-felled, so from the shores of Kenneth Lagoon you couldn't really notice the damage. In fact, despite the fact that this delicate, shallow tarn is bordered by State Forest on one side and private land on the other, it seemed as pristine as ever.

We walked around the back of the flooded marsh, and even the strengthening wind couldn't drown the frog song. The shallows were teeming with small brown trout, most of which weighed less than a pound or so, as always. They were tailing, but not sprinting around as they usually do when the frogs are about. It turned out that they were gorging themselves on snails and amphipods. They were very nervous and extraordinarily difficult to catch.

By now the mist was thickening and the wind beginning to howl. We decided to shelter in the hut on the wooded knoll flanking the northern shore. It lies on private land, but this area is still very remote and only visited by a handful of people each year. We were sure the owners wouldn't mind. Despite the density of the mist, we soon found the grassy vehicular route which leads from the Gowan Brae property, eleven kilometres to the east, past the Kenneth Lagoon hut and on to Lake Ina. A few minutes later, we found that the track passes the hut no more. The shelter had burned to the ground, probably seventeen years ago. The rock foundations were overgrown with moss and grass and the roofing iron had all but rusted away.

The good thing, though, was that the level area in front of the hut, which had once been trampled bare, was now soft with grass and perfectly manicured by the wallabies, of which there were countless mobs. What a perfect spot for a tent, especially since it was so well sheltered from the wind. We lit a campfire—something, tragically, that you are not supposed to do in the Western Lakes anymore—drank wine and made a curry in the wok. The atmosphere was so cosy that we didn't even notice the rain.

The morning was perfectly clear and sunny, and we decided to do a day walk to Lake Ina rather than break camp. We even opted to go the easy way via the vehicular route. Private property actually extends to within two hundred metres of Ina's south-eastern shore and for decades, despite laws against driving off-road in the Western Lakes, the odd vehicle has been taken right to the water's edge. Private land or not, I used to think this track was an abomination, but after yesterday's forestry road it seemed strangely quaint—very grassy and hardly ever used. An even more pleasant surprise was the amount of fresh devil poo deposited along the track, strings of matted fur mixed with splinters of bone. Since 1989 devil facial tumour disease has devastated most of Tasmania's devil populations. Here, at least for now, things were as they should be.

We stopped to fish the small round tarn halfway up Ina's eastern shore, well away from the vehicular track, and caught quite a few good-sized brown trout, all of which we polaroided as they cruised hard in along the edges in search of frogs. But we forced ourselves to move on, because our real destination was the old rustic hut that lies in a fagus gully at the northern end of the lake, where we first camped alone together.

The last part of the route traverses a rocky outcrop, and has never been easy to follow. Now it was completely overgrown. The sad thing about this was that it was further evidence that ever fewer people walk here. Once the old timers die off, who will care enough to fight against the logging companies and other exploiters? Trust me, National Park status offers next to no protection. I've already seen the inundation of the Lake Pedder National Park, the logging of the Hartz Mountains National Park, and the wanton destruction of other reserves too numerous to list.

Then again, it was good to see so much regrowth, especially since it was comprised mostly of gumtop saplings. The older trees were dying back because of the prolonged droughts which have been a feature of the last seventeen years, but the young trees offered hope that the bush might one day repair itself.

From the outside, the hut looked more snug than ever. Being located in a miniature rainforest, it had always been slightly overgrown with mosses and lichens. Now it had become a part of the bush, like an elvish dwelling in Tolkien's *Lord of the Rings*. Inside, though, things were depressingly dank and musty. The roof obviously leaked and the earthen floor had sprouted luminous mushrooms.

Frances noticed an exercise book hanging from a central post. It was sealed in a plastic bag, but even this had not been enough to protect it from the moisture. The pages were damp, the ink smudged. Still, the entries remained legible. The first page offered a proud proclamation:

LAKE INA HUT
LOG BOOK

THIS LOG WAS PLACED IN 1998
BY THE GIRLS FROM OGILVIE HIGH SCHOOL

PLEASE RECORD YOUR STAY

Ogilvie? Now there was a coincidence. Our daughter was to begin her secondary education there in just a few months' time.

Next, we read an account by Stuart Barry, who had arrived with the original builder of the hut. According to this entry, the builder was an Austrian immigrant, a keen outdoorsman, who arrived in Tasmania in 1961. He started the hut in 1968 and finished it in 1972, with the help of three other immigrants, one Austrian, one German (whom I'd met here on several occasions years ago), and another Scottish. They too walked in from the Lyell Highway via Clarence Lagoon, and carried in the roofing and potbelly stove. In the 1990s, age finally caught up with the builder, and he stopped visiting. But now, fifteen years later, he had returned one last time— funny, isn't it, that we humans have such a finely developed homing instinct? He wanted to remain anonymous, but he asked Stuart to express his hope that other people would learn to love this place as he did.

There was another memo, dated January 2003, from Fred, Chris, Andrew and Rob with notes on their successful fishing and a comment that 'without the information in "Frog Call" we would not know of the existence of this pleasant hut'.

And, on November 2005, Gavin (from WA), Graham (NSW) and Ron (NZ) noted that they had travelled up from Clarence Lagoon and finally found the hut after doubting its existence. 'Read about it in 'Frog Call'.'

Given the parting wishes of the builder, I found these two entries intensely humbling.

That night, back at our idyllic camp near Kenneth Lagoon, Frances and I weighed up seventeen years of change. Were things better or worse than they used to be? The logging and associated roads are devastating. But at least the rest of the bush remained relatively healthy, certainly more healthy than the forests further east. Yes, there were petty rules like not being allowed to light fires, but they were unenforceable and easy to ignore. The trout fishery itself was undoubtedly as robust as it ever was. And, as for us, we enjoyed each other's company as much as ever.

There was a lot to be grateful for.

Silver Plains

IT STRUCK me, on that terrible day in 2004 when I returned to Lake Sorell in Tasmania's Central Highlands, that despite being located in temperate woodland, the Silver Plains camping area was reminiscent of a ghost town in a desert. I don't like clichés and these analogies formed involuntarily like unwelcome mirages, possibly because the lake was such an integral part of my impressionable childhood, a time when I watched too many TV westerns.

I know a lot more about ghost towns now than I did as a kid. When travelling with Julie, my sister-in-law, through the bustling port city of Iquique on the edge of Chile's Atacama Desert, I got a taxi driver to take us fifty kilometres inland to a remote place where there were reputed to be some ancient Incan geoglyphs. He insisted that we make a short detour to Humberstone, a deserted nitrate-mining town. It had been established in 1872, he said, but suffered a dramatic decline in the early 1930s following the stockmarket crash and the advent of cheap synthetic fertilisers, and was finally abandoned in 1960.

When we visited in 1987, Humberstone was not the World Heritage Site that it is today and we were totally alone. Although it had obviously been a sizable town, it seemed to have been deserted overnight. We wandered through the grand old theatre, the workers' quarters, the hotel, the market place. There was even a dry swimming pool, apparently built from metal plates which had been salvaged from the hull of a ship. Everything was silent and sandy. Dunes drifted into hallways, doors squeaked on rusty hinges, breezes corralled tumbleweeds into cracked courtyards. And beyond the town the hills were indeed decorated in geoglyphs, most of which featured parts of huge animals and mysterious symbols. I say *parts* because the nitrate miners had eaten into the hills with no regard whatsoever for ancient artwork.

We didn't bother going to the graveyard—the whole landscape was cemetery enough. It had been forsaken by the Indians, the Spanish and even, it seemed to me, nature itself. The atmosphere was dry and lifeless, and filled with so many natural, cultural and private losses.

Incidentally, my original fascination with South America can be traced back to a Carl Barks comic in which Donald Duck and his three nephews became *Lost in the Andes* while looking for chooks that laid square eggs. I mention this because the year I first read that comic was the same year, 1969, that I first went to Silver Plains and I caught my first lake-dwelling brown trout. I well remember that fishing trip. My father and I drove through kilometres upon kilometres of pastures and pristine woodland where there was scarcely a house to be seen and suddenly, at Silver Plains, there were people everywhere as if we had arrived at a regatta or marketplace. There were cars, boats, caravans, tents, generators and a host of very happy and excited people, mostly anglers with their families and friends. We launched our dinghy and motored around the open water, trolling. I probably hooked my first trout, a small one, about midday but I didn't realise until I decided to check to see if my hook had become fouled with weed, by which time my catch was as stiff as a board. Later I hooked two much more lively fish and even managed to boat one of them. I felt more alive and happy than I had felt in a long, long time. Indeed I almost forgot the terrible burden that clouded my days and nights.

The Silver Plains campsite, happy though it was, was too busy for me and Dad. We ended up finding a more secluded site under a huge cabbage gum near the old accommodation house at Interlaken, which had originally been built by the government in 1907–08, but was now unaccountably abandoned. It was already falling into disrepair, like a typical hotel in a typical ghost town, and I was scared of it. It hinted of decay and loss.

For many years, despite its naturally milky water, Lake Sorell was the only lake I fished. The gnarly trees and harsh rock outcrops flanking the shores made me think it was immortal. Why not? It had existed for thousands of years, long enough for an isolated population of climbing galaxias to evolve into a completely unique fish, the locally endemic golden galaxias. It was big, too, even to a boy who lived on the east coast and was used to fishing in the Mercury Passage. Once, in a steady chop, I forgot where I was and began automatically looking for our couta lines, which made Dad laugh. And that night I caught Dad pulling the dinghy up the shore above the 'high tide mark', which made me laugh. It felt good to feel like laughing.

Despite the oceanic feel, there was less water in Sorell than I imagined. Even when full to brimming, the lake had a maximum depth of just over four metres and average depth of about three metres. It seems amazing to me now that I wasn't worried that one day the water might dry up.

Why would you worry about such a thing? you might ask. *Adults couldn't have predicted what was to come. And you were only seven years old.*

Many seven-year-olds think more deeply about life, the universe and everything than many adults would ever care to believe. And many withhold their dark thoughts from condescending grownups; from everyone. The things that ate into my mind like cancer were not the sort of things that adults believed should, would or could bother children. But I had a passion for nature, a love of people and an enquiring mind.

On 20 July 1969, just after our grade-two primary school class had watched Neil Armstrong set foot upon the moon and we were being invited to say what we thought about it all, I asked how much rubbish the astronauts were going to leave there. I guess this must have seemed petty to the other kids, because they laughed at me cruelly. Our teacher came to my defence though, and steered the class into a discussion on the topic of pollution. We quickly canvassed litter, and water contamination, and smog, and then our teacher gave us a reasonably detailed overview of the phenomenon we now know as climate change. Remember, this was 1969. The enduring image in my impressionable mind was of icecaps melting and everything being inundated in a flood of biblical proportions.

Standing at Silver Plains in 2004, looking back, I guessed that it was the biblical analogy that compounded my childhood fears. One morning, a few months before the moon landing, I happened to ask myself, *What if God doesn't exist?* I tested the hypothesis in my head, and could find nothing to give me solace. I began to doubt that it would be possible to produce a rational reason why a benevolent god would allow elephants to be poached, or children to starve in Africa, or innocents to be killed in earthquakes. Then I wondered: if there was a god, and he liked to send disbelievers to hell, would I be amongst them? I mean, I didn't choose to disbelieve—I desperately wanted to have faith. Was it my fault that the existence of god made no sense to me?

The nuns visited our small country school once or twice a year, and we children of Catholics were ushered like lepers out of class to 'special lessons' in the hallway. During one such session, I mustered up the courage to ask one nun why God allowed children to be born in places where there was no access to the Bible. She said 'There are missionaries in remote places so everybody has access to the word of God, if they want it. Some people, though, don't want to listen to God, and they will burn in Hell'.

'What about the children that were born and died before you had missionaries everywhere?' I pleaded.

She smiled. She probably thought her manner comforting, or at least benign. I found it condescending. It made me realise that she had never asked these questions of herself, and that she was not about to think about them now, not even for the benefit of a child in agony who desperately needed answers and reassurance. In that moment, not only did I lose all faith in her God, but, much worse, a good deal of my faith in adults. I can't possibly explain how devastating this was, how it sent me spiralling into deep depression.

I became so sick that between ages eight and eleven I literally shat water. Eventually, out of sheer desperation, but not before my mother had already noticed that something was up, I confessed to her my fear of climate change. It felt good to have said it out loud, but I knew she didn't understand and I made her promise not to tell anyone, especially not Dad because I couldn't bear for him to think I was stupid.

A week or two after my confession, as Dad and I were trolling around Lake Sorell, he said 'You know something? When I was kid I used to worry about the polar icecaps melting'.

I was instantly angry with what I saw as my mother's betrayal of trust. I was equally annoyed by my father's clunky attempt at empathy. I would have steadfastly said nothing, but my rod suddenly bent double and I was soon so busy playing a big, strong trout that the topic died a natural death all of its own.

Over the next few days I realised I was feeling better. Perhaps it was because Dad hadn't ridiculed me. It became apparent to me that in his own clumsy way he cared, that he might even know something of the hell I was going through. Perhaps my situation was not as abnormal or hopeless as I had feared. It took time, but within a year, I had completely overcome my depression. Better still, it never ever came back. I wonder where I would be now without the bush, without the fishing, without the water?

Every day since I turned twelve, I have liked to boast to myself that the happiest time in my life is *now*. It would be absolutely true if it wasn't for those unavoidable hiccups that blight every life. Like when my father was diagnosed with cancer. I was twenty-two at the time and suddenly it was my turn to take him to Lake Sorell. Late in the afternoon of the last day of that long weekend, he caught a big brown trout, silver like a sea-runner. He tenderly ran his fingers over the fish's skin—as smooth as the bark on the gum tree by which we camped, he noted—and kissed his catch. I knew that he knew it was the last trout he'd ever catch.

I fished Sorell hard in the years after my father's death, and learned to use flies. I mastered the use of wet flies for catching frog feeders in marshes too shallow and weedy for trolling. I learned that all those rising fish which refused to eat metal lures were suckers for dry flies. I even began using flies to catch fish that *would* eat lures, like the browns and rainbows that were always charging about after golden galaxias on the shallow reefs.

During this time I became an adult—I learned to ignore warning signs. Even as heat and drought killed off the Lagoon of Islands and Lake Dulverton, I never suspected that anything would happen to Lake Sorell. How could it? It was one of Tasmania's most popular trout fisheries, perhaps the most popular. The bustle of people along the camping grounds was unmatched even by standards set at the modern-day Arthurs Lake. It was unthinkable that it could die.

I began to notice a decline in the number and condition of brown trout in 1992. By the 1995–96 season there were large numbers of fish in very poor condition in the lake, and everyone was complaining to the authorities. The problem proved to be the result of a succession of years where winter flows in Mountain Creek were insufficient to permit effective spawning and/or the survival of fry— a phenomenon which resulted in the lake carrying a diminishing population of old, lean fish. Rainfall soon began to fail at other times of the year too, first in spring, affecting the recruitment of rainbow trout; then in summer and winter, affecting water levels.

Very low water left the marshes exposed, causing the amphibious weeds to die off, and permitting wave action to churn the bed of the main basin, turning the water to mud. Warm, muddy water resulted in further dieback of aquatic weeds and the release of nutrients into the water. The darker water absorbed ever more heat, exacerbating losses through evaporation.

Severe water-level problems became apparent in 1997, and were compounded by relentless pressure to draw water for agricultural and domestic requirements in the rural communities of Bothwell and Hamilton. The angling community left overnight, like the residents of Humberstone. The fishery has never come back, nor the people. Ironic, isn't it, that after my fear of a biblical flood, the most immediate threat was drought. Though in truth my primary school teacher had predicted this too.

In 2004, on the twentieth anniversary of my father's death, I drove back to Lake Sorell. The pristine forests were being logged to within an inch of their lives, and on the radio a 'climate sceptic' was opining that environmentalists weren't really concerned about environment or people, they were just waging an ideological vendetta against capitalism and consumerism. 'How come a lame-arsed idea invented in the early 1990s has so quickly become an accepted truth?' he frothed. 'Where's the proof?'

I pulled up at Silver Plains. They were silver alright. Not with light reflected from wet marshes, but with grey dusty silt as far as you could see. It was the height of the fly-fishing season yet there was no-one there, no-one at all. The silence was absolute, ghostly. It took a while for me to pinpoint what was really wrong. There was no frog call. How could it have come to this?

I suppose if you don't love wild places as much as fly fishers do, there is nothing immediate at stake when the bush begins to die. And if you live in the city and only go camping now and then, it is hard to differentiate cyclic changes from devastatingly permanent ones. But those of us who live in the bush day to day, season to season, year to year, decade to decade, eventually become acutely aware of abnormalities.

I noticed that the eucalypts surrounding the lake were sick with dieback. The high branches were dead, and clusters of juvenile leaves were sprouting desperately from lower down on the trunks. The silence, I realised, was more than the absence of people and frogs—it was the sound of the forests panting with thirst, gasping their last breaths.

I walked kilometres around the lakeshore to the big cabbage gum near the accommodation house, which was even more like a prop from a ghost town than ever before. The dear old tree was dead, the trunk grey, dry, cracked and weathered. Actually, on closer inspection, it wasn't quite dead. On one side was a thin cord of shiny living bark that went halfway up the trunk and ended in a meagre flush of bright leaves.

I couldn't allow myself to weep. This was Lake Sorell, where I had learned not to be overwhelmed by depression, where I first came to accept the death of things I dearly love.

I ran my fingers over the strip of new bark, smooth as trout skin, and kissed it.

Ross Bridge

MY FAVOURITE place in the world is Tasmania's Western Lakes wilderness—incorporating the Walls of Jerusalem National Park, the Nineteen Lagoons and the Chudleigh Lakes—where I have bushwalked and fished for almost thirty years. On my most recent trip I took my son Tom and his mate Jake, both aged sixteen, and on the drive from Hobart along the Midlands Highway we stopped for refreshments in the charming village of Ross, where we enjoyed a somewhat impromptu picnic on the grassy riverbank beside the famous Ross Bridge.

'You wouldn't believe the history of this bridge,' I said.

'Go on,' encouraged Jake.

So I told them how in the 1980s, when coming back from a folk festival a bit hung-over and vacant, a bunch of us called in to Ross for some snacks, and sitting on this very same piece of riverbank, Ric noticed a bloated dead sheep snagged on the pin rushes and strapweed, hard up against the first sandstone arch. Naturally we all wandered out onto the bridge and began pelting it with rocks. When Jock finally got a direct hit, the sheep's gut exploded, and we retreated back to the esplanade, retching and laughing the whole way.

After the sheep incident though, inertia set in, so I wandered off alone for a fish. When conditions are perfect, the Macquarie River's red-spinner mayfly hatches provide some of Tasmania's most spectacular fly fishing. Everyone else went off to the pub where Calvin, for a lark, rubbed out the menu on the black board and wrote:

WET T-SHIRT
COMPETITION !!!
Ross Bridge
Today, 2.00 pm

No sooner had he sat down than a bunch of bikers, fellow veterans of the festival, walked in, and for some unfathomable reason their girlfriends decided that getting their breasts appraised by a bunch of vacant drunks was a pretty damned good idea.

Soon everyone had reassembled on the riverbank. About a dozen bikie molls had lined themselves up for a dousing, as well as a local barmaid, two international travellers, and several passers by. 'Who's runnin this show?' demanded the biggest, ugliest biker, looking directly at Calvin, who was sitting on the tailgate of Ric's panel van.

'Ah, me,' Calvin conceded reluctantly. He wanted to explain that it was supposed to be a joke, but it was far too late for that.

'Well you better get ready to throw some buckets of water on the bitches' titties then. What's the first prize?'

Calvin glanced around for anything of value and was relieved to notice two slabs of beer in the back of the van. 'These,' he said with feigned confidence. The biker nodded a begrudging approval.

By the time I returned from fishing, Calvin was collecting bucketsful of water from the Macquarie. I sat down on the tailgate beside Ric, and once I'd been informed of the afternoon's happenings, I settled back to revel in Calvin's discomfort. Presently he threw water over the first of the giggling girls and enthusiastically shouted out the score. 'Nine out of ten!' I ripped open a carton of beer and passed tinnies to everyone nearby.

'Nine out of ten!' Calvin shouted again, this time at an older woman, who immediately rushed at him and kissed him hard on the lips. Everyone laughed and clapped. Except Beatrice. Stoically, Calvin regained composure and issued another bunch of nines-out-of-tens before finally sloshing the head-biker's moll and pragmatically declaring 'Ten out of ten!'... to muted applause.

A few minutes later the biker strode towards Ric and I and, after seeing that the two cartons had been partially consumed, he yelled 'Where's me beer?'

Ric, thinking quickly, replied 'We'll buy you three cartons at the pub, but we thought we'd put Calvin on the spot'.

I was relieved that the bikie appreciated the joke and managed to laugh.

Jake appreciated my story too, but wanted to know if the bridge had a *real* history, 'not just the one invented by you and your mates'.

'Look at the sandstone masonry, the quality of the carvings, and tell me if you think it's historic,' I replied melodramatically.

The Ross Bridge was built in the 1830s on orders from Governor Arthur, and is the third oldest bridge in Australia. It is essentially the work of two convicts, James Colbeck and, more famously, the former English highwayman Daniel Herbert, who was freed after the bridge was finished and now lies buried in Ross' Old Cemetery.

'The carvings—the animals and people—are a bit worse for wear,' Tom noted.

I explained how many of the sandstones in south-eastern Tasmania incorporate a type of clay that makes them especially prone to erosion. 'The carvings have been sprayed with silicone, originally in 1994, once or twice more since then,' I said. 'That will help preserve them, but eventually they will crumble. It's just the way of living things. Dust to dust, ashes to ashes.'

'What do those carved symbols mean?' Tom asked, pointing back to the bridge.

'God knows,' I said. 'They're Celtic. The learned father of one bloke I knew was convinced that they were prophetic. The usual guff—the end of the world is nigh, and so on and so forth.'

'And all this amazing stuff is really going to be allowed to rot away?' Jake wondered.

'Maybe. Maybe not. Over the years many authorities, including town mayors, heritage engineers and archaeologists, have proposed that the carvings be removed to a museum and replaced with replicas.'

'Makes you wonder why anyone bothers putting sculpture in the real world at all,' said Tom. 'If everyone's so afraid of it aging, why isn't there a law that all good art be hermetically sealed away in storerooms. I wonder what the mayors and heritage engineers think of chalk art on footpaths, sand sculpture or those Buddhist mandala things?'

Jake laughed out loud. 'Surely it would make more sense to put the replicas in the museum and leave the originals where they belonged.

Penny for your Thoughts

IF YOU like, you can drive up to the edge of the Chudleigh Lakes via a Hydro road and begin your bushwalk across the stark highland plateau from the enlarged Lake Mackenzie, formed in 1972 as a result of the inundation of the natural Lake Mackenzie, Sandy Lake and the Pine Marsh. I prefer to walk up the Great Western Tiers via one of the old stock routes, all currently managed as walking tracks. When I say *old* stock routes, I mean it. While formal surveys of pastoral leases were not carried out until 1850, most of the moorland was being utilised long before then.

As for trout, the Chudleigh Lakes system was first stocked in 1895, seven decades before there was a road to Lake Mackenzie. It was a local initiative for the benefit of farmers, villagers and tourists alike—and hugely successful. A public hut for visiting anglers was completed at Sandy Lake in 1904. Another was constructed at Lady Lake in 1911–12. Yet another at Lake Nameless in 1916. By now hundreds of anglers were walking into the area annually, and interest only declined when, in 1921, a road was completed from Deloraine to the phenomenal Great Lake. It was a temporary lapse though. Enthusiasm for the Chudleigh Lakes revived as the Great Lake fishery went into decline during the 1940s and 50s. The devastating wildfires of 1960–61, which raged unchecked for months, probably represented the greatest disaster the Chudleigh Lakes had faced since the retreat of the icecap some fifteen thousand years ago. They burned much of the region back to bare rock and clay and destroyed the fishing huts, but failed to stem the rising tide of interest.

Today the area is revered by locals. For many families, access to the Western Tiers and Chudleigh Lakes has become a rite of passage, a recreational and cultural imperative. Higgs Track is the biggest and most popular track. It leads past the Lady Lake Hut (reconstructed 2002–04) and on to the Ironstone Hut at Lake Nameless (reconstructed in 1995). The fact that these huts have been rebuilt is testimony to local passions. Don't be fooled by bureaucratic revisionism which wants you to believe that such projects were joint initiatives between government departments and the Deloraine community. The locals had all the initiative, and they had to fight the bureaucrats tooth and nail for the things they achieved. Those of us who believe that access to this area is a right, not a privilege, owe such people a debt of gratitude.

Despite the popularity of Higgs Track, I personally prefer to use minor tracks like Parsons Track, Sids Track and the Western Creek Track. For a start, they're much less steep, though you wouldn't credit it to look at the contours on the map. Moreover, they are stunningly beautiful, passing tunnel-like through dense stands of stunted myrtles and King Billy pines and, near the top, offering views that are to die for.

It was drizzling when Jake, Tom and I arrived at the lonely little carpark, and a pair of expensive walking boots lay forgotten on the muddy gravel. We put them out of the rain under the car where they would be visible to the owner when he returned for them. Which he surely would do, because almost everyone who uses this track lives within an hour's drive of it.

It only took an hour to scramble up through the forest, but we rested on the escarpment anyway, regaining our breath; and I pointed out that somewhere below us, beyond the dense grey mist, the descendants of the original leaseholders were toiling on properties that had been in their families for generations. 'They took stock up here,' I said. 'Sheep.'

'Difficult to imagine,' Jake responded sceptically and not unreasonably. But within a few minutes, as we were clambering off the boulder scree onto the sodden moors, he exclaimed 'There *are* sheep here—one, at least'.

'Wonder if it's the grandkid of one of the originals or a stray from the lowlands,' Tom marvelled.

It was my turn to be sceptical. How could they see anything at all through the dense drizzle, now thickening into rain? I could scarcely make out my own feet.

'There it is again,' implored Jake. 'Listen…'

I heard it—a plaintive bleat—and laughed, not at their mistake, but at myself for taking such an astonishing sound for granted. 'That's the Tasmanian froglet,' I said knowledgeably. '*Crinia tasmaniensis.*'

By the time we arrived at the hut, the rain was torrential. The shelter was crude, but dry and welcome. We threw our packs into the lean-to woodshed, and went inside. The room was so small that we couldn't help but jostle each other as we attempted to extract ourselves from our wet jackets, and Tom, who's a shade under six foot, kept scraping his head on the crude log rafters. We stood there dripping, glancing around at the four rustic bunk beds and the exposed studwork, each hoping that one of the other two would volunteer to get wood for the firebox.

'You're right about the locals being proud,' Jake declared all of a sudden. He was reading from a laminated A4 sheet, newly pinned to the wall since my previous visit a couple of months beforehand.

How the hut came to be.

Many years ago Reginald Bernes had the land lease up here and brought his sheep up to graze. A few years later a friend of his Norm Whiteley asked if he too could graze his sheep up here. The two men would come up together grazing hundreds of sheep in this valley. The Lady Lake hut had burnt down sometime earlier, the tin had been blown all over the area. In 1967 they gathered the tin while tending and moving the stock by rolling it up and taking it back on horseback to where you stand today. They cut down some trees and started building the hut. Over time they brought more stuff up to add to the hut by horse or foot. They got sand from one of the lakes and brought up cement to make the floor, they made the beds, they had a camp oven for the outside fire (Not allowed to do that any more) they made it their home away from home.

By Hannah Bernes (Granddaughter of Reg Bernes)

Beside it, clearly in response, was a courteous but firm refinement from Peter Lee, also laminated:

Hut History cont. (1980 onwards)

After legislation stopped stock grazing the hut had very little use for a number of years. Some of the burnt roof sheeting from Lady Lake Hut had deteriorated allowing water to enter causing some of the corner stumps and roof beams to rot.

After having to abandon a number of fishing trips to the Chudleigh Lakes area in the late 70's due to bad weather and no shelter in the area (Nameless and Lady Lake huts both in disrepair) Geoff and Peter Lee started using Sids Track. This allowed Whiteley's/Burns' Hut to be used should the weather turn bad. By 1980 a new track was completed and the hut was used regularly for fishing/hunting and family camping.

In 1985 as the hut was being used quite often by Geoff and Peter and families it became obvious major repairs were necessary. Enough "new" second hand corrugated iron to re-roof the hut was carried up the tiers. With the help of Don Youd the hut was completely dismantled [and rebuilt].

***

'Is there a hut logbook?' said Jake, his interest piqued.

'Don't get Dad started,' Tom warned.

'Logbooks have been removed from most backcountry huts and replaced with registration ledgers complete with a list of bureaucratic demands: To be filled in by the leader of each walking party! Name of leader! Postcode! Number of people in group! Destination! Duration of trip! Purpose of walk! Bloody soulless crap. And guess what—ninety percent of people actually respond to such guff...'

'Told you not to get him started,' said Tom.

'If you want to have a permanent record of a logbook, you can always photograph the pages,' I preached. 'The real thing belongs in the place it was written. Taking such curios away to protect them makes about as much sense as protecting an animal by shooting it stone dead so that it can be entombed in some sterile museum...'

'This isn't one of those registers you were complaining about,' said Jake, brandishing a Student Notebook. I realised he was flipping the yellowing pages at me, and I became somewhat mesmerised by the flutter of inky scrawls. Soon Jake was sitting on a stool reading the most recent contributions. Suddenly he was laughing. 'Those boots belong to two blokes called Ras and Snotty—at least, they were the last to leave the hut, only hours before we arrived... and here's another note from Miss Bernes.'

25 February 2007

Hanna, Kev, Pam & Max. Well we made it. Bigger walk than expected. My Grandfather will be "proud" as he was one of the 2 men who built this hut even though it is called the Norm Whiteley Hut my Grandfather also built it. But he doesn't get much recognition for it. So his name is Reginald Bernes. Many a night he spent in this hut many years ago. He is now a 92 year old man and it hurts him that noone knows that he also built this hut so I'm on a mission to let people know about his part in building this hut that so many people use. So here I am pop I've made it to the top and seen your hard work What a trendy little hut it is I dont know if I will ever come back up again (Kev will) But I have been & taken a lot of Photo's for you.

From Hannah Bernes,
Granddaughter of Reg Bernes

Tom, looking over Jake's shoulder, began cherry-picking his way back through the entries, reading aloud some of the more interesting ones,

· *Artificial* ·

and I realised if I didn't light the fire no-one would. As I walked out into the rain the boys laughed in unison and Tom said 'It's another note from our barefoot friends.'

24 July 2004
Hugh "Snotty" MacKinnon + Ras
MLC Hall once again off poodle faking jolly
First time in fifteen years of going to Whiteley's that there's been no wood in lean-to when we arrived. "Enough said".

'Has anyone been coming here for longer than that?' Tom wondered, and the boys set about going back in time.

Jake began laughing ever more enthusiastically. 'Here's one by a little kid.'

14 January 2004
We arrived after 2 hours of pain suffering and degradation! It was a hard walk (more like a bloody hike) and all for a tiny hut that smells funny & looks like a sick old man has died in it.

I had the fire going by now, and the ingredients of a curry in the wok, and we pulled our seats closer to the heater. It was raining heavily on the corrugated iron. I poured myself a large whisky, and small ports for Tom and Jake.

'There's an awful lot of references to someone called Penny Lee,' Jake noted. 'Apparently she's a legend.'

'Holy cow!' Tom interjected. 'Listen to this:'

Wednesday 29 May 2002 10.00 am
A tribute to the four brave souls who survived in -4°C for over 6 hours after their helicopter crashed at 5.00 pm Tue 28 May 2002.

To David—the pilot who crawled on his side over ice covered rock attempting to make a phone call out.

To Calvin Howe who lit the fire the rescue helicopter spotted, made his companions as warm as possible and kept calling until help arrived—one tough bloke. He was still standing and calling when rescuers arrived.

To Pat Frost who was making her first trip into the area, was thrown from the chopper on landing and called for hours, kept talking and was braver than any normal soul during her treatment and evacuation by chopper.

· 273 ·

To David—the passenger, who despite severe back trauma, kept talking and dealt with his pain with courage.

'That's not your mate Calvin from Strahan is it?' asked Tom.

'No, but I know something about those four. They were part of the team involved in rebuilding the Lady Lake Hut, not far from here.' I pointed to Hanna Bernes' laminated A4 history. 'Remember: old roofing from the original Lady Lake Hut was used to build *this* hut. Anyway, believe it or not, the press reported that the pilot had forgot to fill the copter with petrol.'

Jake, mildly annoyed that Tom had somehow managed to commandeer the book, began poking around under a crude bench and managed to find two more diaries. The first entry in the oldest proved to be from Peter Lee—he of the second laminated sign—on 28 January 1983 in response to a previous entry from an even earlier logbook, now missing. 'I guess we can expect much better facilities by Gary Wright (27/1/83) in the near future.'

'Wonder what that was about?' said Tom.

The second entry, dated 4 February 1983, was signed by Warren Lee (aged eight), Penelope Lee (aged seven) and Janelle Lee (aged eight). Geoff, Helen and Peter Lee had written their names, but not their ages. 'They must be the adults,' reasoned Tom. 'Funny isn't it how little kids always write how old they are. I wonder what age you are when you stop that stuff?'

'Ten,' said Jake knowledgably. 'Anyway, looks like the Lees have been coming up here longer than Ras and Snotty.' They continued to read selected accounts out loud.

6 April 1983

For the record, my comment of 27-1-83 was not a criticism of the shack as such but ... is it really necessary for Anybody to satisfy their creative urge by decorating the bush outside the door with used teabags.

Gary Wright

30 April to 1 May 1983

Penelope Lee—7 years
I am sorry that my Christmas tree up set Mr Wright.

'Imagine,' said Tom, 'that little girl would now be…' he paused to do the maths, '… thirty-one. Her whole life-history is probably in here.' The boys began scouring the books for more entries by Penny Lee, reading them out aloud as they went, but unable to resist other passages if they were interesting enough. It soon became clear that they hadn't been the first to do this.

1 to 2 February 1984
Penelope Lee 8 years old it was a great day.

Great had originally been spelt *Grate* but had been blotted out and studiously rewritten.

5 to 6 September 1985
Penny Lee—9 years
Nice stay but the only bad thing was that dad snored all night.

The quality of Penny's printing had suddenly gone from spidery to competent, but she was still young enough to boast about her age. We huddled closer around the fire: me cooking, the boys reading, the rain thundering.

24 to 25 January 1986
Penny Lee—10 years
Good tucker and a loud dog. Uncle and brothers both stupid. Dad okay only because he cooked the tucker.

13 July 1986
Penny Lee—10 years
A lot of snow and a lot of wet socks. Only stayed for the day.

12 to 13 September 1986
Penny Lee—10 years
Went fishing on Friday (no luck they didn't like us)
Went up Ironstone on Saturday. It was great day for skiing. (used a plastic bag).

4 to 5 September 1987
Penny Lee.
I had great fun sliding down snow slopes on my brother's sled. A good idea when

there is snow and you feel like a drink, is to put some snow into a cup and add some cordial and then you'll have a Slush Puppy the cheap way (a Slush Puppy for people who don't know is an ice drink).

'You'll note that she has stopped telling us her age,' Jake noted as if he were Nostradamus vindicated.

4 April 1988
Age 12
Penny Lee came for the day, went to the lakes for lunch, came back here for tea. Brought the dog up for the first time.

Jake noted that Penny's cousin, Janelle, reckoned 'the dog was stuffed'. Tom noted, gloatingly, that Penny had re-declared her age.

30 June 1990
P. Lee
Disappointed to find shed in a mess. No wood, no sticks.
Dirty mugs, pots and frypan! And some blankets left on the floor.
WAKE UP YOU USELESS BASTARDS!

Jake laughed and said 'Penny's growing up'. He seemed to like the way she had become independent, proud and feisty. Perhaps he was becoming a bit besotted; plenty of other visitors to the hut had gone down that path.

'It's not Penny's writing though,' Tom observed. 'P. Lee must be Peter.'

'Bugger,' said Jake.

15 to 16 November 1992
Penny Lee—17 years
What can I say—how nice it is to be back here! (Isn't everyone just sick of hearing about Penny Lee!)!!

'Apparently, for girls, the obsession with age never stops,' said Jake.

'You seem to be obsessed with her age too,' laughed Tom. 'Have you forgotten that she's not seventeen in real life anymore?'

• *Artificial* •

7 January 1993
Kerry Dick + Tony Dick
From Ulverstone
Game Fishing + Shooting
Couldn't find a Rats ARSE

Subsequent visitors had added their own comments with arrows pointing to relevant parts of the Dicks' text. 'Sucked in.' 'Keep away you fucken Murderers. Leave animals alone!' 'Sounds like all the Dicks were here.'

2 May 1993
Penny Lee should be made a permanent fixture as the night's up here are now getting cold (you can't beat a woman to make the bed for you).
    Mark Grove

5 June 1993
Penny Lee was here I'm not going to write anything … except to say that Mark Grove has got "buckleys"!!

The last exclamation mark had a large asterisk where the dot should be.

13 June 1993
Penny Lee—17 years old
There is a lot of snow (and I made a 'slush puppy'.)
Peter Lee 47 years old
I made a slush puppy too.

26 June 1993
<u>God's</u> <u>Country</u>
Sitting on a block of wood adjacent to the door
I scratch my head, I'm thinking, I'm looking at the floor
I'm thinking about the mountain, it's called the Great Western Tiers
And it's been my love and hiding place for the last eleven years
I think about hidden lakes and spots I've seen trout
Mobs of hundreds of kangaroos, and antiques I've found about
History of this place I'd love to know it all
I hope the tourists stay away, they'd prefer it in the mall

• *Artificial* •

I've picked up a lot of litter, as I've walked around
I hate to see this rubbish, left scattered on the ground
My pop came up here, loved to catch big fish
Sometimes he'd cut them in half to get them in the dish

'There's pages and pages of this poem,' laughed Tom. 'Let's cut to the end.'

There is a young lady, her name is Penny Lee
I think she seem's to hate me, but with my idea's she must agree
  Mark Grove

'God's Country' marked the end of book one and Jake said 'Imagine, if this log had been removed from the hut as soon as it had been filled, there would have been no foundation for books two and three. People's whole lives would have changed'.

3 September 1994
Have been visited by 'Russel the Rat' (who is also known as Gary the Rat) and 'Holly the Huntsman'.
  Glen Butler, Basil Kohl

6 September 1994
Penny we didn't get to meet. Well we will one day I hope. I would love a guided tour of this place.

'This prat has supplied his name and phone number,' Jake scoffed.

28 September 1994
No sign of Gary Rat (We still call him that despite argument with Basil to the contrary!)
  Penny Lee

'I bet Gary Rat was named after Gary Wright,' laughed Jake.

21 November 1994
Came for a walk to relax after finishing uni exams.
  Who did it? Who killed Gary the Rat? He is lying tummy up in the middle of the floor, looking oh so innocent and peaceful. I think he deserves a dignified burial

as he had become a household pet, rather!

Gary so peacefully lies in grave with a head piece on the southern side of the hut. The service was attended by myself, who expressed my utter most sorrow of his departure. He rests in Peace.

Penny Lee

15 December 1994
[Penny Lee climbed up falls with Mark and Anita.]
Saw a goat (?!) on other side of gully below falls. Hope his future holds something better than Gary's.

'Who's Mark?' Jake wondered. 'Presumably it's not 'God's Country' Grove.'

'Probably not a goat either, just the bloody Tasmanian froglet,' said Tom.

'Not according to Mark,' said Jake, reading on:

I saw this goat, and don't laugh it really was a goat—a white one and it appeared rather young. Any suggestion on where it came from.

Another diarist had obligingly written 'Out of its mother, probably.'

19 to 21 December 1994
Pretty pretty Penny Lee
How I wish you would kiss me
Pretty pretty Penny Lee
Brent Atkins

A different hand had appended 'Liar write your own poems'.

22 December 1994
Penny Lee
Her long blonde hair makes me shiver
I wish that I could be with her
Lovely lovely Penny Lee
———/———— —
No doubt about it she is legend
More beautiful than I'd imagined
I can't believe she is so nice

Perhaps some day I'll meet her twice
Pretty Pretty Penny Lee
———————/———————— —

Unfortunately it is my fear
That you feel that I am not sincere
So here the poetry will end
Pretty Pretty Penny Lee

It was signed 'GUESS WHO?' all in capitals, and some wag had added 'probably some git called Brent Atkins'.

22 December 1994
Hey you with the crush
We don't want this kind of mush
Why this is enough to make one sick
So go away you little ...

20 July 1995
The Lees have been here
for many a year
Perhaps as a result
The rat died in fear
Anyway wouldn't you know it
They still can't work out
Who is the poet

Someone else had written 'Personally I thought it was obvious but perhaps it's better Penny doesn't know'.

23 July 1995
Not very imprest with the resent additions to the book, the poets work has gone downhill rapidlly. Brent Atkins did not write the poetry and wont lay claim to it.

19 August 1995
I've returned Pen, & what a charmful day to return.
We're going on to Ironstone Lake then to Nameless for lunch
The "crawlys" of the hut no longer scare me.
Ps. Pen. I'm real jealous of your poems.
  Kate Mirowski

28 October 1995
The hut rat has been reincarnated, as another rat
  B M How

29 August 1999
It was a real adventure
With Randal and Brent
These blokes tried pretty
Hard to get us all bent

And so ended book two. 'Time now for the final instalment,' Jake declared enthusiastically.

6 December 2000
Alana Howe
I am a little concerned about Brent's fascination with Penny Lee!?

'Sounds like Alana has a fascination with Brent,' said Jake.
  'Sounds like you've got a fascination with Penny,' said Tom.

26 December 2001
Helen Lee and Peter Lee
Grant Armitstead Penny Armitstead

And an exclamation in different ink, 'Someone caught "The Legend"!!'

6 January 2002
Hugh Mackinnon, Roly Mackinnon, "The Galoot Simpson", Charlie Lewis +
Greg Hall

They were lamenting that overnight a devil had chewed their meths bottle and new Lecki walking stick, and that it had made an attempt on Roly Mackinnon's ear. 'Serious!'

29 March 2002
Rumour has it that the famous Penny Lee is now married and I still haven't had the privilege of making her acquaintance. Bugger!!
  Randall Turner & Shannon Barwick

2 June 2002

*Came up to have a look how Dad, Pat, Dave and the pilot battled for many hours.
They are 4 very lucky people. Dad will tell a bigger story everytime he tells the tale.*
  Ellie Howe

2 June 2002

*I needed to come to see the spot where Calvin has left a part of his spirit. Right now
he's badly bent and broken but his sense of humour is still intact. I know he will be
back one day to collect the part of him that he left here a few nights ago.*

  *Its going to be wonderful party when we get Calvin, Dave, Pat and Dave and
all their rescuers together again.*

  *Thanks to Ellie, Alana + Brent and Gump for making the trek in with me
today.*
  Margaret Howe

2 June 2002

*Made the trek today to see what is left from Tuesdays disaster. I know that, as mum
said, dad will be back one day to visit the site again—an area he has always loved
and will no doubt continue to.*

  *Thank you to everyone who was involved in Tuesday nights rescue. I know Dad,
Dave, Pat and the pilot were glad to see you arrive. I know our family back home
were certainly glad to hear you had made it to them. Look forward to meeting you
all in the future.*
  Alana + Brent Atkins

18 August 2002

Tundra Howe.
*I would have got up here quick but I had to wait for Alana, Brent and Penny the
Dog.*

26 January 2007, Australia Day

Caitlyn Webster—8 years
Quite fun but not when I trip over all the time.
P.S. Penny Lee is my Aunty. Woohoo

There used to be log books like this in all the bush huts. Many of
them are now entombed in the Department of Primary Industry and
Environment's library, dying of asphyxiation, accorded no more
respect than some academics would allow for the sandstone

sculptures on the Ross Bridge. Will you go into an office block to read them? Would you prefer to stumble upon such nuggets of intimacy by accident in front of a fire drinking port while the rain tumbles down on a corrugated-iron roof?

15 September 2007
Snotty and Ras, we have your boots. We will give them back, providing you tell us what 'Poodle Faking' is.
   Tom Latham, Jake Long

Classified

BIRTH NOTICES
CALVIN AND BEATRICE ARE PLEASED TO ANNOUNCE
THE ARRIVAL OF ARTHUR.
MOTHER AND BABY DOING WELL.
MANY THANKS TO THE MIDWIVES AND SUPPORT STAFF AT
ROYAL HOBART BIRTHING CENTRE.
NO THANKS AT ALL TO LESTER JONES
AND THE ANSELL COMPANY.

Revenge

WE WERE at The Pook when Budgie arrived with the newspaper, the one with the article about Three-toe—Scarface's cousin, the bloke from West Coast that Calvin hated so much—being released from gaol, and another smaller item in the world news describing how a fly fisher drowned in a European river after his raft had been vandalised by an animal liberationist.

'Every credo attracts its share of lunatics,' Budgie lamented. 'The right has right-to-lifers who'll happily execute a doctor who tries to save a mother's life by helping her abort a non-sentient cluster of cells. The left has animal-rights activists who'll happily kill an angler as if people weren't also animals and didn't have any rights whatsoever. That's the trouble with irrationally passionate people. They become so convinced of their own rhetoric that they end up not being able to think straight. Extremists often end up so far to the left or right that they end up merging with the opposition, usually on the dark side of the world at the point of fascism.'

'You're too bleak, Budgie,' said Beatrice. 'What hope have we got if that's the distillation of our common humanity?'

'Well, all those fascist bastards will be first against the wall when the revolution comes,' said Lester, trying to cheer us up. Then as an afterthought 'Well, second against the wall—after I've finished with the council planners and building inspectors'.

'Who do you think is going to give you a permit to build the wall?' Budgie laughed.

'Anyway, revenge is useless,' I suggested. 'I bet that activist was thinking that it would be good for an angler to know what it's like for a fish to be hunted, good for him to feel the same pain that he inflicted upon so many trout. His hope, expectation, would have been that the angler, in his final moments, would finally come to understand that hunting fish was inherently evil. The critical thing, as far as the activist was concerned, was conversion.'

'And punishment,' insisted Calvin, almost sympathetically.

Budgie was aghast. 'You subscribe to that hellfire and brimstone rubbish?'

'Nothing wrong with revenge,' said Calvin bitterly.

'But what's the point of revenge?' I argued. 'It certainly doesn't bring about conversion. If that nutter had vandalised my raft, I wouldn't be thinking as I drowned, *Oh my God, now I see the light.* I'd be thinking, *you bloody nutter.* I don't believe that it is possible to convince me that fishing is akin to murder. I don't believe that humanity should deny or atone for its primal imperatives.'

Lester was keen to play devil's advocate. 'So you're suggesting that paedophiles and murderers simply don't feel guilty about what they do? That people like Three-toe are morally innocent?'

'The trouble is, Trout,' Calvin exploded, 'you are emotionally removed from it all. That bastard ruined the lives of so many of my friends. I reckon that The Taxman was so emotionally scarred by what Three-toe did to him as a kid that he didn't really care about living anymore. That's why he took risks like wading the Henty as recklessly as he did. Three-toe didn't just take The Taxman's innocence; in the end he took his life. I hate the bastard so much I scare myself.'

'What's the advantage of Three-toe rotting in gaol,' Lester posed. 'He's been declared safe to society and...'

'Safe? My arse!' Calvin declared. 'Anyway, gaoling Three-toe forever would make other bastards think twice about doing the sorts of things he did.'

Lester wasn't convinced. 'I've studied all the research. When it comes to crimes of passion, the threat of punishment, even capital punishment, has no deterrent effect whatsoever.'

'The way we punish people makes no sense anyway,' I suggested. 'Surely it's the act, not the consequence of the act, that lies at the heart of it all. If I do drugs and fall asleep at the wheel then narrowly miss hitting an oncoming car, I get a slap on the wrist. If I do drugs and fall asleep at the wheel then hit an oncoming car and kill the driver, I go to gaol. My culpability in both instances is the same, surely? The crime was driving inebriated. The consequences, mere fate.'

'You're forgetting that people need revenge,' said Calvin. He was being serious.

'Pah,' said Lester. 'Revenge shouldn't come into it. The only criterion to be considered by a judge or jury or board of review should be whether the offender is likely to reoffend. If he isn't, he is rehabilitated and should go free. Revenge is illogical, destructive.'

'You don't really believe that, Lester.' Calvin was angry now, really angry. 'If that was the case, I'd be free to track down Three-toe and kill the prick in cold blood. God knows I've thought enough about it. The instant I'd disposed of him, I'd never be at risk of killing anyone again. I'd be rehabilitated. Wouldn't even need to go to court. And where would that leave his family?' I realised that Calvin was crying. For The Taxman.

And I thought, what if he is right? What if revenge is an essential part of the grieving process? What would that say about humanity's humanity? About our ability to avoid war and Armageddon?

And then I wondered why I should care about emotive responses overriding rationality when I've always said that we should celebrate our bestiality.

Hut

I WAS walking in a remote untracked part of the Western Lakes, lamenting all the restrictions that have been placed on being human: no dogs, no campfires, no building shelters, no collecting food from the bush. You might be able to argue that some of these ideologies are justifiable in the interests of sustainability, but you can't pretend that they enhance our relationship with the bush. And surely you can't pretend that they are necessary outside of wilderness areas.

Just before I headed out on this walk, I learned that legislation was about to be introduced into Parliament that would make it illegal for me to build a shack for a friend like Lester. Or even homes for my children. The problem, so far as our government saw it, was that too many Tasmanians were building their own homes, taking too many jobs away from industry. So from now on you would have to pay a huge fine for the privilege. You would also be forced to do a tedious and expensive building course even if, like me, you were already a qualified builder but not currently working in the industry. And even then you could build no more than two dwellings every decade. There was no suggestion that owner-built houses were sub-standard—that was almost impossible given that we already had to submit to thousands of petty design requirements and have all our work inspected and reinspected. In fact, rather than complaints about owner-built houses, the industry was overwhelmed with complaints about shoddy workmanship from so-called professionals. The only reason for the new regulations was that in Tasmania, under Labor or Liberal governments, industry always comes first. I guess it won't be long before we won't be allowed to cook our own meals lest we take jobs from the catering industry, or grow our own vegies lest we impact on multinational farming interests. If so, the justification will be the same as always: the new laws will be sold as something necessary to guarantee public health and safety.

I was angrily rehashing all this in my head, thinking about how nice it would be to do something, anything, without bureaucratic interference, when I began considering the practicalities of building my own little hut in the wilderness. The area I was walking in would be a prime location for such a shelter. It was many hours cross-country from the nearest road or walking track, the fishing was superb, I came here often. But where exactly would you build it? It would have to be reasonably close to a good trout lake, but far enough away that other anglers might not stumble upon it by accident. In fact, it would have to be secreted away in a clump of dense forest so that it couldn't be seen from a distance, or even from the air. There would also have to be dead pencil pines nearby, because they would be the best source of framing and cladding.

Suddenly I realised that the perfect spot lay just a few hundred metres away at the end of the plain I was already in the process of traversing. Now that I thought about it, there was probably no more practical site in all of the Western Lakes. I walked over to the edge of the little rainforest. There was a fringe of long-dead pencil pines where, in the early 1960s, a fire had burned up to the tree-line before dying out. I continued on past the spars, pushed my way through a dense wall of tea-tree, and suddenly I was inside a closed-canopy myrtle forest. There was no understorey, only deep green moss on the ground, on the tree trunks, and on the limbs and branches. I could see a long way ahead, all the way to a little rise—where stood the most beautiful little hut I have ever seen, as exquisite as a gingerbread house. I approached reverently. The dwelling hadn't been here long; a couple of years at most—the timbers were still pink. But a few mosses and lichens had already settled in; soon enough they would envelop the place like vines over a sandstone manor. It reminded me of Mark's Japanese retreat in the hills behind Niigata, the way caring craftsmen had breathed life back into dead trees.

By now I was certain of two things: that construction of the hut had not been officially sanctioned, and that it had been built by a fly fisher. I flapped my arms up and down at the sheer audacity of it all.

I realised there was a time when the discovery of such a hut would have been an affront. After all, if we all demonstrated such lawlessness the wilderness would soon be overwhelmed with shacks, would cease to be remote and unspoiled. But nowadays, in addition to my fear of us losing our wild places, I have become even more fearful of us losing our wild selves. Petty laws and mindless compliance have reached epidemic proportions, as if Australians are now quite prepared to be subsumed by bureaucracy. This hut gave me hope that there was a Resistance.

I walked closer. The roof was clad with split shingles, so too were the walls. The door was actually two, one above the other—the same stable-style utilised in the Meston, Junction and Malbena huts. The fireplace and chimney were made of dry-stone laid by a craftsman almost as talented as the best of the ancient Inca stonemasons. Shivers rippled through my torso, like when I saw my first Chippendale furniture, my first Monet painting.

The hut was unlocked. The wooden latch opened smoothly and the doors swung easily on their hinges. The floor was natural, an almost perfectly flat dolerite shelf. The hut had been built to fit the available floor space, extending right to the edges of the rock platform so that rain dripping down the outside of the walls could not flow back inside. This meant that, in plan, the hut was a rugged pentagonal shape. But the roof was a single gable, so the walls varied in stature, from shoulder-height at the lowest point, to a little over seven feet at the ridge. The hut oozed quirky charm at every juncture. On closer inspection, it was obvious that the battens had all been split with an axe and straightened with an adze. There were no chainsaw marks. The only artificial materials, the only imported ones, were galvanised nails, and the brass hinges on the door.

Even the furniture was delightfully rustic, the bunk beds being similar to those in the Malbena hut, the chairs cut from single logs. There was also a rocking chair framed from saplings, its seat woven from wide hessian straps. A cushion had been placed on the rocker in an upright position for airing. It was upholstered with wallaby skin, and stitched together with sinews. Everywhere, the craftsmanship was exquisite.

Finally I noticed a note pinned above the fireplace:

Welcome!

No doubt you are a fly fisher, well acquainted with the trophy fish in the lake at the foot of the hill. Enjoy your stay! There is a bottle of whisky under one of the bunks. Please replace what you drink next time you visit.

PS: Be very careful who you tell about this hut. If the authorities find out, they'll pull it down for sure.

I wasn't sure that the authorities would pull down the hut, as much they might like to. The Parks and Wildlife Service now suffers from the same malaise that affects all big government departments— chronic inertia. Every decision has to go through committees, legal processes, public consultation, more committees. A hut that was discovered at Tiger Lake in the Walls of Jerusalem in the 1980s, the Solitary Man's Hut, is still there precisely for that reason. It has now become so well known and loved that getting rid of it would be fraught with political risk. But I wasn't about to test that precedent, nor betray the builder's hospitality and trust. Let's face it, the anarchy of the situation was a big part of the hut's attraction.

I explored the surrounding forest and almost couldn't find the spot from where the timber had been gathered. The dead pencil pines had been completely removed, so that there were no obvious stumps. All that was left were a few muddy patches where the roots had been, and these were already partially overgrown with sphagnum.

I realised that the builder was right to assume that the only people who stood a chance of finding his hut were dedicated wilderness fly fishers, because even if other walkers set out to find it, they would miss the vital signs, the cryptic clues that are only meaningful to other anglers.

Common ground

HOW LONG must you live in a place before you can legitimately call it your own? For eternity, like the Africans? Forty or sixty thousand years, like Indigenous Australians? Less than a thousand years, like Maoris? A generation or two, like the Jewish settlers in Israel or the Chinese settlers in Tibet? Most of one lifetime, like my association with Tasmania's Western Lakes? A single day, like the first time I visited the Gordon River?

And when your attachment to the land *is* ingrained, soul deep, how long does it take to breed it out? How much time needs to elapse before indigenous people, pagan ones, can be considered sufficiently civilised that their attachment to the land can be deemed so worthless that it need not be considered by modern land managers?

Is it wise, or even possible to divorce ourselves from the very things that made us human in the first place—fire, dogs, freedom of spirit?

In the 1990s, the Tasmanian Parks and Wildlife Service tried to impose restrictions on who could and couldn't go into the bush. It proposed that to walk overnight anywhere you'd have to book in advance and be subject to severe quota restrictions. It was an inherently silly idea, like advocating abstinence as a solution to the HIV epidemic. Indeed, overviews of such carrying-capacity management strategies in North America, where the idea originated, have demonstrated quite clearly that they never achieve their objectives. In fact they often have a negative impact on the environment.

For me, the Parks and Wildlife Service's proposal was a multi-pronged attack on my very essence. The bureaucrats were demanding that I divorce myself from the bush. That I recognise fishing to be an illegitimate pursuit. That I cease writing about wild places. That I abandon spontaneity. That I stop interacting with nature. That I embrace bureaucracy and submit to Big Brother. In effect they were telling me that I should feel privileged to commit suicide for a cause I was utterly opposed to.

At first I thought it remarkable that the proponents of the permit system, all self-confessed left-wingers, were advocating such draconian measures. But, of course, everyone has little things, like the ones I've just listed for myself, that they simply cannot abandon without risking their sense of self. Is the fact that the Wilderness Society wants to stop people going into the wilderness really any different to the fact that most anglers don't want anyone to fish where they fish?

The reality is that everyone wants to dictate terms and conditions to other people. Right-to-Lifers want to dictate their morals. Professional builders want protection from home builders. Botanists want to tell you what you can and can't put in your garden. Animal liberationists want to stop people eating meat. Certain environmentalists don't want people to have cats and dogs.

I don't lament this diversity of opinion. What frightens me is when the ideals become so perverted that they end up becoming more important than the people that lie at their centre. It happens all the time. Worthwhile concepts such as gods, communism and economics are frequently perverted to the point where they are no longer seen as servants of the people, but become omnipotent entities in their own right.

I don't pretend to have lots of appropriate answers. I don't even pretend to have enough appropriate questions. I am too aware of my personal hypocrisies, my peculiarly left-wing ones. I'll even list a few for you...

Indigenous people have the right to determine their own futures, but people in Borneo must not cut down their rainforests.

Freedom of speech is the basic tenet of civilised society, but anti-vilification laws are a pretty good idea.

Basic human dignity dictates that we maintain the right to have children free of government interference, but if we are to a avoid a global human catastrophe, compulsory population-control is probably long overdue.

This is why I am less pious than some about the hypocrisies of the right. Things like the fact that there's a subset of Christians who have the audacity to preach 'Thou shalt not kill,' while at the same time glorifying war and advocating the electric chair.

What I have become certain of, though, is that emotive issues are the only ones worth fighting over. And that emotive arguments should never be lightly dismissed.

I suspect that if we are ever to learn how to live together, we will have to accept that there is no absolute truth, no moral high ground. Only then will we be prepared to look for the common ground.

Cold Trail

IT WAS the end of April and things were colder than usual. Lester and I had gone with our kids to the local swimming pool, heated of course, and having done a few laps we retired to the edge. 'Budgie's been quite sick,' I said. 'Flu and depression I think. Sometimes I wonder if there's something even worse wrong with him that he's not telling anyone about.'

'Where is he?' Lester asked.

'He went off bushwalking. Nobody knows where.'

'You don't think he'd do anything silly do you?'

'I am worried,' I admitted. But I was pretty sure I knew where he'd gone to. He had always been fascinated by the story of the abandoned tent in *Frog Call*. He once told me that he reckoned he knew where it was, but I didn't confirm or deny anything.

Suddenly, I made up my mind. 'I'm going to go looking for him,' I confided.

***

The evening had been perfectly calm and I had half-heartedly tried fishing, but the water proved to be a tiny but critical fraction of a degree above freezing. The PVC flyline became glacially cold as it sailed through the air, and when it settled on the water, ice crystals sprouted along its length, filling the night with delicate crinkling sounds. When the line was tugged back across the lake surface, the brittle ribbon of ice adhering to it began to fragment and fall away. But as the line passed through the guides, crystals stuck to the guides anyway, and the accumulation on the rod-tip quickly attained the size of a giant hailstone.

I gave up. I walked off across the moor to a little trapper's hut, an ancient thing neatly hidden in an improbably stunted clump of rainforest. I lit a fire, cooked a meal, drank a bladder of port, and went to bed. Early.

In the morning, the billy was frozen solid. For a moment I thought I saw icicles hanging from the mantelpiece, but it was just wax from last night's unattended candles. They must have expired sometime in the middle of the night—lucky I didn't burn the hut down. Outside, ice had heaved the bare patch of dirt near the doorstep. The air was crisp and dry. I headed off to where I thought Budgie might have gone.

Crossing the sphagnum moors is a chore normally akin to trudging over soggy doonas, but today it was as easy as walking on tundra. The moss was as solid as the surrounding sheets of exposed rock. Everything was white: the moorland, the cliffs, the trees. I remembered my son, Tom, being two-and-bit years old on his first skiing trip and remarking incredulously of the Ben Lomond plateau 'It's pitch white!' How cold did it have to be for this frost to be as white as that? Was it as cold as it was in 1929 when the Central Plateau froze so badly that in many places the snow gums died, their sap frozen in their veins. I recalled iconic photos, taken by photographers Sterling and Beattie, of people ice skating across Great Lake, of great veils of ice extending horizontally from tree trunks. I looked at my blue hands, considered warming them with my breath, and promptly shoved them into the pockets of my polar-fleece jacket.

Eventually I reached the shoreline leading to the resting place of The Tent.

Clearly, last night hadn't been the first cold snap of the season. The water must have frozen over a few days previously. Then, sun and wind must have caused the thick icy skin to fracture and crumble. Pentagonal fragments, pushed by the breezes and currents, had collected into bays where they piled up almost vertically, one against the other. Last night these fragments had frozen together forming gigantic columnar sculptures—perfect representations of the dolerite landscape.

The ice in the lee shores, though, was flat and clear like plate glass, with only a few air bubbles trapped within, so you could see right through and watch giant pre-spawned trout flirting in the shallows flanking the inflowing gutters.

Here and there the ice was punctuated with curious circular holes, and water pulsated in them like the bells of living jellyfish.

I threw a rock out into the lake where the ice was thin. It punched a perfect hole through the lake's skin, and pulled a comet-tail of air into the water. The air flattened out amoeba-like against the underside of the ice. I watched as it drifted slowly, chaotically, this way and that. A white wraith imprisoned in a netherworld, looking longingly out at its old life, the better one, searching with wretched futility. Searching, searching…

The sky was grey now, and snow began to waft. There was no wind, no sound. I had to find Budgie quickly.

I recalled a fifty-year-old bricklayer—who had lived in Hobart all his life—turning up to work at the Salmon Ponds one morning exhilarated about a car trip he had taken with his son 'all the way' to the top of Mount Wellington. Snow, he exclaimed, was fluffy. Budgie had been aghast at his ignorance, had said so loudly and rudely.

I remembered the day when Hobart City Council banned people from driving down Mount Wellington with snow on their bonnets. Budgie was glad to see everyone enthusiastically flouting the new law. It was a good day—the kids making snow angels, us making snow angels, everyone snapping off icicles from beneath overhanging boulders and sucking them like icy-poles, making slush-puppies by pouring raspberry juice over cupfuls of fresh snow, sliding down embankments on sheets of Forticon.

Budgie had said to me that before he got too sick to fend for himself he'd go to the Western Lakes and walk—walk and walk and keep on walking—until he was peacefully overwhelmed by cold and exhaustion. I knew he had been fascinated by the story of The Tent. But would he actually have come here? Sure, he had done a bit of grave digging in the past, but was he a grave robber?

If there was anything at all left of the tent, it would surely be nothing more than a skeleton. For a while after the fabric had fallen away, the spring-loaded poles would have remained domed over one another like the frame of a tribal hut in the style built two centuries before on the wild south coast. But this was not the south coast. Here, there were never any domed huts, much less any aluminium-alloy. Would Budgie have been struck by the thought that the thing he sought was alien, artificial, out of place? Would he have felt that it didn't belong here? Would he have felt, finally, that he didn't belong here?

The end

BUDGIE WAS nowhere to be found. When I came out of the bush I went to his place, and there he was sitting in front of an open fire, cup of tea in one hand, a novel in the other, as relaxed as I had ever seen him. I didn't know whether to be happy or angry.

We sat around talking, starting off with light stuff—the frosts have been spectacular of late, haven't they—then me saying that I went into the bush—really? Me too—then me admitting I had been looking for him, and gradually our conversation began drifting into deeper darker territory. I got the feeling that, for the first time since I'd got to know him, he was prepared to get some stuff off his chest. 'What actually happened to Lai,' I ventured.

'Lai? She got crook.' He didn't say what illness. He said nothing at all for long, long minutes. 'She didn't have the will to fight it. I blame the bureaucrats...'

'Budgie, come on, get real. You can't blame the system for Lai's death, no matter how full of little-dick men it is.'

Budgie turned on me with the full brunt of disappointment, disbelief and accusation. 'Come on now, Trout, you of all people know what it's like to have your soul wrenched. You know that when you are incarcerated from the things you love, you slowly starve to death...' Then he continued in a more appeasing tone. 'You know what humanity is. How it arises from the depths of time. You say that anthropologists have proven that fire and dogs were critical to civilisation, that they lie at the heart of what makes us human. There's more to it than that... *Everything* you and I treasure is disappearing. No fires. No dogs. No pets. No access to wilderness without some bureaucrat's permission, and then only if you win a lottery. No bush left to access anyway. No hunting fish to eat. No guiding. No fishing at all. No freedom of speech. No incorporating any aspect of another person's work into your own. No building your mate's house. No building your own house. No serendipity. The culture of self and conformity is much more aggressive than that of mateship and outrage. I worry that things artificial will soon assume absolute victory. What next? No kids without a licence? No growing your own food?'

In a lot of ways Budgie reminded me of Len, the Doukhobor. And, of course, myself. 'You've never got over you and Lai not having kids, have you?'

'I think that the thing that softens death, or most drives our will to live, is the knowledge that you can pass your loves and passions on to other people. I don't think her inability to have children would have mattered that much if she had more freedom to share her world with others. It was the anti-guiding laws that hit her hardest.'

He told me how she had set up a successful, and immensely rewarding, business guiding fly fishers on some of British Columbia's best steelhead fisheries, including the Dean River, and how arbitrary quota systems, aimed at interstate and international visitors, destroyed her business overnight. I thought of New Zealand's Fish and Game department's lamentable attitude to guiding, and of my own recent experience on British Columbia's Elk River.

The atmosphere swelled with anger, sorrow, regret, despair.

'I'll tell you something worse,' Budgie sighed at last. 'I'm not sure anymore that there is any point in passing on our passion and knowledge. If our kids are condemned to live in a contrived world where an affinity with wild things and wild places is regulated to death, to pass on our passion is to tie one of Coleridge's fuckin albatrosses around their necks.'

'Do you think it might be worse *not* to pass on what you know, to keep on pretending that you're a heartless grumpy old bastard. They say you don't miss what you've never known, but you, of all people Budgie, know that's a lie. I know how much you miss your father. You've already told me that it would have been easier for you if you'd known him and lost him, even if he died when you were still a kid.'

'I'll tell you something,' Budgie lamented. 'Everyone wants to bequeath the things they know and cherish to the ones they love. That's what gives us immortality. When you can't pass those things on, what then? Imagine how it felt to be among the last tribal Aborigines, like King Billy's dad. It would have been just as hard for the last generation of family blacksmiths or cabinetmakers. And things change so fast now that there are *no* family skills or traditions. Sometimes I think that there is nothing of value left for anyone to bequeath to anyone.'

There was yet another very long silence.

'Why did you come back?' I asked at length. 'Why didn't you just sit there until the cold overwhelmed you? You always said that's how you wanted to go, and I know you've got the determination, single-bloody-mindedness, bravery, stupidity to do it.'

'I realised where I was,' he offered. 'You know, the place of The Tent. It was his place, not mine.'

'That's not the real reason.'

'There is no real reason. Tell you what though, I was agonising about things on the lakeshore, alone in the biting cold, when I saw a fin in the shallows. Christ it was big—like a shark. I put my rod together in a flash, but by then the thing had disappeared. I stalked the bank for more than an hour, and then there was a break in the clouds and for the briefest moment I could polaroid. There it was: ten metres offshore, twenty-five to the right, cruising ever so slowly along a fringe of overhanging tanglefoot. We've both seen twenty-pounders. This was bigger than that. True! It was disappearing into shadows. I had one chance. I did a perfect double haul. The fish didn't have to deviate, so there was no body language to judge if he had taken the nymph. I had to time the strike by pure intuition.'

I didn't need to ask whether he was successful.

'It felt good Trout, real good. I'm good at what I do, and I don't want my skill and passion and knowledge to die with me. '

Sensing that now was an appropriate time to be positive, I said 'You've always talked about writing a book. Why don't you write about all the stuff you tell me. I mean, it's a lot more real than your science-fiction ideas and stuff'.

'I haven't got the energy. Anyway, I don't suppose I'll have to.'

It took me a while to realise exactly what he was saying. 'Hey, don't rely on me to do your dirty work for you. Anyway, I could never do it justice. I'd get it wrong. It wouldn't be the same…'

'No doubt about that,' Budgie admitted. 'It'd be crafted well enough to make people think it was the real thing, but it'd be exaggerated, flashier than real life, *artificial*. Sad thing is, I'm sure your book would have far more takers than mine.'

Acknowledgements

ARE THE stories in this book true? The short answer is yes, they are. But although most of the stories are designed to be perfect imitations of the real thing, they can't help but be representations, and I suppose if you look too closely you might find flaws.

In other cases, in order to protect the guilty, I have changed names. Have you ever read John Birmingham's *He Died with a Felafel in His Hand*? (The share-houses he describes are uncannily like those I've lived in.) In the movie of the book, the number of characters is reduced, and some people become amalgams of several others. This increases the pace of the story and allows the scriptwriters to weave tighter threads amongst the remaining cast. The result is a story even more enjoyable than the book, but the film can hardly be described as unfaithful to the source material. I have employed similar techniques in *Artificial*, and I believe that this has enabled me to be more bold, truthful if you like, than I was in *Frog Call*.

One of my primary objectives in writing this book was to record *my* Tasmania—sometimes I wonder that other Tasmanian authors are living in the same universe, let alone the same State. I suppose, though, that the Tasmanians I know are mostly dedicated fly fishers, and that probably makes them different from everyone else.

Fly fishers can no more control their own lives than they can control the seasons or the weather. No matter how hard they wish or pray, they simply cannot make the whitebait run, or the duns hatch, on the weekend of their choosing. They can't even pay someone to make it happen for them. In this sense, class and wealth count for nothing, and everyone starts off equal. Success is largely dependent upon passion and talent.

Is there a downside? I suppose that it is precisely because trout foods and behaviours are so unpredictable that my lifelong fly-fishing friends, in addition to being obsessive, are quite cranky, even downright weird. Such adjectives are also properly descriptive of my friends' long-suffering partners, though it's hardly their fault—I suspect it comes about either by osmosis or as a by-product of years of uneasy accommodation. In any case, I have at my disposal a menagerie of screwball characters whose barely credible stories don't so much hold a mirror as a magnifying glass to all that I find good

• *Artificial* •

and tragic about life and humanity. I thank the following for permitting me to recount their indiscretions and misadventures:

Alan Board, Andrew Koch, Bob French, Brad Harris, Chelsea Long, Chris French, Danny Rimmer, Deborah Dowling, Don Wiggins, Frances Latham, Halla, Hayley French, Isabelle Vescovo, Jac Gibson, Jake Long, Jane Andrew, Jane Latham, Jane Meiklejohn, Julie French, Karen Ziegler, Katie Rimmer, Kelvin Barrett, Kevin Lange, Lester Jones, Lily Steele, Marc Laynes, Mark Bradford, Mary Latham, Meree French, Michael Nolan, Mick Hetherington, Paul McCosh, Penny Armistead, Philip Weigall, Ric Dowling, Rob McDonald, Rob Sloane, Russ Trand, Stewart Long, Theo Steele, Tom Latham.

Tracking down Penny Armistead proved easier than anticipated. I was recounting 'Penny for your thoughts' to a fishing friend, Simon Taylor, and it turned out that only the day before he had been at her place for tea. (This sort of intimacy is one of the many reasons I love Tasmania.) Not only did Penny give me permission to recount her life story, but her email provided some wonderful quotes: 'The hut has always felt like it was our own, years ago it was extremely rare to see another walker in the area. My father and his cousin Geoff put the Western Creek track in a couple of years before the visitors book started—I was about 5 years old. This track was secret for many years until the forestry found it and named it … I have not managed to convert my husband into a walker, and have had two children who are now 4 and 18 months. Dad and I have just recently decided that it is time for my eldest, who has only been carted up in a back pack, to have his first overnight trip … Thanks for recording such a special part of my life in your book.'

Unfortunately, many of the people I've met while travelling have family names which have escaped my knowledge or memory. My gratitude for their contributions to my life are heartfelt nonetheless, so sincere thanks to:

Adrian, Anna, Bryce, Chuck, Don, Jefferson, Len, Liat, Patricio, Phoebe and Ryan.

I am also exceedingly grateful to those who offered, and gave, direct help with this book. I am most indebted to my long-time

• *Artificial* •

partner Frances, who is not only a proficient proofreader but also brave enough to tell me when my stories don't work, especially when she finds that I am descending into pure rant or being unnecessarily offensive. I value her opinion at least as much as my own. I value her company above everything.

I am also beholden to my long-time friend Rob Sloane, editor of *FlyLife*. I am never all that confident about my writing, and without his feedback, encouragement and painstaking editing I doubt the manuscript for this book would ever have been completed, much less published.

Jane Latham took three of the black and white photos—the raccoon, the bear with a salmon and the bluetongue. Alan Waugh and Melissa Waugh supplied the picture of the silhouette.

Finally, thanks are due to those brave souls who volunteered to test-drive the early drafts, especially Lester Jones.

Each of the following pictures relate to a specific
chapter of *Artificial*.
For more clues visit:
newholland.com.au/artificial

30/4/83 TO 1/5/83
Penelope Lee - 7years
I am Sorry that my
Chistmas tree up 3M Sct
Mr wright
WarrenLee.
PETER LEE. GOOD WEATHER, CALM NIGHT, NO FISH!!

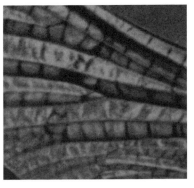